WHAT'S ALL THIS GOT TO DO WITH THE PRICE OF 2X4S?

LEGACIES SHARED SERIES

Janice Dickin, series editor ISSN 1498-2358

The Legacies Shared series preserves the many personal histories and experiences of pioneer and immigrant life that may have disappeared or have been overlooked. The purpose of this series is to create, save, and publish voices from the heartland of the continent that might otherwise be lost to the public discourse. The manuscripts may take the form of memoirs, letters, photographs, art work, recipes or maps, works of fiction or poetry, archival documents, even oral history.

What's All This Got to Do with the Price of 2x4s?

BY MIKE APSEY, C.M., R.P.F. (RET.)

as told to Ken Drushka
and Matt Hughes

UNIVERSITY OF
CALGARY
PRESS

Published by the
University of Calgary Press
2500 University Drive NW
Calgary, Alberta, Canada T2N 1N4
www.uofcpress.com

We acknowledge the financial
support of the Government of
Canada, through the Book Publishing
Industry Development Program
(BPIDP), and the Alberta Foundation
for the Arts for our publishing
activities. We acknowledge the
support of the Canada Council for the
Arts for our publishing program.

LIBRARY AND ARCHIVES CANADA
CATALOGUING IN PUBLICATION

Apsey, T. M. (Mike)
What's all this got to do with the price
of 2x4s? / by Mike Apsey ;
as told to Ken Drushka and Matt
Hughes.

(Legacies shared ; 19)
Includes index.
ISBN 10: 1-55238-188-9
ISBN 13: 978-1-55238-188-5

1. Forest policy – Canada.   2. Forest
conservation – Canada.   3. Forests
andforestry – Economic aspects
– Canada. I. Drushka, Ken
II. Hughes, Matt   III. Title.
IV. Series.

SD129.A67A3 2006   333.75'0971
C2006-900026-3

Cover design, Mieka West.
Internal design & typesetting,
zijn digital.

 This book is printed on
acid-free paper.

Printed and bound in Canada by
Houghton Boston.

TABLE OF CONTENTS

INTRODUCTION

People write their memoirs for all sorts of reasons: to set the record straight or to settle old scores, to relive their best moments or their worst, to instruct the young or to indulge their contemporaries' taste for nostalgia.

My motivation is different. I have never been interested in blowing my own horn. I have spent most of my life as a perennial staffer, advising others on the situations before them and the options they might choose from. Those who then make the decisions on the basis of that advice receive – and deserve – whatever credit or blame may accrue. The staffer remains in the background, ready to congratulate or console as appropriate.

So I was placidly making my way through my seventh decade with neither the intention nor the desire to put down what had happened in my life and what I might have thought it all meant. Then a friend and colleague of many years, a distinguished writer and fellow lover of the forest, Ken Drushka, let me know that he had contracted cancer and that it was not likely he would survive it. He had made a list of the things he wanted to accomplish in the time remaining to him and one of them was to get a book out of me. I was also encouraged to take on this task by Ike Barber, founder of Slocan Forest Products, and by Dr. Peter Pearse, whose 1976 Royal Commission on the BC forest sector had been a milestone in my career.

Ken Drushka, 1940–2004. Lover of the forest, writer, friend.

And so Ken and I began a collaboration, getting together and talking about where I had been and what I had seen and done. We filled many pages with transcripts of our pleasant conversations and occasional (and enjoyable) arguments. Ken was ably assisted by Anne Rees, who had often worked with him and whose contributions I know he would have wanted to see recognized in these pages.

Sadly, the cancer would not allow Ken the time to fulfil his wish. He became too ill to continue and I completed the book with Matt Hughes, a writer who had sometimes helped me prepare speeches when I was at the Council of Forest Industries.

Ken Drushka died in May 2004. This book, which would not have come into existence without him, is warmly dedicated to his memory.

My grandmother was once no more than a stone's throw from Winston Churchill. Luckily for him, she didn't have a stone.

"Michael," she told me, in the strong Scottish burr that she never lost through all her years in British Columbia's Okanagan Valley, "I winged the man with a tomato."

I was a young teenager when she recounted the tale of her brush with one of the great men of the twentieth century. The Second World War was a living memory for me, because I'd grown up in Vernon, BC, site of Camp Vernon, one of the Canadian military's largest training camps. I'd lain awake at night listening on a crystal radio set to the CBC's Lorne Greene – dubbed "the Voice of Doom" – describing the setbacks and victories of those six long years. Winston Churchill was the indomitable spirit of the British Isles, where my father and both sets of grandparents had come from, as close to a sacrosanct figure as my boyhood world could provide.

And yet my teetotalling, devout old Granny had flung a rotten vegetable at him, splattering his arm with dripping red juice and little green seeds. Today, we would say there is a "disconnect" between these two images. In the early 1950s, I was simply confused. I had yet to learn that, sometimes, context is everything. To understand, you must widen your scope.

My grandmother, Elizabeth (Lizzy) Apsey: (left) As Winston Churchill knew her. (right) As I knew her.

In the years after the turn of the twentieth century, Winston Churchill was a brash and rising politician who had lately jumped from the British Tories to the Liberal Party. But his liberalism had not yet extended to the radical notion of giving women the vote. My grandmother was then a fiery young Scots suffragette – not to mention a temperance crusader – and to her Churchill was just another man standing between her and her rights as a citizen. So she hurled that overripe tomato and only regretted that her aim was slightly off.

Perhaps that jarring image of her and Churchill that my grandmother set before me was what sparked a lifelong urge to grasp the larger context, to see the big picture. Certainly, as I look back on a career spent in coming to terms with the forest, I see that one common theme is that I have always been seeking a wider scope, a longer view.

This book is about understanding the forest, because it turned out that that is what my life has been about – and still is. I offer in these pages an argument for a point of view about how we should relate to the forest, and I tell the story of how I came to hold that point of view.

This is also, of necessity, a collection of the kind of anecdotes that tend to stick in the memory of anyone who has spent his life among the breed of people who make the forest their life and livelihood.

And, in the last chapter, I offer a vision and some thoughts for where I believe we should go from here.

Finally, a few words about what this book is not. It is not the kind of book that relates in detail a scheme for the reorganization of the tenure or stumpage regimes in British Columbia; indeed, I make no comment on whether they even need reorganizing. Nor is it one of those books in which an author picks at old wounds or takes revenge on aging enemies. To the best of my knowledge, I have acquired no enemies and can recall no wounds.

Last of all, this is not one of those books in which, with the perfect vision of hindsight, today's knowledge is used as a lens to magnify the imperfections of the past. The people who came before us took the facts as they knew them, applied the understanding that their experience and their values had given them, looked up the road as far as they could see, and made their decisions. It is not my place, standing a little farther along the road, armed with a few more facts and a different set of experiences, to scorn either their efforts or their results. They did the very best they could with what they had. We can do no more in our time.

WHAT'S ALL THIS GOT TO DO WITH THE PRICE OF 2X4S?

CHAPTER ONE

The Dairy Drive-In Decision

I was born in Vernon, British Columbia, on April Fool's Day, 1938. My father, who had also been born on April 1, had told my mother that it would be advantageous for tax reasons to bring me into the world on March 31, but she was unable to comply. Every joke and trick applicable to the day has at some time been played on me.

My father, Jim Apsey, was a bookkeeper for Associated Growers in Vernon. He had come to the Okanagan Valley as an infant, the child of Thomas Apsey, an English coachman from Taunton in Somerset, who had married Elizabeth Millar, a Scottish suffragette and housemaid. My mother, Doreen Woods, was born in Kelowna of Irish and English immigrant stock. Her father, Patrick Woods, had been a well-known rugby player in Ireland and was meant to have gone to medical school, but for financial reasons he ended up emigrating to Canada. I never knew my mother's mother; she died in the great flu pandemic that followed the First World War.

Nor did I ever really know my paternal grandfather. Thomas Apsey died when I was very young. As a boy, I knew my paternal grandmother as a strait-laced, teetotalling little old lady who never missed an opportunity to warn me of the dangers of strong drink. "Michael," she would say, "always remember that drinking is evil." At Christmas, she prepared a bowl of punch well laced with vodka but she would not take so much as a sip of it.

She did, however, have me add a jar or two of maraschino cherries and as the annual family visit wore on she would send me to bring her half a dozen of them at a time. By the end of the afternoon she would be dancing a highland fling. I did not realize it at the time, but my grandmother was teaching me a valuable lesson: life has its rules, but some of them are less obvious than others.

My father was a quiet-spoken man. I never once in my life heard him swear, not even so much as a damn. As a child, he had had polio. It was not uncommon then; they called it infantile paralysis and even the Churchill's American friend, President Franklin Delano Roosevelt, had had it. It gave my father a crippled leg but he did not let that prevent him from walking and bicycling all over. Most people did not have cars in those days; we did not own one until well after the Second World War.

He would take me on hikes into the hills around Vernon. The Okanagan Valley is actually a high, wide plateau between mountain ranges that scrub the moisture out of the air before it arrives. The land is dry, and down south toward Osoyoos it becomes Canada's only desert. Dry country is rattlesnake country, and my father taught me what to do if I happened to hear that unmistakable sound while walking through the brush.

He was not a man to prod his children into one direction or another. He was subtle in his messages, but one piece of advice he gave me has stood me in good stead all my life. He told me, "There is no end to the good you can do in this world if you don't care who gets credit for it."

There was no spanking, nor any threat of it in my upbringing. My sister and I were expected to do as we ought, and if we didn't there would be a quiet talking-to. That had not been how it was in my father's boyhood. He'd been unable to sit down for days after leaving on a teacher's desk a biscuit tin that contained a dead rattlesnake. She was new to Canada and had expressed an interest in seeing a rattler. But even a thoroughly dead snake can twitch as its tissues contract, and my father's offering unfortunately gave a rattle-shaking spasm just as the teacher lifted the tin's lid.

I had a happy childhood. I did well enough in school, though I would probably have done better if no one had ever invented hockey and soccer. Like most small-town Canadian boys of the forties and fifties, I lived an energetic, outdoorsy life. In the winter we would play hockey on homemade rinks in our back yards or out on frozen Kalamalka Lake. One year we put a goal at one end of the lake's thirteen-mile length, imagined a goal at the other, and off we went. We ended up miles down the lake, too tired to make it home and someone had to drive out and rescue us.

I was better at hockey than I was at girls. My sister Bette (the best sister anyone could ever have) used to worry about me and would try to fix me up with her friends. Nothing much ever came of it. Besides, in the summers, we local boys were always at a significant disadvantage. The big training camp at Vernon that had readied troops for the Second World War would take in an influx of cadets and all the girls would go for the boys in uniform. One year, a friend and I launched a counterattack: we put on our hockey uniforms and paraded around the streets. We soon learned that not all uniforms are created equal. The boy soldiers just laughed at us, and so did the girls.

One summer in my teens I went down to the Kelowna Regatta with three friends. We met four girls and divided up into couples. The girl who ended up with me was very pleasant. She invited me home for a Coke. I was sitting on her living room couch while she arranged things in the kitchen when her mother walked in. Some pointed questions ensued. When I revealed my name, the mother's face acquired a quizzical expression then she told me to wait while she went upstairs and came back with a big photo album.

She opened it to a picture of a young couple dressed in the beach styles that had been popular twenty-odd years before. The young woman in the old photo was obviously the mother of the girl with the Cokes. She pointed at the young man and said, "Is that your father?"

It was indeed. My father had a few secrets, it turned out. One of them didn't reveal itself to me until another ten years or so had gone by. I was in Vancouver's Gastown district, buying a rocking chair as a present for my parents' twenty-fifth wedding anniversary. Suddenly, for the first time in my life, it occurred to me to calculate the number of months separating the date of their wedding from the date of my arrival.

All at once I understood why, although we were high church Anglicans, my parents had eloped to Kamloops for a quiet little wedding. The highlight of their honeymoon had been to attend a local softball game.

Even before I was legally old enough, I began to work in the summers. The work ethic was very strong in my family, as it was in most people who had come through the Depression; if you wanted something, you went out and earned it through honest labour. There were many Japanese-Canadian farmers and orchardists around Vernon and I was close friends with a number of boys whose families grew fruits and vegetables on their own lands as well as on lands leased on the Indian reserves. In the summer, there was all the work you could want for twenty-five cents an hour, and often less.

One thing I learned is that farming is hard. It was fun being out with my friends in the Okanagan sun, and I enjoyed learning about their ancestral traditions (all that "anti-Jap" wartime sentiment was soon forgotten), but those summers lugging buckets of tomatoes – I was never much good at picking – taught me that I did not ever want to be a farmer.

Today, much is made of how Canada has become an example to the world of a successful multi-ethnic society. In my youth, the Okanagan was already mixed. There was still a British flavour to the place, with plenty of English, Irish and Scots, but I went to school with young people whose ancestry was Japanese, Chinese, German, Ukrainian and what we then called Indian.

The Indians had been kept separately at schools on the reserves or at the now-infamous residential schools. But sometime in the fifties there was a change in policy, and one day a bus pulled up outside Vernon High School and out came the new kids. It wasn't long before they blended in with the rest of us.

One of the new arrivals was Len Marchand, future Member of Parliament, cabinet minister and senator, the first "status Indian" elected to Parliament. He was a year or so ahead of me, but we got to know each other. Years later, our paths crossed again when he was Pierre Trudeau's Minister of Environment, with responsibility for federal forestry programs, and I was deputy minister to Tom Waterland, BC's Minister of Forests.

One spring I got a job spraying pesticide on fruit trees. The farmer had a huge tank of the stuff mounted on a trailer. He would hitch up the tractor and drive it slowly up and down the rows while I walked behind the trailer and used a high pressure pump to spray the white stuff until the trees had a thorough coating. No mask, no goggles, no hat or gloves: after a while my hair would turn a different colour. To this day, I've not seen any ill effects, but that was a few years before Rachel Carson let us know what DDT was doing to the birds.

The past is another country, someone once said; they do things differently there. DDT was a miracle in those days. It killed the bugs that brought malaria and typhus; it kept other bugs from eating the food we grew before we could eat it. Today, we know better, but that does not give us the moral right to look down on the people who made and used DDT. They did what they thought was right, based on the best information they could get at the time. That is all any of us can ever do.

I have regular medical check-ups. When a man is my age and size, doctors have a tendency to look for problems, sometimes in the most uncomfortable areas of the anatomy. They don't find much amiss, however, and I sometimes wonder if that might be because of DDT's fifty-year half-life – my tissues must hold a reservoir of the stuff that I acquired in my teens and perhaps it kills off anything that attacks my body.

I have raised the question with my doctors but for some reason medical science steadfastly resists this novel theory. I sometimes meditate, however, on the truth that much that was considered good for us when I was growing up – bread and butter, a well-marbled steak – is now on the don't-touch list. Doctors even used to advise anxious people to take up smoking: "It will calm your nerves," they would sagely counsel. No doubt many of the things we are advised to do today will horrify our grandchildren.

Through all of my growing-up years, I was scarcely aware of the forests or the forest industry. I had no particular career plans, although I wouldn't have turned down a rookie position in an NHL team. In fact, when I took the standard aptitude tests they gave us in high school, the results put me in line for a lot of ribbing from my friends – it turned out I was most suited to be a nurse.

In my mid-teens, I met a fellow on the street in Vernon who offered me a summer job with the BC Forest Service. My parents weighed the man up and decided it would be all right for me to go, and I spent the summer at a place called Burton, on the Arrow Lakes in the Kootenays.

I must have been quite young when I got my first glimpse of the BC forest industry. I saw a friend of my father's whose face had been roughly rearranged. "Dad," I said, "his nose is funny and he has a black eye. Did someone beat him up?"

"I'm afraid so." "But why?" "Well, you may be too young to understand, but you've seen those trucks with logs on them?" "Yes." "You know they go to sawmills to be turned into lumber?" "Yes." "Well, the Forest Service holds auctions where they sell those trees." "But what's that got to do with your friend's black eye?" "People are only supposed to go to the auctions when it's their turn. But my friend wanted the trees so he went when he shouldn't have."

People who believe that selling timber at open auction would be a panacea for the BC forest industry's troubles should take note. ∎

I was part of a volume-and-decay crew. There was a faller and two or three of us with measuring tapes. We felled trees then measured them to develop statistical tables that could be used by timber cruisers – men who estimated the quantity and quality of wood in a stand.

Driving from Vernon to Burton, passing through the Monashee Mountains in a Forest Service truck, gave me my first up-close look at logging operations. Or they may have been bug-kill sites, the trees having been cut down to prevent the spread of bark beetles or some other such pests. Either way, I remember thinking, "This is an awful mess." But I didn't say anything.

The Kootenays are over the mountains to the east of the Okanagan in an area called the Interior rain belt. I spent a lot of that summer in the rain, but I didn't mind it. I later learned that, in his end-of-season reports, the crew chief added a notation to mine: "He sings in the rain."

The next summer, a Forest Service crew chief in the Kitsumkalum country named Vance Stewart came across the singing-in-the-rain report and decided I would fit into his operation. I reported to a tent camp a little north of Terrace. It was volume-and-decay work again, and over the summer I learned two things that have stuck with me.

When I arrived at the Kitsumkalum camp the crew was waiting for me. "Apsey?" somebody asked, when I got out of the truck. "Yes, Mike Apsey." He showed me a board and said, "We have a tradition here, Apsey." I look at the board. It had marks on it. Beside each mark was a name. "Undo your fly and lay your thing on the board," another of them said. "Excuse me?" But they meant it. I did as instructed and the measurement was made and my name was added. Then I noticed that each of the other names had two marks whereas mine had only the one. "Now, Apsey," I was asked, "do you see that lake?" "Yes." "Time for a swim." "I don't want a swim." But again I was brought to understand that there was a tradition to uphold. I stripped off and went into the water. It was only the first blush of summer and the lake was fed by glaciers. It was freezing.

After a few minutes, someone called, "All right, come out of there." I hurried toward my clothes. "Not so fast, Apsey. Back to the board."

A second measurement was taken. It fell short of the first.

To this day I am not sure what this had to do with volume-and-decay. But at least I learned to take traditions seriously. ▪

The first came after I had encountered an unfriendly plant called devil's club. It came equipped with large, sharp spikes that had no difficulty penetrating work shirts and jeans. To avoid having to wade through the devil's club that flourished in the sites where we were working, I convinced the faller to lay the trees down so that the trunks provided safe walkways over the spikes.

One day I was working on one of those trees, a big spruce, when I heard one of the other crew members shouting at me, "Apsey! For God's sake, look out!"

"I'm busy," I said. I was balanced on the tree trying to measure its circumference and diameter without toppling over into the devil's club.

"Behind you! Behind you!"

I looked. Just down the trunk, staring back at me, stood a full-grown grizzly bear. Now, in the stories of Robin Hood, I had always identified with Friar Tuck, because like him I am large and affable. But this was a clear repetition of the episode in which Robin Hood and Little John met on the narrow bridge and I was wise enough even at a young age to cut to the chase. I dove into the devil's club and let Mr. Bear go on his merry way.

From that experience I learned to choose the lesser of two evils.

The second thing I learned came when I was at Terrace and saw logs that were being hauled to the dissolving pulp mill down on the

Today's kids seem to have only celebrities to imitate. In my youth we had heroes to look up to. But, for some reason, I fell naturally into the role of side-kick.

When we played together, my cousin Tad was the Cisco Kid, dashing and dapper, while I was his faithful companion, Pancho.

I was the Lone Ranger's Tonto, Hopalong Cassidy's Red Connors, Wild Bill Hickock's Jingles. Later, when I read Don Quixote, I was Sancho Panza, the guy who plays an indispensable part but neither gets nor wants the glory.

It was a frame of mind that came naturally to me throughout my career. ■

Don Quixote with Sancho Panza Apsey.

coast at Prince Rupert. The logs were on trains, stacked on flat cars that seemed to go on for as far as the eye could see, huge lengths of valley-bottom spruce. There is no finer softwood timber in the world. This was the wood that had been used to build airplanes that had helped win the war. And they were going to a pulp mill.

I was not a forester then. I had not developed that sense of the romance of the forest that is part of every forester's soul. But I knew there was something wrong about those magnificent trees going to a chipper so they could be turned into cellophane. Even in those days there were better markets for those logs, even if it was just to hew them into squares and ship them to sawmills in Japan.

I also spent one summer working for the BC Ministry of Highways as a helper to an engineer. From that experience I somehow developed the notion of becoming a surveyor. I applied to a technical school in Calgary, was accepted and planned to go there after high school.

But then I happened to be at the Dairy Drive-In ice cream stand up at the top of the hill near Camp Vernon and I ran into my friend George Trachuk. He was two years ahead of me and had just completed his first year studying forestry at the University of British Columbia. The substance of our conversation was that the girls were very pretty in Vancouver and that being a UBC forestry student involved attending a great number of parties at which a good time was had by all.

In that moment I changed my career plans, and after a summer spent stacking hundred-weight sacks of fertilizer in sweltering hot boxcars at Cominco's Kimberley operations – an activity that burned off fat and muscled up my back and shoulders – I reported to UBC and began a career that would, literally and figuratively, take me far.

I did not learn my father's last secret until after he died. My sister and I talked with his doctor. The doctor asked us, "Did your father ever complain of pain?"

"Never. Why?"

"When I performed a post-mortem I found that, because of his lifelong limp, he had worn down three of the vertebrae in his back. He must have been in constant pain. Every step he took, every turn of a bike pedal, every time he threw a curling rock down the ice, he was in great pain."

I thought of all the times we'd gone hiking together. My dad had never said a word. My love for the man soared. And, at the same time, my love for my caring mother soared. ■

My mother and father, Doreen and Jim Apsey, on their fiftieth wedding anniversary, 1987.

CHAPTER TWO

Hooked on the Forest

I had been to the coast only once before, in my early teens. My father had driven us all down in his old '46 Dodge but we hadn't stayed more than a day or two. Compared to today's version, the Vancouver of 1957 was a pokey little provincial city, but to me it was a huge and exciting place, full of tall buildings and four-lane thoroughfares choked with rush-hour traffic. There were also plenty of beer parlours where, if I undid the top buttons on my shirt to show my chest hair, I could buy a glass of ten-cent draft despite being shy of the legal drinking age.

In one of the places around Main and Hastings they had a machine that let you test your strength by lifting a steel bar. My summer of the fertilizer bags must have put more muscle on me than I realized: I yanked the thing right off the floor, breaking a board or two. The proprietor was not impressed, however; my friends and I were asked to leave. We transferred our allegiance to the pubs on Granville Street, the Castle, the Cecil and the Yale. It was, after all, a shorter walk back to the UBC campus on Point Grey, a journey often made necessary by the fact that by the time the beer halls closed we were either out of money or the last bus had already left.

But, although the lure of pubs and parties had prompted my decision to attend UBC, I soon found myself fascinated by the science

I had come to study and by the men – it was an all-male faculty in those days – who taught it.

First among them, in my estimation, was Dr. Vladimir J. Krajina, a man who was quietly brilliant and brave. He was a Czech who had fought in the resistance during the Nazi occupation of his country, was captured and barely escaped execution. After the war, he was elected to the Czechoslovakian parliament. As the general secretary of the main opposition party, he was a prime target for arrest and imprisonment when the Communists took power in 1948. He fled to Canada where his reputation as a full professor at the Charles University in Prague won him a post as a special lecturer in botany at UBC. He later became a full professor and his researches developed the bio-geoclimatic mapping system that is now used all over the world.

He was a wonderful teacher, yet he didn't teach by giving us dry lectures; it was more as if we were receiving good advice politely offered by an old-world gentleman. Dr. Krajina taught me how to think, partly by instruction but more by the example he set as a scientist. He also taught me how lucky I was to be a citizen of a free country where all I had to do was work hard and I would be rewarded.

I wanted to do my undergraduate thesis under Dr. Krajina. I envisioned a comprehensive review of all the world's pines, starting with our BC species then going on to the fast-growing pines in the United States, the Russian species and so on. He thought it would be a worthwhile project and encouraged me to do it. Then one day he spoke to me after class.

"Mike, I'm sorry, but you cannot do your thesis with me."

I was crestfallen. "Why not?"

It turned out that Dr. Krajina was not a member of the Faculty of Forestry but was with Arts and Science, and the former would not let him supervise a forestry student's thesis. Here was a man who had faced down Nazis and Communists, but against the "silo" mentality of the academic world he was powerless.

In the end I did my thesis under Dr. Harry Smith. He was a fascinating person. He taught a wide range of forestry courses, everything from silviculture to the economics of the forest sector, and I had taken many of his classes.

For my thesis, I chose a practical problem: was it possible to measure the volume of wood in a stand based solely on aerial photography? Stereoscopic imaging from twin cameras mounted on the bellies of aircraft had been perfected during World War II. It was possible to fly over a forest and make precise measurements of the width of the trees' crowns and their heights, but timber volumes could only be calculated from a measurement of the width of their trunks at breast height plus their heights. I wondered if there was a mathematical formula that would correlate the sets of figures; if so, foresters could estimate the amount of timber in a stand from aerial photographs, and save themselves a lot of foot-slogging through rough country.

I decided to use red alder for the experiment, because there was lots of it about. I had by then inherited my father's old '46 Dodge and spent a fair amount of my free time driving about BC's Lower Mainland to find stands of the chosen species and measure them.

To discover the height of a tree, you use a clinometer, which is an instrument that you look through to gauge the angle from where you are on the ground to the top of the tree. You then measure your distance from the tree, apply a little Euclidian geometry and calculate the height.

I was fortunate to have been assisted in many of these tree measuring forays by a young woman I had met at a campus coffee shop, who was studying to be a school teacher. Her name was Sharon Meagher. When I met her she was in the company of some fellow who was introduced as her boyfriend. Not long after, she and I decided that it would be much better for both of us if she married me instead, and we became engaged. We spent every weekend for months driving about southwestern BC, measuring literally hundreds of red alders.

I cannot say if such a beginning is a sure guarantee of marital bliss, but we have been together ever since.

Once I had the raw measurements, I had to deduce the formulae that linked heights with crown and trunk widths. Today, a student would crunch the data through his notebook computer and have the answers in seconds. But I was working in an age when computers were something you saw mostly in science fiction movies. Still, in 1957 – the year of Sputnik – UBC had acquired a computer of its very own, an Alwac III-E from California. It used vacuum tubes as switches and had a memory capacity of 32 bits. It also filled a good-sized room.

I had been introduced to Jozsef Csizmazia, who had access to the Alwac III-E. He helped me enter all the data onto punch cards. Then we stuffed the cards into a hopper on the machine and he threw some switches.

The computer began humming and sorting, and he and I went for coffee. When we came back, the results were printed out. Jozsef immediately scooped up all the punch cards, put them back in the hopper and threw the switches again.

"Why do we have to do it again?" I asked.

"To see if we get the same answer," he said.

We did, and I went on to complete my thesis. I turned it in to Harry Smith who in due course called me into his office, where books and journals were stacked perilously high on every flat surface. He returned the paper to me, and I saw that he had given it a very good mark.

"I guess now you think you're very smart," he said.

"Well, sir," I said, "it's you who gave me the mark."

He laughed at that. Then he turned to one of the stacks and riffled his fingers down its length as if they could read the layers. He found and retrieved a paper and handed it to me. It was by a Danish forester who, back in the 1800s, had made the same connection as I between crown diameter and width at breast height.

I was flustered. "Why didn't you tell me about this?" I asked him. "I could have worked on something else."

"But, Mike," he said, "you were having so much fun."

A couple of years ago, in a Seattle bookstore, I came across a book on red alder. There in the reference notes was a citation of my thesis – my first contribution to the profession had at least been useful to someone.

I kept in touch with Harry Smith after leaving school. I read the papers he published and would run into him at forestry gatherings. He became a mentor to me, a relationship that continued for many years after I had begun making a career in forestry. I could always ask his advice, he would always give it and it was always worth hearing.

Classes were small and students had regular, easy contact with our professors and lecturers. Any forestry student who had a question or a problem could sit down with the Dean, Dr. George Allen, for a chat. We were fortunate, those of us who studied forestry at UBC in those days, to be taught by some interesting characters. One was Bob Kennedy who, for an exam, presented us with a crossword puzzle based on terminology he had taught us in his wood technology class. The clues were tough.

Ken Graham introduced us to the subject of forest entomology by asking for our assistance. Before his opening lecture he told us that he had one of the world's largest collections of insects and similar critters, but that there were a few gaps in it. He was missing a specimen of phthirus pubis, the human crab louse.

He placed a small jar on the corner of his desk and said, "I'm pretty sure one of you in this room has the crabs. I don't want to know who you are, but I do want your crabs. So after your colleagues have all gone, I'd like you to come back and take this jar home with you.

"I want you to take a razor and shave one half of your pubic area. Then strike a match and set the other half on fire. When the crabs run into the clearing, hit them with a spoon and while they're still stunned put them in the jar. Then when no one is around, leave it on my desk. You'll help me complete my collection, for which I'll be enormously grateful."

I doubt that anyone took him up on the offer. I don't remember anyone walking funny for a few days, which would have been a clue. ∎

Another was Malcolm Knapp – Pappy Knapp, we called him – who taught us how to build logging roads and bridges. As a class project in one of his courses, I chose to design a bridge. The design had to be handed in on April 1, and I thought it would be fun to play a little prank on Pappy: I designed a magnificent bridge, using my best drafting skills; then I had a friend, Tachi Kiuchi, one of the first Japanese students to come to UBC, replace all the writing on the drawings with their Japanese equivalents. I handed it in and in time it came back with Pappy's comments, "I don't understand a word of this, but it looks like a good bridge," and a good mark. Kiuchi, the son of a senior Japanese diplomat, later became chairman and chief executive officer of Mitsubishi Electric America. Lately he has been writing books urging business to live up to its environmental responsibilities and is the Chair of the Future 500 organization.

UBC was a much smaller place in those days and still a little rough around the edges. Instead of today's high-rise concrete dorms we were housed in renovated Army huts that had been hauled to the campus then subdivided into rooms for one to four students. We performed our ablutions in communal showers and ate in a mess hall, sitting on the same benches and eating off the same tables that soldiers had used before us. There were a number of "camps" – mine was called Acadia – and they were of course strictly separated, male from female. They were not segregated as to faculty, however, so the next generation of foresters, scientists, doctors, lawyers, and all the rest were mixed together. It gave us a wide exposure to each other's worlds.

My years at UBC coincided with a unique offshoot of the Cold War. In 1956, the Hungarians had risen against their Communist government and the Soviets had invaded to crush the revolt.

At the University of Sopron, close to the Austrian border, the professors and students of the forestry faculty resolved that they would not live under Soviet tyranny. One day the entire Sopron Forestry School – about two dozen faculty members and some two hundred students – crossed the Austrian frontier.

Sopron was a distinguished forestry school, very old by Canadian standards, having been founded almost sixty years before Canada became a country. The thought of the students and faculty being stranded in an Austrian refugee camp had an impact on Dr. George Allen, UBC's Dean of Forestry. He was an early UBC graduate who had done his post-graduate work at Berkeley, California, and had been brought back to UBC by H.R. MacMillan, BC's first chief forester and founder of the province's greatest forest company.

Phone calls flew between UBC, Ottawa and the Canadian embassy in Vienna. The entire Sopron School was invited to re-establish itself at UBC. Harold Foley, president of the Powell River Pulp and Paper Company, offered the Hungarians accommodation in Powell River until classes could begin.

The Sopron students completed their education on a parallel track, their classes separate from the rest of us in the Faculty of Forestry. But on graduation they received UBC degrees and many of them went on to make their careers in British Columbia, contributing enormously to their adoptive province. As my own career moved forward, I came to know and work with many of the "Hungarian mafia" as they were affectionately known. ▪

In my first summer after starting at UBC I wanted to work for the Forest Service but there was some problem about hiring students. I went to work instead as a compass man for the Highways Department around Revelstoke. I assisted an engineer whose task was to lay out new work and to check the work that had already been done.

These were the grand old days of highway construction in BC, with first-class new roads opening up the Interior of the province under the direction of the legendary Minister of Highways Phil Gaglardi, the MLA for Kamloops. The legend said that "Flying Phil" had never met a speed limit he couldn't ignore. Highway construction zones throughout the province were dotted with large signs bearing the minister's name and the closing words, "Sorry for any inconvenience."

One day the engineer was ill, and I was asked to take his place doing the instrument work in a steep and scary stretch of landscape that offered falling rocks on one side and a sheer drop on the other. After a couple of days the engineer was back and called me into his office. He congratulated me on having done a pretty good job but he had a question about some of my figures. They accurately defined a curve around the mountainside, he said, "But then you come around the curve, and all of a sudden there's a hundred foot drop," he said. "What do you propose to do about that?"

"Well," I said, "we could always put up a sign saying, 'Sorry for any inconvenience.'"

A few weeks later I was working way up at the top of a slope when I saw a black car drive up. A man got out and approached the engineer. I couldn't hear their conversation but I could see that the visitor was getting more and more agitated at whatever the engineer was saying. Finally they were both waving their arms and yelling at each other.

I came down the slope to see what was going on but by the time I was at the bottom the angry man had jumped into his car and roared off. "What was all that about?" I asked the engineer.

"He wanted to know what I thought about the way the Department of Highways is run."

Plainly the man hadn't liked the engineer's answers. "Aren't you worried?" I asked.

"Why should I be?"

"That was Phil Gaglardi."

I don't know if the engineer found his career cut short, but it may be that the highways minister's example had an effect on my own course through life. Or maybe it was all the times I accompanied my father to other people's houses and businesses when he was moonlighting as a preparer of tax returns. Either way, I was never happy sitting behind a desk receiving reports from afar. I always had to go and see the situation at first hand. In later life that habit would take me up jungle rivers and across the windswept plains of Anatolia. And sometimes, as with Flying Phil's encounter with the engineer, I would be lucky enough to meet people who would reward me with that rare commodity, the unvarnished truth.

By the end of that summer, I was glad to get back into school and again take up the study of forestry. Indeed, I have never regretted choosing forestry as my career; it is a varied way of life, no one day exactly like another. I could never have spent my life laying out one mile of highway after the next, each with exactly the same width and depth of asphalt, or overseeing the production of an endless stream of identical ingots.

And I could not have met and associated with a better class of people than foresters. No matter where I have gone in the world, no matter what problems I have encountered, I had only to find my way

Grandmother Apsey expressed a genteel sense of alarm when she heard that I was going into forestry. My studies at UBC coincided with the infamous bribery scandal which resulted in BC Forests Minister Bob Sommers, who had grown much too close to some members of the forest industry, becoming the first cabinet minister in the Commonwealth to be sent to jail.

"Are you sure?" she asked me.

"I'm sure."

"Well perhaps I'll have a word with McGregor about it."

It was not until long after that I realized that this acquaintance of hers named McGregor was British Columbia's Chief Justice Gordon McGregor Sloan, whose 1945 and 1956 Royal Commissions on the province's forest sector laid the basis for BC policy for over thirty years. ▪

to the nearest forester to receive instant help. We are a worldwide community.

I have never met a forester who did not love the forest. No forester was ever trained to destroy a forest, but to preserve and value it. Some foresters, especially in the developing world, can find that our expert championing of the forest is not enough to override the greed and short-sightedness of those who hold economic and political power. It is an imperfect world, but the forester's love of the forest is nonetheless as perfect a love as we fallible humans can manage.

I spent two summers working with the Canadian Forest Service. The first year, I was stationed near 100 Mile House in the BC Interior, part of a small crew of students under the direction of Peter Paul, a CFS forester. He was conducting research as part of a project to establish a fire-hazard rating system.

We were situated outside of town in tents by a small creek, with a trailer in which we cooked and ate most meals. For supper we would go to the 100 Mile Lodge, which was owned by a religious cult called the Emissaries of Divine Light; in fact, just about everything in 100 Mile House except the police station and the forest service office was owned by the Emissaries, who were led by a British aristocrat named William Martin Alleyne Cecil, Marquess of Exeter, a descendant of Queen Elizabeth I's favourite privy councillor. He had a large cattle ranch in the area.

I had taken an English course at UBC that examined utopian societies in literature. Now I was seeing one in the round: the Emissaries shared their possessions communally – even their spouses, I was told. One of them, a young woman who sometimes prepared our lunches, took a shine to me. One day, she put four hardboiled eggs in my lunch bag, each bearing a single word that together formed the sentence, "Mike, I love you." As luck would have it, my lunch bag ended up in the hands of one of the other guys on the crew, exposing me to considerable teasing but possibly saving me from a life spent among the Emissaries of Divine Light.

As part of our research, we went out to observe fires as they were happening. At one fire, near Tatlayoko Lake in the Chilcotin country, bulldozers were gouging fire lines through the bush and we followed into the heart of the fire zone, measuring temperatures and humidity and making notes about what kind of vegetation and debris was on the ground as well as the type and age of the forest and other factors relevant to how the fire might spread.

Since we were there, the fire boss decided we might as well be useful and asked us to set some backfires. These are controlled burns that are deliberately set to consume fuel in front of the fire so that, when it arrives, there is nothing to keep it going. Despite the images of water bombers and tanker trucks that the reader may have seen on television, very few forest fires are ever put out the way house fires are; unless it is caught almost immediately, just about the only thing to do with a forest fire is to contain it with fire lines and back-burning, then let it burn itself out.

One of the tools fire fighters used for controlling backfires was a metal backpack filled with water and fitted with a hose and a pump much like a bicycle air pump. The operator pumped and the water squirted out. I had the bright idea that we could more easily get the backfires going if we filled one of these tanks with gasoline; then, while one of the other crewmen held a burning stick in front of the flow, we would have a home-made flame-thrower. We tried it and it worked well, spewing flaming liquid that ignited the brush.

The fire boss wanted us to start the fires in the evening around the edges of the area he had selected, so that they would burn overnight; when the temperature rose in the morning, the fires would move toward the centre of the selected zone. He had also assigned a couple of young Aboriginal men to work with us. While we budding forest scientists lit our fires with my flame spitting invention, they went about assembling piles of twigs here and there and getting them started. We sniggered at their feeble efforts. But when morning came, our flame-thrower ignited blazes had all burned out overnight, while theirs were flaring up nicely and doing the job the fire boss wanted done.

There was a lesson there that I was to see repeated in other parts of the world, once – in a Colombian jungle – to my great benefit: people who live in and with the forest, as their ancestors have done for millennia, can be the inheritors of knowledge that may not yet be dreamed of in our philosophies. We would be wise not to scoff and snigger, but to open our minds to traditional knowledge.

Another day that summer, one of our crew, Jenji Konishi, came across a fire that had been started by a lightning strike not far from our camp. We all rushed into town to report it to the forest service then drove back to study this blaze that was just getting up a head of steam. We forestry students were out in the middle of the fire,

I was driving along a country road in Manitoba when I passed an Indian man and woman. He was riding a horse. She was trudging along behind, carrying all of their belongings; they were piled on her head, tucked under both her arms, strapped to her back.

I had to stop. I went over to the man and found myself at a loss for words. I finally managed to sputter out the obvious question.

He looked down at me and replied, in a way that said the answer was equally obvious, "She got no horse."

Sometimes the way you see the world is just the way you see it. ■

taking measurements and jotting down notes, when the Forest Service arrived with a gang of freshly conscripted fire fighters.

In those days, regulations granted BC Forest Rangers the authority to draft any able-bodied man to fight a fire. In 100 Mile House that day, the ranger had used a time-hallowed method of drafting a crew: he went into the men-only section of the local pub and ordered everybody into the trucks. The conscripts were delivered to the fire site, handed tools and told to get to work.

Many men conscripted into fire fighting under those circumstances were not unhappy about it: they were in the beer parlour in the middle of the day because the woods were too dry for logging, and fire fighting was paid work. But it turned out that two of the draftees had been meeting in the pub to sign the papers that would see a new sawmill built in the area. They did not appreciate being put to unanticipated manual labour, and even less did they want to see healthy young men apparently larking about twirling odd-looking instruments – for measuring humidity – over our heads. Only some very fast explaining spared me from a shovel across the side of the head.

For my next summer, the Canadian Forest Service sent me to the southeastern corner of Manitoba. The place where we stayed, Dawson Cabin, is a historic site on the old Dawson Trail, which was the main route between Lake Superior and the Red River before the CPR was built.

I was teamed with a young forestry student from Laval University in Quebec. We dug soil pits in various types of forest in the area, part of a research effort to determine the relationships among soils, forest productivity and what is now called biodiversity. I am sure that the data we collected was useful to someone, somewhere, but the knowledge I retain from the experience is that in a southeastern Manitoba summer, a new type of insect appears every couple of weeks. Each new arrival is meaner and nastier than the one it supersedes, mosquitoes giving way to no-see-ums, no-see-ums stepping aside for horseflies, and so on in an unending concatenation of appetites for the flesh and blood of innocent forestry students.

The worst of them were the ticks. Other biting insects are hit-and-run raiders; ticks want to move in for the duration. I had had some experience of ticks in the Okanagan, and once assured that the Manitoba variety did not carry Rocky Mountain spotted fever, I was less worried about them. But at the end of every day out in the woods my fellow research assistant and I would have to strip off and inspect each other closely, applying a just extinguished match to our new tenants, that being the only way to evict them. I felt more sorry for the wildlife and the dogs on nearby farms which would become infested. We spent some time trying to de-tick an occasional dog, never with much success.

But for me the real lesson of my summer in Manitoba came from going there and coming back on the train, seeing the immense size of our great country as it constantly unrolled outside the window of my rail car – and the size of the forest that stands on it in all its glorious variety. By the end of that summer, ticks or not, I was hooked on the forest. I knew it would offer me a fascinating way of life and an opportunity to go out into the wide world and meet a lot of interesting people.

I went back for my last year of university with a clear sense that I had found my path and that I was on my way. I had made another decision, too. I went to Winnipeg and visited some Millars from my grandmother's side who were in the jewellery business. I picked out a nice diamond, carried it back to Vancouver and placed it on the finger of the lady with whom I wanted to share my life. Fortunately, she was of the same mind.

I graduated in 1961, wearing an academic gown, a new jacket on my back and the unaccustomed sensation of a tie around my neck. I walked across the stage in UBC's old armoury and Chancellor Dal Grauer tapped me with his hat to signify that, for the first time in recorded history, an Apsey of my lineage had earned a university degree. My parents had come down from the Okanagan for the occasion. They were proud of me and I was proud to have made them so.

I had a job to go to before I received my degree, not an uncommon circumstance for university graduates in those days. During exams, a recruiter from the provincial government came looking for me. I believe he had got my name from Harry Smith.

Like many students, I was not at my most presentable during exams. There was a tendency not to sleep very much, nor to attend closely to the civilized arts of washing, shaving and putting on clean clothes. I came to the interview looking as if I might have spent the night under the Georgia Viaduct.

The man from the government was not put off by my appearance. In a lengthy interview he told me that his office, the Bureau of Economics and Statistics with the Department of Industrial Development, Trade and Commerce, was looking for a bright young man. The job would be that of an economist and statistician, preparing materials for Crown corporations or private companies that wanted to start up or expand their operations in BC. I would also be required to prepare the forest industry sections of regional economic development surveys.

Most of my friends were lining up jobs with forest companies or the Forest Service and there was a lot of talk about how much they would be earning. The $130 a month that the man from the Bureau was offering me was less than my classmates would be getting, but I wasn't concerned. My standard of comparison was what my father had earned as a bookkeeper, and I was already ahead of him.

Besides, it wasn't a question of money. My course work had developed in me an inclination to see big pictures. Designing forest roads and bridges or developing harvesting plans for this or that stand of timber was good, but I wanted to spend my career enjoying the view from atop the highest hill I could climb. I wanted scope.

There was another reason: it's a cliché that knowledge is power; it's a less recognized fact that knowledge is also a lot of fun. It was fun to be in the know. I liked knowing what was happening. I enjoyed working out what ought to come next and then seeing if it did. The Bureau of Economics and Statistics sounded like not only a place from which I would see a pretty big picture, but an opportunity to get paid for having fun. I took the job.

I moved to Victoria, leaving my fiance Sharon in Vancouver, where she was already teaching at an elementary school. At first I shared an apartment downtown with a succession of other young men who were starting out in life, but soon after I moved to an apartment across the street from Beacon Hill Park. Then as now, Victoria was home to many retirees and I was the youngest person in the building.

My office was in the Douglas Building, near the Royal British Columbia Museum and across the street from the Legislature. I shared space with another young man starting out on a career in public service, Larry Bell. Later, he would become Premier Bill Bennett's indispensable "Deputy Minister of Everything." As I write this, he is Chairman of the Board of BC Hydro.

The work was even more fascinating than I thought it would be. There has never been such a time in the history of British Columbia, nor do I believe its like will ever come again. The great post-war economic expansion was in full flow and our province was racing forward in all directions: hydroelectricity, transportation, lumber, pulp and paper, mining and smelting, construction. Every sector of the economy was taking off.

The government of W.A.C. Bennett was doing all in its power to urge on the good times. The Premier, a self-described "blunt businessman" who had built up a chain of hardware stores in the Okanagan, had a clear vision of where he wanted to take British Columbia. He had recently "provincialized" the BC Electric Company and renamed it, and now BC Hydro was embarking on an epic series of dam-building projects. The province had also bought the Pacific Great Eastern Railway and was resolved to push its lines into the far north. I'd already seen at first hand the network of new blacktop and bridges that was opening up the Interior.

There was no part of the province that wasn't being seriously looked at for development. Although W.A.C. Bennett was the undisputed leader of his party and government, his cabinet was full of forceful

Years later, while serving with the UN in Turkey, I met former Prime Minister Lester Pearson when he was chairing a World Bank commission on international development (he was recommending that the industrialized countries should increase their resource transfers to low-income countries to a minimum of 1 per cent of GNP as rapidly as possible; that target remains unmet). At a reception, I found him alone staring out a window and we had a good, long chat about development and forests and so on. At the end he asked me, "Where are you from?"

"British Columbia," I said.

He praised the beauty of my home province and asked what town I came from.

I told him that I was born and raised in Vernon but that my parents now lived in Kelowna.

"Oh,' he said, "his town."

I knew he meant Premier Bennett. Before I could say anything, Pearson said, "That man will go down in Canadian history as one of the finest premiers that the country has seen. But, Mike, he's not my kind of people." ■

ministers, all of them strong advocates for growth. My department was under the leadership of Robert Bonner, one of the most senior members of the cabinet. Ray Williston, Minister of Lands and Forests, was another force to be reckoned with.

There was a lot of action and I felt myself to be part of it. I have some sympathy for those who are doing that kind of government work in today's economy. Forty-odd years ago, British Columbia was still a frontier province; people were still pioneering, building mills and mines and whole new communities, opening up great stretches of land to new development and settlement. Whole new industries were being born in the Interior. It was boom times, year after year.

Ray Williston was perhaps one of the last of the fun-time forest ministers. Until the sixties, the forest industry of British Columbia was primarily a coastal industry. The coast was where the big trees grew and where there was easy transportation for a product that could float down a river or be towed by a sea-going tug. The trees in the Interior were smaller and of different species and the rivers did not run toward the markets of the US Midwest and east coast.

But technology had been driving change since the end of the Second World War: tougher trucks, powerful chainsaws, more sophisticated mills. Meanwhile, the markets for wood products continued to grow with the general expansion of western economies that had been building all through the 1950s.

Forest Minister Ray Williston was in the fortunate position of having a largely untapped Crown resource at a time when proponents of resource projects were figuratively lining up outside his door. All he had to do was allocate harvesting rights and the entrepreneurs would run out and build a pulp mill and a town to go with it. People would flock to the new venture to take high-paying union jobs or open businesses to serve all those thousands of new workers with their well-filled pay packets.

The minister brought in a new form of licence, the Pulpwood Harvesting Agreement, which ensured a wood supply for those who wanted to build pulp mills in the Interior and made the projects attractive to investors. Ray Williston got a lot of credit for that instrument, and rightly so. But those who look back on those days as a guide to how we should conduct forest policy today are letting nostalgia cloud their view of reality.

In the early sixties we hadn't yet bumped our heads on any lids to growth. The sky was the limit and the British Columbia frontier offered the opportunity of prosperity for all – what W.A.C. Bennett would come to call "The Good Life." Today, it is a much different matter. Some forty years on, forest ministers have no new trees to bestow; the job now is to allocate a limited resource among contending uses, taking into account many non-commercial values that were not even contemplated in Williston's time.

I was a forest economist working in a government department dedicated to fostering economic growth, in a time when young men seeking careers were being drawn into government and industry. I often found myself seated down the table from the high and mighty of the day, including Premier Bennett, his senior ministers and important visitors from overseas – Europe and Japan were increasingly seen as promising sources of customers and investment. My role in these meetings was not to offer opinions, but whenever a policy discussion required a leavening of fact and figure, I was expected to provide it.

As the man with the numbers, my stock in trade was the line graph. It was soon made clear to me that Premier Bennett had strict rules regarding any graph that might be presented to his gaze. It must proceed from left to right and it must show an upward trend.

When faced with a raw mass of statistics, part of my job was always to see which of them could be arranged so that the graph would go up and to the right. The sole exception was a graphic depiction of unemployment, which the Premier preferred to see in decline.

When the push was on to develop the hydroelectric potential of the Interior, someone far above me in rank came to me and asked, "Mike, we're going to build this huge dam. How many pulp mills can we build using the power it will generate?"

"None," I said.

"What do you mean 'none?'"

I explained. "Pulp mills don't need hydroelectric power. They can generate their own power by burning waste from the mills."

"No, you don't understand. I need to know how many pulp mills could be powered by this dam?"

So I gave him a number in the range of forty and he was happy. ■

I was not a close confidant of the Premier, and cannot report any secrets that have not already found their way to the light of historians' scrutiny. I can say, however, that he was a good man to work for. To begin with, I was slightly in awe of him, of course. But I found him to be open and unaffected. Rather than offer a perfunctory handshake and move on, he would stop to talk even with someone as far down the precedence totem pole as I was, and if he asked a commonplace question – "What are you working on?" – he seemed genuinely interested in the answer.

In our more complex era, the years of the first Bennett government are viewed by some as a time when government was run on a seat-of-the-pants basis. Major projects were supposedly calculated on the back of an envelope. I can testify that such was not the case. I was continuously involved in developing our department's report on the economic conditions in the province that went to cabinet every week. Another prime objective was to improve the statistical base from which we could understand and predict what was happening and what would come next.

My focus was mainly on the forest sector, and I worked with the Forest Service on developing statistics on harvesting, silviculture and other areas of interest – Larry Bell, at the next desk, was doing equivalent work on other issues – but I also found my scope expanding. There is nothing like being an analyst in a bureau of economics to teach the truth of what Lenin once said, though he had another

I was often invited to the formal events when the Premier and his ministers received visitors from abroad. One of the first I attended was for a large group of Europeans in a spacious dining room at the Empress Hotel.

It was a full-fig formal banquet. I was seated with some distinguished European gentlemen at a table right in front of the head table, where Premier Bennett sat with the senior members of the delegation. Before me on the snowy white tablecloth were more pieces of cutlery than I had ever seen assembled around one plate. There were knives to the right and forks to the left, several of each, with various spoons to back them up. There were some pieces of cutlery I could not even identify.

My grandmother, better versed than I in such matters, had advised me to start at the outside and work my way in. I was doing well enough until they brought the soup. It came in an odd looking bowl that had a small handle on either side. I chose a spoon and set to, but it soon became difficult work because of the shape of the bowl.

I decided to watch the Premier and copy his moves. He was using the same spoon as I and could soon see that he was having the same difficulty as he got to the bottom of the bowl.

Then he put down the spoon, picked up the bowl by its handles, tilted it up and drained it down. I looked around and everybody else was doing the same. I followed suit.

When I got home I looked it up in Emily Post and, sure enough, it was proper etiquette. But I bet if I'd done it in front of my grandmother she'd have rapped my knuckles. ■

context in mind: everything is connected to everything else. I developed linkages with my counterparts at the Dominion Bureau of Statistics, as StatsCan was then known, preparing briefs for federal-provincial conferences on forestry and forest products. I worked with other producers of numbers in industry and the academic community to pull together interesting information and turn it into useful publications. I also connected with people doing similar work in other provinces, though there wasn't much inter-provincial cross-fertilization in those days. I thought we should know what the competition was doing.

Knowledge is fun. More knowledge is more fun. The more you understand your options, the better your decision-making. Sometimes a little more knowledge, just a few facts and figures that nobody has yet looked at too closely, can open a whole new range of options. Five hundred years ago, people could go out and discover whole new continents. Today, there are no more continents to find, but whole new worlds can still open before us if we ask the right questions – especially if we ask questions that begin with "What if...?" Questions like: what if we made dimension lumber out of lodgepole pine. The answer is: you get a whole new lumber industry in the Interior. Nowadays it's called lateral thinking or thinking "outside the box." In my time at the Bureau, it was just called asking questions. And answering them was a lot of fun.

This was my first real job, working with trained people who were older than I and more experienced. Going in, my natural concern had been whether I could cut the mustard. But I worked hard and learned fast and within a short time I knew I was pulling my weight. My work was appreciated.

Besides developing confidence and experience, I was also finding my own style. Although I was an economist and analyst, I didn't want to sit in an office surrounded by the ebb and flow of nothing but numbers, drawing conclusions and making recommendations solely on the way things came out of the calculator. I had an urge to go and take a look at the reality behind the stats, and I began to travel up and down Vancouver Island – to the mills at Crofton, Chemainus, Nanaimo, Port Alberni, Campbell River – then over to the mainland. I would look things over, talk to the people who worked the machinery, get a feel for the place, a grasp of the way things worked. Back at the office, someone might have asked, "Where's Apsey?" But they soon got used to my forays.

The centerpieces of BC's development plans in those days were dams and highways. Both meant the loss of forest lands. People recognized even forty-odd years ago that flooding a valley to create a hydroelectric reservoir means drowning an ecosystem, even if words like ecosystem and biodiversity hadn't come into the public lexicon then. But we knew that we were trading a forest and all that went with it for a source of electricity.

People were – and still are – less aware of how much forest has been taken away to make room for those smooth, wide highways that we love to drive on. But every thousand kilometres of hundred-metre wide road allowance is a hundred square kilometres of land. In British Columbia, most highway rights-of-way go through forest, because forest covers most of British Columbia. Add in the railroads, the pipelines and the hydroelectric transmission corridors, and you find that we've turned tens of thousands of square kilometres of forest into transportation corridors. Then add all the forest land that's been cleared for farms, towns, cities, and all the other uses we have for formerly forested land, everything from garbage dumps to golf courses, and it's a staggering amount of land that used to grow trees for harvest.

Even back in 1961, with the memories of the clearcuts I'd seen in the Kootenays and those great spruce logs going to the pulp mills, I was asking myself whether we were doing right by the forest. It was a question any forester couldn't help but ask. The answer grew on me, gradually, when I looked at the question from the forest's point of view.

We humans think that we're the dominant form of life on planet Earth. It's a natural mistake that comes from looking at the world from our point of view. From the point of view of the forest, the real dominant life form for the past 250 million years, we're just another passing nuisance. It will be here long after we are gone.

Most of us are familiar with images of Mayan cities buried in jungle, eerie stone temples wreathed in creeper vines with trees growing out of what were once vast plazas paved in flagstones. Exactly the same thing would happen to most of our cities if we walked away from them. It would take longer, because northern tree species are slower growing than those of Yucatan, but the end result would be just the same.

Consider the walkway outside my house in a rural suburb of Victoria: it's made of concrete; every now and then I have to scrub away the green film of moss that springs eternal on the walk's pebbly surface. If I stopped doing it, the moss would thicken and deepen. Its detritus would accumulate and become soil. Grass and other more complex plants would eventually crowd out the moss, and the humus of their generations would make yet more soil. Eventually, when things were right, the trees would come in, and a forest would grow.

Does it sound too far-fetched, to go from moss on bare concrete to trees growing in rich soil? Then consider this: only some twelve thousand years ago – an eye blink in the life span of much of the earth's forest – it was under hundreds if not thousands of metres of solid glacial ice. When the glaciers melted, do you think they left topsoil behind? No, they left rocks and pebbles and grit and sand that was soon colonized by opportunistic moss and lichen. As soon as these pioneers had done their work, the grasses and ground covering plants moved in, only to be crowded out in turn by fast-growing trees which in turn were edged aside by the big, slow-growing cedars and firs and pines.

The key fact about the forest is its resilience. It takes a great deal to kill a forest and even then – witness the survival of the cedars of Lebanon – it comes back. It is relentless and it is renewable. Our help can speed things up and, by silvicultural techniques, we can leapfrog the regrowth cycle over the phase of fast-growing "weed trees" – i.e., trees for which we don't yet have an economic use – but whether we help or not the forest will come back.

In the early 1960s, I hadn't come to that conclusion, but I was beginning to understand that there was more strength to the forest than many of us realize. The forest is the natural inheritor of any landscape that is not too high, too dry or too cold – and that includes most of the surface of this planet that we think we own.

In April of 1962, at a small church in White Rock, Sharon and I were married. For our honeymoon, we drove down to the Oregon coast, a suitably dramatic seascape of crashing surf and wave-washed rocks in which to begin a lifelong adventure in matrimony. After a day or two, Sharon noticed that she had broken out in small red spots and wasn't feeling too well. It was measles, an occupational hazard often faced by teachers of young children back then.

We cut short our honeymoon and came home. Sharon was still living in Vancouver because she had to finish out the school year. I went back to my bachelor apartment across from Beacon Hill Park and subsequently found myself daubed with red spots. I quarantined myself, lying in bed and coping as best I could with the disease's fever and cough. Then one day I heard a timid tapping and dragged myself to the door.

I opened it. There was no one there. I peered around the jamb and saw, as far away as the length of the hallway would allow, two of my neighbours, a pair of tiny spinster ladies of advanced age. They had deduced that I was ill and offered to help me if they could, though they would come no closer than their present distance. I have never been sure whether the space they wanted between them and me was for protection against the measles virus or just because I was a man, but I lived on the soup and groceries they left on my doorstep, always skittering away before I came out to get the food. It was an act of kindness for which I was grateful. Apart from the normal childhood ailments, I had never had anything more serious than flu and had not experienced the loneliness that comes from being ill and on your own.

As I was nearing the end of two years with the Bureau, a married man with the future to think of, it seemed a good idea to take a post-graduate degree. I applied for and was awarded a fellowship at the University of California at Berkeley. I resigned from the civil service and Sharon and I went south.

We rented an apartment in Oakland. I then went to the university to claim my fellowship and begin instructing in forest economics. But it turned out that the system among academics in California was more competitive than I had understood; I was told that I was a few days too late and that all the fellowships in forest economics had already been handed out.

They did have a fellowship in dendrology and, having studied under Vladimir Krajina, I felt up to the challenge. They put me in charge of a lab group of young students. I showed up in a suit and tie, as any instructor – and many of the students – would have done in

There didn't seem much point teaching dendrology in a classroom when the Berkeley campus offered a magnificent variety of tree species. I asked the campus gardeners for a map and assigned an individual tree to each of my students.

"Over the course of the term," I told them, "I want you to make regular observations of your tree and record any changes that you see. Make notes and turn those notes into written descriptions which you will deliver in class. I also want you to make drawings."

One of the first students to make his report, a young man of considerable artistic skill, presented a well-realized and detailed drawing of his tree on a large sheet of paper.

Underneath the tree was an equally explicit representation of a young couple making love.

It was Berkeley and the sixties were about to burst upon us. ∎

my UBC days. I was the most formally dressed person in the room. The seeds of the sixties counterculture were already sprouting at Berkeley; two years later, in 1964, they would blossom into the Free Speech Movement when some of the campus's students, freshly back from "freedom rides" into the segregated American South, took on the university's administration over the question of whether they had the right to distribute political pamphlets outside the Berkeley gates.

I liked the work, but it soon became clear that the botany fellowship was not enough to live on. It occurs to me to wonder what might have happened if I had arrived at Berkeley a little earlier and obtained that fellowship in forest economics. Many people who were at that campus in the following years found their lives drastically altered. Berkeley was a prime source of brave young men and women who went down into their country's southern states to march with Martin Luther King and sit in at lunch counters where America's black citizens could not get service. The treatment handed out to those Freedom Riders, as they were called – the beatings and roustings by Ku Klux Klanners and racist cops – radicalized many of them.

It's hard to imagine Mike Apsey as a beaded and bearded student activist, but stranger transformations have occurred.

As it was, Sharon and I packed up and came back to British Columbia. I felt I had seen enough of the government side of things for a while and began nosing about to see what kind of job I might be able to get in the private sector.

CHAPTER FOUR

What a Hell of a Way to Run a Company

Not long after I returned to BC and let it be known that I was looking for work, I was approached by Archie McGougan, a senior officer of the pulp and paper group at MacMillan Bloedel and Powell
River Ltd. (later to become just MacMillan Bloedel Ltd.). When I'd
been working for the government, I'd regularly been in touch with
the company to gather information and occasionally to trade in
that essential commodity. I've always believed that the more knowledge that's in circulation the better it is for everybody; it's the data-
management equivalent of the economic maxim that a rising tide
lifts all boats.

So Archie McGougan knew who I was and what I could do and
he thought that I would fit nicely into his market research group.
After a lengthy discussion, I came to the same conclusion and took
the job. I went in as a junior analyst and came out five years later as
the senior man.

The company was then housed in an office building at Pender and
Bute, with the pulp and paper marketing team occupying the third
floor. One of the marketing managers at the time was Ray Smith,
who later went on to become MB's president and chief executive officer and ended his career as chairman of the board. When I met him
he was the man down the hall whose office door was always open to
young staff who needed advice or an intelligent sounding-board. He

was a gentleman in the old-fashioned sense of the word, who became a mentor to me throughout my career. I was not unique in that distinction; Ray Smith helped many people make their way in the BC forest sector. We could always count on him to offer sage advice, suggest a name to make contact with or ask an insightful question that unexpectedly threw clarifying light on a dilemma.

The man at the top of the company pyramid in those years was the president, Charlie Specht. I didn't have much contact with him, but one time I did have occasion to go up to his office to introduce a senior high school student named Greg Holmes. A number of us in the company were involved with the Junior Achievement program and Greg was president of one of the entrepreneur groups we sponsored.

I thought it would be instructive for him to meet a titan of industry so I took Greg up to the ninth floor to the president's office so that he could offer Charlie Specht a share in the students' small enterprise: the manufacture and sale of wooden tie racks.

The company president handed over the one dollar share price and received his certificate. As we were leaving, he said, "I suppose that's the last I'll see of that dollar."

Even though I'd been vetted and accepted by Archie McGougan, I still couldn't be officially offered the job until I'd been looked over and approved by Gary Bowell, the pulp and paper group's senior vice president who later went on to run a number of different companies in Vancouver. A Rhodes scholar and a graduate of the Harvard Business School, he was very many rungs above a junior market analyst. He asked me only one question: "What do you want from this company?"

I looked about his office. It seemed very pleasant. "I think I want your job," I said.

"Then get to work," he said. ▪

Charlie Specht, me, and Greg Holmes. MACDEL – A Junior Achievement Company Counselled by MacMillan Bloedel Ltd. "Company of the Year – Best in Area," 1967.

But the kids worked hard. They researched and learned how to cut costs and went out and sold. When the project was wrapped up, I escorted Greg Holmes back to Charlie Specht's office where he handed the investor a cheque for $1.30, after tax.

"A 30 per cent return on investment," MB's president said. "I wish we could do that in *this* company."

During the five years I worked there, MacMillan Bloedel was a company in transition. Over the previous ten years it had more than doubled in size, amalgamating – in a merger-turned-takeover – with the Powell River Pulp and Paper Company, a long-established pulp and paper producer. The restructuring that followed the amalgamation had not been painless.

I was part of the chain of people who worked through the company's highly detailed process leading to capital expenditures above a certain limit. One thing I soon noticed was that whenever the purchase of a new piece of equipment was being considered, the argument in favour of the new technology always predicted large net returns on investment – as much as 25 to 30 per cent. Strangely, though, when the new equipment was bought and installed, overall ROI remained flat.

In a meeting where one of these acquisitions was being discussed I piped up and asked why there was this discrepancy. The manager who wanted to make the purchase looked down the table at me and said, "Apsey, why are you always asking these kinds of questions?" and the discussion moved on.

Still, I continued to do rigorous, all-encompassing analyses of the effects on the company of buying individual pieces of production machinery. On the other hand, sometimes word would come down from the highest echelons of management that, without warning, MB had just bought another entire company.

"Fit it in," the bosses would say. And we would. ■

What we would now call the corporate culture of MB was changing. The old, top-down management style, with reporting relationships functioning on almost military lines, was giving way to a more modern spirit. My own hiring, while certainly not a significant step for one of Canada's largest forest products companies, was still a small straw in the wind that was beginning to blow through the industry. I had developed the beginnings of a reputation for asking original questions and coming up with novel proposals, and one of the standing orders given me by Archie McGougan was, "Mike, we want you to use your imagination."

A lot of people in MacMillan Bloedel were exercising their imaginations through the mid-sixties. The company was expanding in several directions. Oddly, though the BC Interior was then blossoming with new pulp mills and sawmills turning lodgepole pine and Interior spruce and fir into dimension lumber for the booming US housing industry, MB had no interest in going over the mountains to where so many others, like Poldi Bentley of Canfor, were finding opportunities.

But the forest industry in BC had begun as a coastal industry and MB was a coastal company. It never went into the Interior, though it went to many other parts of the world. I wouldn't say that the senior management and directors had a blind spot about the Interior, but they consistently found more attractive opportunities on the other side of the continent or across the oceans.

The expansion was a combination of vertical and horizontal integration, both of which were considered good things in the sixties. MB horizontally expanded into pulp and paper production in eastern Canada and in Europe. New machines went in at the company pulp and paper operations in Powell River and Port Alberni. The wood products group – especially plywood – was aggressively seeking new markets. The company invested in vertical integration: corrugated box companies in Britain, and Royal Dutch Paper Mills on the continent, plus a linerboard plant in Alabama that was a joint venture with the United Fruit Company. MB even had specialized importing companies in Europe and the US to bring in and market the company's products.

The business decisions behind all of this constant growing and changing were based on a sophisticated matrix of facts expressed in numbers, and my job was to build and maintain part of that matrix. It was more than just being able to generate the internal statistics: figures on production, sales, costs of the past, present and future. I was responsible for creating an accurate numerical portrait of our competitors in Canada and around the world, their planned expansions, their customer bases, both actual and potential, the products they made now and the new products they might make later, and the even newer products that were just glimmering on the horizon.

It was the kind of work I very much enjoyed. I'm sure I inherited from my father a talent for numbers. They were never just marks on paper. They sang to me. But I understood from early on that numbers are more useful for understanding history than for projecting the future. I could get a lot out of the business journals and the figures generated by governments and industry associations, but there are always facts that don't find their way into the columns of numbers. I was often out of the office in search of those facts.

Just as at the Bureau of Economics and Statistics I took every opportunity to get out into the field. To me, second-hand information was always second-best. It's fine to sit in an office and think about numbers and develop cases and models, but it's all academic until you go and actually talk to people in the mills and the woods and the marketplace. That's where you get the context, and context is everything. A key part of the context was the people who were in and around the issues I was dealing with – not just mill managers or marketing executives, but the mayors and councils, the local business owners.

If you're going to do market research, you have to go out into the market. I did a lot of travelling in the United States, already a prime market for MB and with plenty of room for future growth. I was looking for the settings into which the statistics would fit, the changing conditions that can bend the line on a graph projection far beyond what mere numbers may indicate. I went out and talked to consumers and buyers, got a sense of what they were thinking and what they wanted to see happen.

And I went more than once, because the world was changing even as I studied it. Today's world changes even faster, and even more profoundly. There is a lot more to be understood and a much more pressing need to get it right. Look around in today's business environment and you can see the companies that are good at market intelligence; the reason you can't see the ones that didn't get it right is because they no longer exist.

I had plenty of work to do at MB and I found it engrossing. I conducted studies of major pulp and paper products, which in those days included kraft pulp, sulphite pulp, dissolving pulp, linerboard, sack kraft, newsprint and fine papers. I had to identify expansion opportunities and profitable marketing strategies.

I also prepared a wide range of regular reports, such as long- and short-term demand forecasts as well as production and capacity surveys. I did a survey of the effects of free trade following the then recently completed Kennedy Round of international tariff reduction agreements.

I examined the forests and forest products capacities of other countries, to forecast what they might bring to world trade and how that might affect MB's interests. I performed the same kind of analysis and assessment on individual forest products companies. Someone would say, "Mike give us a report on the Company X," or "Take a look at the potential for eucalyptus pulp," and I would gather all the information I could, make sense of it in my head, then apply insight and imagination to see where it would all lead to in five or ten years.

A lot of my work factored into the continuous expansion that was the major focus of MacMillan Bloedel in those years. One project I worked on, for example, was the joint venture with United Fruit to build a linerboard plant at Pine Hill, Alabama. The economics of that project were heavily influenced by the availability of generous state and county grants and low-interest loans. I got a good grasp of the extent to which US forest companies were subsidized, a subject that was to take on ironic significance years later when I was involved in fighting the lumber wars against US protectionism.

On the other hand, not all of my good ideas became company policy. I prepared what I considered a very persuasive report entitled "Lumber Wrap – Potential Usage in BC," which argued that paper-wrapped lumber was definitely the coming thing and that it would be a good idea for MB to get in on the ground floor. But someone above me in the chain of command said, "I don't think so," and it never became a staple product of the company.

But there were plenty of other products and places to expand into in the sixties and, like many corporations, MacMillan Bloedel was committed to the idea that bigger was better. Corporate leaders were beginning to see the world as a global marketplace – a cliché today but still only an emerging reality then – and the thinking was that having operations in different parts of the world or branching into different product lines would offer more balance to the balance sheet. A drop in sales in one sector or an economic downturn in one region would be counterweighted by improvements in other parts of the company's broadly based interests.

Eventually, however, the conglomerate comes to be seen as too broadly based. "We've got to get back to our core business," becomes the phrase of the day. "Stick to your knitting" becomes the advice from the same management consultants who earlier urged expansion and diversification. Then the ancillary operations are sold off and the corporation goes back to doing what it knows best until the next cycle of expansionism seizes the imagination of boards and CEOs, and off they go again. I've seen several of these cycles over the past forty years and I expect to see more of them.

One thing that my years at MacMillan Bloedel taught me was an appreciation for the importance of research and development or "science and technology" as it is referred to these days. MB had a fine research and development component, where some very able scientists and engineers were constantly researching ways to improve production processes and to develop innovative products. It was a shame that, shortly before the company was sold to Weyerhaeuser, the R&D group was disbanded. I now believe it was done to "tidy up" the company so that it would be easier to sell.

I suppose the R&D outfit must have looked like one of those unnecessary cost centres that could be dispensed with. That was, of course, within the company's purview. But I think the easy dissolution of a first-rate research and development facility bespeaks a short-sighted attitude that is all too common within the Canadian forest sector.

We have had a far from exemplary record when it comes to doing science and technology research in our own industry. There have been some strong actors who have maintained an effort over the long term – MB was one of them until the decision to sell the company was taken – but mostly it has been a hit-or-miss business, without enough long-term commitment.

I don't know why it is this way. Canadian corporations in many other sectors of the economy – like telecommunications, health care technology, transportation – have maintained strong commitments to R&D and have become world leaders as a result. Forest-related companies in Scandinavia, the United States and other parts of the world have done well out of developing and exporting technologies. But in Canada, the attitude is, "Oh, someone's developed a new machine? I'll buy the Mark II version." We wait for the second-generation technology, and see no problem in letting the scientists and technologists of other countries do much of our R&D for us. All too often those researchers are talented Canadians who have had to leave their own country to find a place where they can put their brains to work.

I wish I could pinpoint the problem. Is it the tax regime? Is it something in the psychology of those who rise to the top in the corporate hierarchies of our forest firms? Is it just a lack of original thinking? I don't know, but I have sat on a number of committees and attended any number of conferences to discuss the sad state of forest-related research and development in Canada.

We get together in some convention hotel or government conference centre and review the history, speculate about the future and produce our recommendations full of bold wonder. Then we disband until someone calls another conference and we come back and do it all over again.

The reason that we have had to do it time and again is that there is usually no follow-up plan. We throw our expert recommendations out into the world of the Canadian forest sector, where they fall to the ground and lie there unnoticed. There is no implementation plan, no "who's going to do what and by when."

It's fun to go to conferences, to argue and predict and prognosticate, but these days I'm far too busy to spend my time just having fun. I want to see the prospect of real results. I want to see visions that meet the "Apsey test" of being not only bold but doable, and not only bold and doable, but also "buy-in-able" by those who can commit to make things happen.

This is a subject I'll come back to again later in the book. But the roots of what I have come to believe about Canada's forest and the forest sector go all the way back to my years as a young man at MacMillan Bloedel.

There was an old man at MB in those days: H.R. MacMillan, the grey eminence of the British Columbia forest community, first chief forester of the province. He was not "running the outfit" – Charlie Specht was – but he was still a director of the enterprise he had founded and though his office was up on the ninth floor he was a palpable presence in every corner of the company headquarters at Pender and Bute. He didn't have much to do with us junior staff, but the brief conversations he might strike up with us in an elevator or hallway were usually instructive.

I found out how omnipresent old H.R. was the evening of my first day on the job. I had finished my work, arranged my papers tidily on my desk so that I could begin anew in the morning and walked back to our apartment in Vancouver's West End. Shortly after I walked in the door the phone rang. It was one of the people from my section.

"Mike," he said, "there's a whole bunch of material on your desk."

"Yes," I said.

"You have to come back and put it all away in the vault."

It didn't occur to me to ask why and indeed I did not know the reason for the urgency in my colleague's voice until a few months later when, one day in the office, H.R. MacMillan's personal assistant, Dorothy Dee, suddenly appeared in front of my desk. She was almost as intimidating a presence as the old man himself.

"I've come for the pictures of the golden spruce," she told me, indicating the two oversized photographs on the wall behind me. They showed a magnificent tree that grew in the Queen Charlotte Islands, a genetic oddity whose needles were colored gold. The photos had been framed and given me by friends in the BC Forest Service when I left the Bureau of Economics and Statistics.

I was very fond of them and that gave me the courage to tell Dorothy Dee, "But they're mine."

"Mr. MacMillan only wants to borrow them," she said.

He wanted to use the images on his personal Christmas cards. I, of course, assented. It was not until later that it occurred to me to wonder how the legendary H.R. MacMillan would happen to know that one of the most junior members of the headquarters staff had those pictures on his wall. I asked my colleagues what they thought.

After they stopped laughing they said, "At night after everybody else is gone home he prowls the building. Remember your first day? We had to get you to come back and clear your desk before H.R. saw it. He doesn't approve of papers being left out overnight."

Whenever one of us in the pulp and paper group had a birthday, the others would organize a little celebration over coffee and donuts brought up from the cafeteria.

On one such day, another junior member of the staff flipped a coin to see which of us would go for the donuts. He lost and went downstairs. When he came back a few minutes later he was pale and trembling.

He'd been waiting for the elevator on the main floor, the bag of fresh donuts in his hand. The elevator had come up from the basement parking levels, the door had opened and there, standing dead centre in the middle of the car, was H.R.

My colleague got in and pushed the button and stared at the floor indicator while the yeasty aroma of donuts filled the confined space.

"What's in the bag?" came the voice from beside him. No "Good morning." No "Pardon me, but." Just, "What's in the bag?"

When he heard the answer, H.R. said, "A whole bag of donuts? What for?"

The young man stuttered out an explanation involving birthday rituals and coffee breaks. By the time he got to the end of it, the elevator arrived at the third floor and he could make his escape.

As the door closed behind him he heard the voice of authority say, "What a hell of a way to run a company." ■

Outside the corporate world, it was the sixties and things were changing. Inside MB there was an effort to keep some things just the way they were. There was a dress code; it was unthinkable that any executive would show up for work without a tie or wearing a shirt that wasn't white or a suit that wasn't blue, black, grey or brown.

At one point a recently arrived American named Nairn Ward came to work for our group. As he was getting settled in, Archie McGougan called him to a meeting and asked me to sit in as well. Archie spread a map of Greater Vancouver on his desk and said to Nairn, "You haven't bought a house yet, have you?"

Nairn hadn't. Archie took a pen and drew a line around the exclusive Shaughnessy neighbourhood. "You can live here," he said, "or here," drawing another line around West Vancouver's British Properties, "or here," indicating part of West Point Grey. The message was clear, MacMillan Bloedel was comfortable with the idea of telling its senior people where it was appropriate for them to live. For Nairn Ward to have bought a house in Marpole or Mount Pleasant might not have been acceptable.

I was puzzled at first as to why I had been asked to sit in, since I had no role to play in the meeting. It was only later that I learned that Archie McGougan was signalling to me that I was considered an up and comer in the company and that he was gently initiating me into one of MB's unwritten rules.

Another time he called me in and offered me coffee. I sat there wondering what was going on, since my manager had not been asked to the meeting. Archie said, "Mike, I had a conversation with my wife this morning and your name came up.

My wife said, 'Apsey? I wonder if he's related to Jim and Doreen. I went to school with Doreen.'"

"I'm their son," I said.

We then had a brief and pleasant chat during which he relayed a number of complimentary things that his wife had said about my mother. From his tone, I had an odd sense that I now somehow enjoyed a sort of a quasi-family relationship with the McGougans.

As I was about to leave his office, he said, "Mike, you should always remember, it's not what you know. It's not even whom you know. It's about whether you come from good stock."

Vancouver was becoming a bigger, more cosmopolitan place in the sixties, but in the corporate community – especially in companies like MB, where the directors represented a selection of the city's old guard, the old ways were hanging on.

The mills and logging camps had been unionized for decades, but the headquarters staff and administrative employees were now becoming the targets of union organizing efforts. The company responded by bringing in a US consulting firm.

The consultants had all of us non-union employees summoned to a hotel ballroom set up like a university examination room. We were asked to fill in a detailed questionnaire that would tell upper management what we truly thought and felt about MB. No need to put our names on the paper, we were told; the exercise would be completely anonymous, so we could feel free to speak our minds.

But the first question on the form was "In which of the company groups do you work?" The second was "How long have you been with the company?" From there it wouldn't have been too hard to identify each and every respondent. It was a clumsy effort, but I think there was behind it a sincere intent to get a handle on the changes that were shaking Canada's old top-down authority system and probably mystifying a lot of the people up on the ninth floor.

During the five years I spent at MacMillan Bloedel, I had a life outside of work. Sharon and I settled into a good and loving marriage; as proof, I offer the fact that we are still together after forty-four years. Our two daughters were born – Susan in 1964, Jill in 1967.

I had given up sports. A doctor had told me years earlier that I had a choice: I could continue to play hockey or abandon it in favour of being able to walk without crutches in later life. I had given up soccer before leaving Victoria after I was invited to show up at a park to try out for the senior amateur team and found myself run off my feet by younger men. I had taken up photography, though, and was becoming an accomplished amateur.

I also passed through a doorway that awaits all of us at some point in life: the day when you find out what Shakespeare meant by "the ills that flesh is heir to." One winter morning, I sat down to eat my breakfast cereal. With the first spoonful, milk dribbled from the side of my mouth and wet my shirt. I took a sip of coffee and the same thing happened.

I didn't have time to wonder at why I was suddenly so clumsy. I had to get out of the apartment and walk to work. Later that morning, when we were gathered for a coffee break, someone told a joke and we all laughed. I remember the laughter draining from my colleague's faces as they looked at me.

"What's wrong?" I said.

Somebody said, "Why is only half of your face laughing?"

I went to the washroom and looked in the mirror. When I tried to smile, only the left side of my face crinkled up; the right side was frozen.

"Oh, my god," I thought, "I've had a heart attack."

Which shows how little I knew about the things that can go wrong with the human body. What I was actually having was a case of Bell's palsy.

The doctor I took my face to diagnosed the condition after poking and prodding and asking a few questions. He said that the seventh cranial nerve in my face had been damaged and the result was paralysis of some of the muscles. Nowadays it's believed that the same virus that causes cold sores is responsible for Bell's palsy. In those days, they had noticed that it struck people whose faces became chilled by cold, wet and windy weather – exactly the kind offered by a Vancouver winter to those of us who walked to work.

I went to that doctor's office every day for the next few weeks to receive heat treatments and megadoses of vitamins. The condition mostly cleared up, although I smiled funny for years afterwards and had to explain to people that I had had Bell's palsy. Often they would say, "I had an uncle..." or "I knew this guy..." I've looked it up on the Internet and have found that it gives me something in common with Jean Chrétien, George Clooney and Gordon Lightfoot.

There's a postscript to the story: years later, when I was in Colombia, I accompanied a colleague named Earl Hindley to a Colombian acupuncturist who was treating him for pain. When he was finished the treatment, the man asked me, "What's wrong with you?"

"Nothing," I said. But Earl told him I'd had Bell's palsy.

"But it's gone," I said.

"Smile," said the acupuncturist. I did and he got out his needles. I let him stick them in me, in my wrist and several other places. Only one of them hurt.

Then he took them out and said, "Smile."

I did, and for the first time in years I had wrinkles in my forehead.

"Damn," the acupuncturist said.

"What's wrong?" I said.

He'd been so eager to treat a case of Bell's palsy he'd forgotten to take a "before" picture that he could show to prospective patients.

I passed through another doorway in those years, one that is a common marker for millions of people my age and thereabouts. I can still remember where I was the moment I heard that John F. Kennedy had been shot to death in Dallas.

In an age that has seen passenger jets deliberately crashed into office towers full of people, the shooting of one man, even a US president, may not seem so great a calamity. But to us, then, it was as if the ground had fallen away beneath us. Kennedy was the first "television president." To many of us he represented, fairly or not, a new era in the order of the ages. We felt good about the future he pointed us toward: a man on the moon, a new frontier of science and sanity, a better world.

When he was so suddenly, so inexplicably yanked into the darkness, we all lost some of our innocence. And we would never get it back.

After five years at MacMillan Bloedel I was considered a rising young executive. A number of people thought I had a real future in the company. But it turned out that there were some obstacles in my path. I heard through the grapevine that a senior manager in the wood products group had put in a request for me to be transferred over, but pulp and paper had said no.

I was doing too good a job for them and they didn't want to lose me. I can see it from their point of view – why give away a performing asset? – but I would need broader experience in other parts of the company if I was to rise within MB.

This "silo mentality" troubled me. If I could only rise through the pulp and paper group, how was I going to get more scope? It was time to look for other opportunities. And I found one, almost halfway around the globe, that would change my life once again.

CHAPTER FIVE

Scope in Time

One day in the early part of 1968, I had a phone call from Paul Jones, who knew about my background in government and with MacMillan Bloedel. He had gone to work on a United Nations Food and Agriculture Organization project and thought I might be interested in getting involved. It was in Turkey, a place I knew next to nothing about.

I talked it over with Sharon first. Our girls were still young, without a school life to be disrupted. If we wanted the adventure of packing our bags and pitching up in some far corner of the world, now was the time. We decided that that was just what we wanted.

Yogi Berra said, "When you come to a fork in the road, take it!" But first I did what I have always done when I encounter a point of departure on my path through life: I mulled it over with the people whose names appeared on my resume under the heading: references. I talked to my old professor, Harry Smith at UBC, Ian Chenoweth (then a Vice President at the Canadian Pulp and Paper Association whom I had met while with the BC government), my much-missed friends Tom Buell, and Ray Smith, the wise gentleman down the hall at MB.

They were my confidants. They were not there to make up my mind for me, but to be a sounding board for my assessment of the pros and cons and to offer an insight or ask a question I might have overlooked. As I got older and allegedly wiser, I found myself playing the same role for others. Now, after a lifetime of such discussions, my advice to young people starting out on their careers is: make friends with those whose judgements you trust, and keep in touch.

So off to Turkey we went.

The project there was one of several forestry related initiatives being mounted by the FAO around the world in underdeveloped countries that had forests but lacked enough resources to lay out a long-range development plan. They looked at their situations and said, "Here we are with forests but we're importing forest products. We should be able to cut our dependence on imports and instead become exporters. We have some talent, but we need to improve that talent. Over there is the UN with money to assist us." So all over the world, people like young Mike Apsey were being recruited, briefed and dropped into fascinating places among interesting people.

I went first to the FAO headquarters in Rome to be briefed. The Turkish project was already underway but, as often happened with such undertakings, after the Turks had got an idea of what else the FAO might be able to do for them the original scope of the work had begun to expand. So the FAO was sending in three senior people – the three wise men, we called them – to assess the situation and make recommendations. The three were: Peter Vakomies, a Canadian with forest industry experience; Folke Rydbo, the head of the Swedish Forest Service; and Nils Osara, a Finn who was head of the FAO Forestry Department. Briefings had been set up for these and I was slotted into a fourth seat where I got a very good briefing indeed.

The United Nations has taken a fairly heavy drubbing from prominent figures in some countries, mainly I believe because politicians have been playing to domestic political audiences. But, having worked for the UN and having been involved in UN initiatives from time to time in the thirty-five years since I left Turkey, I firmly believe in the UN system. The organization does a great deal of good, often in very trying circumstances, and deserves the support of all of us who are lucky enough to have been born in some of the more comfortable parts of the planet.

I do believe, however, that the forest is so important to the future of the earth – it is where most of the oxygen we breathe comes from – that forestry should have its own directorate within the UN, rather than be a component of Food and Agriculture.

Once briefed, I was off to Ankara, Turkey's capital. The project office was at the bottom of a hill in a nice neighbourhood that was only partially developed. We were looking at some apartments near where I would be working until one of the Turks on the staff explained that it would be better to live further up the hill. "The smog only goes up about halfway," he said.

We moved into a comfortable place up the hill from the Canadian embassy, the Turkish Parliament and the mausoleum of Kemal Ataturk, the founder of the modern Turkish state. We chose an apartment that had western style bathroom fittings as well as the Turkish version – a hole in the floor with foot pads on either side. Our building stood above an open field, beyond which was the Soviet Embassy, surrounded by a high wall and with antennae bristling on the roof. We were one of only two non-Turkish families in the block. The other was that of Alexandre Trouchtanov, the USSR's Second Secretary in Ankara. He and his wife spoke very little English and we spoke no Russian, but we both had small children of about the same age and we all managed to rub along in broken Turkish.

Sharon and I were invited to the Embassy for a reception marking the one-hundredth birthday of Vladimir Illyich Lenin. In the receiving line were the East Block notables then resident in Turkey, including Alexander Dubček, the former president deposed when the Russians invaded Prague after the short-lived "spring" of 1968. They had made him the Czechoslovakian ambassador to Turkey to get him out of the country. It was bizarre to be meeting a man who not long before had been one of the world's best known statesmen and was now forgotten in Ankara; it was even more jarring to see this elegantly tailored personage discover a hair out of place and produce from his jacket a foot-long, bright orange plastic comb – the kind of thing you win in a carnival ring-toss booth – and calmly repair his coiffure.

We noticed that Dubček, the Soviet Ambassador and his entourage were looking at Sharon and me and laughing. Seeing that we had become aware of their attention, they came over and the ambassador, through his interpreter, explained that Sharon had become an object of almost daily speculation among the embassy staff. It had to do with our car.

On our way to Turkey, we had bought a Fiat in Italy. Soon after our arrival in Ankara, it was stolen, and when it was finally discovered, it was missing a few parts. We did the best we could to get it repaired, but it was never the same again. It was particularly difficult to start, and the only reliable way to get it going was to roll it downhill in neutral, then pop the clutch into second gear once it had built up enough speed.

I had a UN truck and driver, so the car was usually in Sharon's hands. She would park it outside our apartment pointed downhill. When she had to go out, she would bundle the girls into the back seat and perform the gravity assisted starting procedure. Her usual route was along a dirt track that cut through the field between our apartment building and the Soviet embassy. At first, the staff had watched with trepidation as the hurtling Fiat built up momentum, fearing that Sharon would fly across the road that separated the field from their embassy and smash into the wall. Once they came to trust her driving ability, they used to lay bets on whether she would turn left or right. She was very popular among those who had bet correctly.

While we engaged in this convivial chat, I noticed that the Canadian Ambassador, Klaus Goldschlag, was giving me the evil eye. I also noticed that he and the Australian envoy were the only western diplomats in the room. On the way to work the next day, I stopped at the Canadian embassy and asked to see the ambassador. I was shown right in.

"Mr. Ambassador," I said, "I have a feeling you were unhappy that the Apseys were at the reception last night."

He said that he was unhappy indeed. There had been some rise in tension between east and west – this was during the middle of the Cold War, remember – and the western diplomatic community had decided to show their displeasure with the easterners by making only a token appearance at the Lenin birthday bash. Sharon and I had broken the rules by showing up.

"But I'm not here as a Canadian," I said. "I'm here as an employee of the UN." The UN was officially neutral in Cold War politics.

Those seemed to be the magic words, and Sharon and I were invited to the next function at the Canadian embassy. The experience was my first lesson in one of the things you have to understand if you're going to be living in a foreign country: everybody else will know the local rules; you have to learn those rules and abide by them. ■

We were advised to hire a maid, which caused a little soul-searching for Sharon and me. We are the descendants of servants, after all. Were we degrading some poor woman by having her tidy up after us? No, we were assured, we would be providing a good livelihood. So we hired a woman named Felize and although we never met her husband she became part of the family. For Sharon, after years of staying home and looking after two active little girls, a whole new world opened.

Traffic in Turkey is a form of organized madness and systematized aggression. Speed is essential, right of way goes to the driver who sees nothing obstructing his path, and red lights and traffic signs offer only "general guidance."

Alexandre Trouchtanov used to say, "If you're not Turkish you can live in this country and drive for ten years. After that, the odds demand that you either leave or give up driving."

In his eleventh year, he was killed in a car crash. ■

The FAO project team was as mixed as any UN group. The leader was Tom Dow, from Scotland. We also had an Englishman named Peter Allen, an Austrian named Harald Sutter and Paul Jones, the Canadian who had brought me in. The project had grown to cover every aspect of the Turkish forest sector, from the forest itself through products to markets and investments. Our mandate was to assist the Turks in developing their forest economy, in whatever ways might be possible. Sometimes this meant tackling matters of great scope, sometimes it was a matter of technical details.

My title was Forestry Officer. Although I had supposedly been brought in to focus on pulp and paper, I soon found myself involved in wider fields. I was assigned a good chunk of the industrial development side of the project, and got to know the Turkish forest sector from top to bottom: timber resources, labour force, energy, technology, production capacity, transportation, the whole thing. I prepared a comprehensive survey of the existing and potential forest industries, from harvesting to wood products to pulp and paper. I also gained a good grasp of ancillary activities, like the box plants that made crates for citrus fruits and the charcoal producers who operated wherever there were trees to be cut.

Like our British Columbian forest, Turkey's timber resources were mostly state owned. Unlike us, however, the Turkish government also arranged for the trees to be harvested. Crews mostly worked for the government, taking the logs to large depots where they were sorted and auctioned off to the mills. I went to a few auctions to get a sense of how business was done. The government always set a floor price for the timber and always the price the bidders paid was that floor or just a little above. I remembered my father's friend who had gone to the auction when it wasn't his turn. Apparently the same unwritten rules applied in Turkey.

The sawmills – there were thousands of them – were mostly very small. Some were just one- or two-man operations, the kind of thing we haven't seen in British Columbia since pioneer days. I saw pit-sawing: a log laid over a hole in the ground while two sweating men

Turkey: Harvesting – "very close" utilization with handsaw. 1969.

used a handsaw, one above, one below, to laboriously slice it into planks.

Turkey had few timber-framed homes, but wooden poles were lashed together for scaffolding on building sites. Heavier poles were used to support the roofs of concrete or mud-brick houses that were still the usual kind of structures in villages.

The harvesting was also like something from centuries past. Trees were felled with axes and hand saws. Nothing was wasted, the trunks being sawed off virtually flush with the ground. The logs were debarked by hand – in one place, I saw it being done by an obviously experienced herd of goats – then bucked into lengths in the forest. Horses or oxen hauled them out to landings where the wood was handloaded onto trucks. I almost never saw a modern piece of equipment. The kind of slash that our logging operations would have left at harvest sites to return its nutrients to the ground by rotting or being burned to ash was instead bundled and sold as firewood.

Turkey: Debarking by hand. Most of the bark collected for fuel. 1969.

Turkey: Debarking by goat! Bark used as Food! 1969.

Turkey: Fuelwood – For heating/cooking and/or charcoal production. 1969.

The Turks were interested in making sure they had enough wood for domestic purposes – including firewood and charcoal, which were important fuels throughout the country. They also had an eye toward export possibilities once they had built up their forest economy. I was involved in a lot of studies that we hoped would lead to investment. Some of them were general overviews, but most were individual projects: should there be a mill in this or that particular location? Our team brought in consultants to handle some of the technical aspects of the work, such as surveying potential mill sites.

Turkey was then still very much a village-based society. They did things differently. One time I accompanied Larry Harris, MacMillan Bloedel's vice president for pulp and paper, out to take a closer look at the forest and some of the places we had identified as potential pulp mill sites.

We went to a village on a hill that I had visited before. It overlooked some flat coastal land near the city of Antalya on the Turquoise Coast. After checking out the harbour and a couple of small sawmills, we stopped to meet some of the local officials. The Turks are a hospitable people; they offered us tea as well as a drink they make out of yoghurt and water. The mixture tasted awful but I had learned to feign appreciation.

While we were chatting a heated argument broke out among some of the villagers who were gathered a little distance away. I asked our Turkish guide what was going on and if it had anything to do with our being there.

He told me not to worry. The villagers were just arguing over who would be manager of the pulp mill and who would be the foreman. Since I had made other visits to the area, it was assumed that the mill was going to be built; it was also assumed that it would be theirs to run, and village factions were contending with each other for the choice jobs.

Larry Harris and I obviously looked astonished, but the local officials told us not to worry. The main issues had been decided after my second visit, although it had taken a riot, the intervention of the police and seventeen arrests to work everything out.

In the meantime, someone had planted cotton on the proposed mill site, a Turkish custom by which nomadic families lay claim to unoccupied land. They expected to make a good profit when investors came to acquire the land. Alas, no mill was ever built at that village. ■

We also looked at forest management practices. The Turks knew how to plant trees and tend them. Near cities they would terrace bare hillsides and plant trees not only for the timber resource but to hold the rainwater that would otherwise have washed away the soil and created floods. One problem I had never encountered before was the threat of goat herders running their animals on replanted land.

The Turks were not unlettered in scientific forestry. They had had a forestry school, modelled on the thinking of European foresters, since the 1850s. The government had a Forestry Directorate which

Goat is a staple of the Turkish diet and the herds can be immense. On one of my field trips, I saw a herd that I estimated at perhaps ten thousand animals, spread over a wide hillside. I asked the man who'd been hired to tend them how many goats were under his management.

He looked thoughtful for a moment then said, "About three hundred."

Clearly the owner of all these goats, sitting in his office in some city, was concerned about the possibility of his herd being taxed. He had told his employee, "If anyone ever asks you how many goats you're looking after, tell them, 'About three hundred.'"

The same thing happened when we sent out survey forms to mills. In one instance I visited a large mill whose manager had sent back one of my survey forms. He had reported that he had forty employees. When I toured the place I saw forty men having tea while plenty of others were at work. I asked the manager why the discrepancy.

"Oh," he said, with a shrug, "we must have made an error." Again, there was always that fear that reporting the true state of affairs would bring a heavier tax load.

Hence my lifelong practice of not trusting the reported numbers without taking a first-hand look at the situation on the ground. ■

later became a Forest Service, and almost all of the country's forest land had been taken into public ownership.

The Directorate had regional and district managers who all knew what they were there for and what they had to do. They were involved in harvesting, in selling forest products and in reforestation. They were very interested in fast-growing poplar and an international poplar research centre had been established at Izmit, about fifty kilometres from Istanbul. Poplar was being planted around fields for soil conservation and poplar plantations were the coming thing.

The forest maps that the Turks could provide were not very good. We received better ones, very detailed, from the US embassy, clearly marked as prepared by the CIA. It was also thought useful to have some aerial photographs and so a German aircraft equipped with special cameras was purchased. Turkey was a front-line state in the Cold War, however, so no one was going to be flying around taking photographs without the approval of the military. After some discussions, the Turkish Air Force seconded a few of its people to fly and maintain the plane and they went off to Germany to be trained.

Months passed and there was great excitement within the Turkish Forest Service the day the plane and its crew were expected back. But then came word that the plane had not landed where it was ordered to but had touched down at another airport. Turkish military police went to see what was going on and discovered that the plane was crammed with refrigerators, vacuum cleaners and other consumer durables not obtainable in Turkey without paying hefty import fees.

The aircraft was impounded for a long investigation and the crew were reassigned. Without pilots, it could not be flown. During all my time in Turkey, we never took a single aerial photo.

I didn't see my job as one of telling the Turks how things ought to be. I am always more comfortable in the role of Sancho Panza, not as Don Quixote. I was there to assist the Turks, helping them figure out what production facilities already existed, what their future pulp and paper needs would be and how they could develop proposals for new mills that would meet those needs and, if things went well, produce a surplus for export. Bearing in mind my father's sage advice – that I could do no end of good in the world if I didn't mind who got the credit – I would lay out options and offer questions that the Turkish central planning officials could consider, letting them work out for themselves the answers that would best serve their interests.

The Undersecretary of the Turkish government's State Planning Organization at that time was Turgut Özal. I worked with him quite a bit and came to know him well. He was an impressively intelligent man, with a sincere desire to lift his country up. He went on to found and lead the Motherland political party and became Prime Minister when his party won the election of 1983. His government built the first bridge to cross the Bosphorus and link Europe to Asia. After six years as Prime Minister he became President of Turkey, then four years later, in 1993, he died of a heart attack.

Turgut Özal would tell me that his goal was to bring Turkey into the first rank of industrial nations, producing world-class products. But in doing so, he would say, "We must not destroy village life." After seeing a good slice of Turkey, I agreed with him completely. Istanbul and Ankara are thriving, cosmopolitan cities, as sophisticated as anything to be found in western Europe. But the soul of Turkish life is in the villages.

I fell in love with Turkey and the Turks. They were and are the most energetic, hospitable, life-loving people I have ever met and I consider it one of the great good fortunes of my life to have been able to spend two years amongst them. I think every young person, before they become too set in their ways, should have an opportunity to be a stranger among people whose ways are different, whose view of the world is informed by a different culture and a different history. There is no better way to discover who you are than to be taken out of your natural setting and put down somewhere completely different.

In Turkey I met and talked with scores of people who were living life as their ancestors had for generations before them. Once, travelling in a truck from somewhere to somewhere else through mountains in the south, we began to run low on gasoline. We stopped a man on a donkey and asked him how far to the nearest village with a petrol station.

"Four hours," he said.

Worried, not wanting to be stranded in the mountains, we nursed the truck along. Twenty minutes later, we came to the village he'd told us about. His only frame of reference had been the speed of his donkey.

The Turks have given their name to steam baths. Once, driving out in the country with Sharon and the girls, we came upon a traditional Turkish bath, a little building established on a natural hot spring.

We asked to be allowed to use the facilities and, as always in Turkey, we were welcomed. But it was strictly segregated: women and girls on one side of the dividing wall, men and boys on the other.

I went in on the men's side and found it a very puritanical experience, the men and even the little boys in bathing suits and T-shirts. Afterwards I waited for Sharon, Susan and Jill to come out of the women's door. I told them about the bundled up men and asked her what it had been like on the other side of the wall.

"They were all stark naked," she said. And they had giggled and laughed when Sharon joined them.

"Why?" I asked.

Lowering her voice, she said, "Their bodies were *totally* shaved!"

While the family and I were hunting for fossilized fish in a gravel bed beside the road, an old man stopped to say hello. He wanted to know where we were from and I told him, "Canada."

The word meant nothing to him. I took a stick and drew a map in the dust. "Here is Turkey," I said. "Then Europe and the Atlantic Ocean, then Canada. I come from British Columbia, all the way out here on the Pacific coast."

"How far is that?"

I worked it out in kilometres and told him.

He gave me a look that said I was either deluded or the kind of young man who tries to fool his elders and walked away muttering in Turkish, "No place is that far away." ■

In Turkey, I discovered time. My first inkling of that discovery came when I was newly arrived, sitting in my office, studying maps of the country and learning some of the place names. Before deciding to come here, I'd known next to nothing about the place. Now I was looking at a map and there, on the Mediterranean Sea at the mouth of the Dardanelles, I saw the site of Troy. That was when it struck me: a name that had formerly existed only in the world of books, in Homer's stories of Achilles and Hector and Odysseus, was a real place. And I could go there.

I looked at other names on the map. There was Gordium, where Alexander the Great had cut an ancient knotted rope, the subject of a prophecy that said he who could undo its coils would rule all of Asia. There was Tarsus, where St. Paul had been born and raised. Scattered across the Turkish map were places, real places, out of history and legend. I would be able to stand where Alexander had stood, walk where St. Paul had walked. I was about to encounter history.

We North Americans have a habit of saying, "Oh, that's just history," when what we mean is, "Oh, that's just the irrelevant past." Perhaps we're like that because we are not far removed from our frontier days. We're more concerned with the future that's beckoning us onward rather than the dusty road that stretches behind us. These days, especially, it seems that the schools do not teach history – not even the simple, romanticized version that was taught in my youth – giving us a younger generation for whom anything beyond their own memories is a hazy mix of vague impressions untroubled by facts.

We British Columbians are an ahistorical people. So many of us are newcomers from other regions of Canada or other parts of the world. And, except for the First Nations, the longest genealogy goes back no further than the 1843 founding of Fort Victoria, less than two hundred years ago.

But in Turkey, history is everywhere. You walk across an empty field, out on the Anatolian plateau, far from any town or highway. You see a block of stone half buried in the earth. Turn it over and you find a cross chiselled into it. A thousand years ago, it might have been a roadside shrine put up by Crusader knights.

Bounce your car up a dirt road to some tiny village, a couple of dozen mud-brick houses and an ancient well. Ask the people there if they know of any ruins nearby. For a few coins the local boys lead you up a goat track, over a hill and around an outcropping of rock and suddenly below you is an ancient theatre, stone seats rising course after course, and down there is the stage where masked actors performed Oedipus Rex to thousands of rapt Greek colonists, back when this was still Asia Minor and the Roman Empire was only a cloud on the western horizon.

We were finishing breakfast in the dining room of a small, back-country hotel before heading back to Ankara when I heard English voices at a table on the other side of the room. The two men seemed to be trying to figure out how to get to a nearby village.

I went over to see if I could be of assistance – and to speak a little English after several days of only Turkish. I sat down with them and we looked over their tourist map then compared it to my own more detailed chart. I was able to set them on the right road.

I rejoined Sharon and the girls and we bundled into the car and set off. But for miles as we drove I kept thinking that one of those men had seemed so familiar, especially his distinctive voice, yet I just couldn't place the face.

Then it hit me: the older of the two was the famous British radio and television commentator, Malcolm Muggeridge. After a lifetime of atheism, he had reconverted back to Christianity and he and his companion, whom I later learned was named Alec Vidler, were retracing the steps through ancient Asia Minor of the Apostle Paul. They later co-authored a book on their travels entitled *Paul: Envoy Extraordinary*.

I was not even a footnote, but at least I'd had another brush with greatness. ■

I had always wanted scope, the big picture. Turkey gave me scope in time. I discovered history in a way I could never have discovered it just through books. I have run my hand over granite lions carved by iron chisels into the gates of a Hittite city that was flourishing when my own ancestors were living in huts of wattle-and-daub and using tools made of stone. I have walked the valleys where Xenophon and the Ten Thousand Greek mercenaries fought their way home from Persia.

I have stood on the walls of castles built by Norman barons to guard the supply routes between Byzantium and the Crusader Kingdom of Jerusalem. I have walked the cliffs of Gallipoli, seen the trenches and the unburied bones of Australians and New Zealanders who died trying to fulfil Winston Churchill's bold strategy. I have touched the columns still standing amid the ruins of pagan temples at Ephesus and the walls of the little home to which Mary the mother of Jesus retired and from which she was taken up into heaven.

The Turks have a folk hero called Nasreddin Hodja, a wise though comic figure who appears throughout Middle East cultures in different guises. I think I identified with him because he seemed to be built along the lines of Sancho Panza and Cisco's sidekick Pancho.

A typical Hodja story: Hodja's neighbour found him searching the ground in the sunlight outside his doorway.

"What are you doing?" the neighbor asked.

"I have dropped my ring," Hodja said.

The neighbour joined in the search. After several fruitless minutes he said, "Where do you think you dropped it?"

"In the house," Hodja said.

"Then why aren't we searching inside?"

"There is more light out here."

Thinking outside the box is not a modern invention, nor a western one. ■

The Turks have a great sense of history and they have done a first-class job of maintaining historical sites, some of them among the most magnificent in the world. Even though I was there for two years and I made a point of traveling the country, what I saw just whetted my taste.

Sharon and I would take the girls and drive. We would pick a road and follow it, away from the places the tourists flocked to, just to see what we could find. We always found something, from a fossil bed to a ruined city. And I began to understand how it all tied together. Once there had been vast forests here, the slopes thick with the fabled cedars of Lebanon that Solomon had imported to adorn his Temple. What had happened?

People had happened, people with needs and plans. They needed fuel to warm their homes and cook their meals, charcoal to smelt metal – the Bronze Age and the Iron Age had both started in what is now Turkey.

Populations grew and so they needed more land for crops and pasturage, more timber for houses, and yet more fuel. They cut whole forests to build the ships that carried trade and supplied the invading armies – Persian, Greek, Roman, Crusader, Turkish – that marched along Mediterranean coasts. When technology changed, it was railroads that carried the goods and troops, railroads that ran on beds of wooden ties and crossed gorges on wooden trestles, while the steam engines ran on lengths of cordwood.

All this had been going on since Neolithic tribes had first given up wandering after herds of horse and aurochs and built humanity's original villages – possibly on a great post-glacial lake that is now drowned beneath the Black Sea. Standing on the ground in Turkey, seeing the forest that remains – even cedars of Lebanon in the mountains – I grasped a real sense of what human history has meant to the world forest.

I also gained an appreciation of the Turks' love of the forest. Because they do love the forest. Turks have taken me into what we Canadians would call an open field with a few scattered trees, none closer than thirty metres to another. The Turks would wave an expansive arm as if to encompass a vista of dense timber and say with pride, "What do you think of our forest?"

The Turks also knew their own history, knew what had happened to their ancient woods, and they were determined to reverse the historic trend. That is why they had called on the UN FAO for assistance.

Another thing the Turks taught me is that behind our commonplace knowledge, the things that everyone (supposedly) knows, some surprising stories may lie.

"Mike," they would say, "what do you know about Santa Claus?"

"He comes from the North Pole."

"No, he comes from Turkey." And they would tell me about Saint Nicholas, a Christian bishop during the reign of the pagan Emperor Diocletian, whose kindness in giving anonymous gifts of gold to a poor man who could not afford dowries for his daughters – the bishop threw them through the man's window and they landed in stockings hung up to dry – led to our tradition of Santa Claus bringing gifts for children.

Or my Turkish friends would say, "Mike, where do tulips come from?"

"Holland, of course."

"No, they come from Turkey." And they would tell me about how Turkish gardeners had long cultivated the flowers before a sixteenth century Dutch botanist received some bulbs and successfully grew then at the University of Leiden in 1593.

The flowers became so popular among the Dutch that a speculative frenzy in new varieties consumed the national economy. For one prized bulb a seller was reported to have received two loads of wheat, four fat oxen, eight fat pigs, twelve fat sheep, two hogsheads of wine, four barrels of beer, two barrels of butter, one thousand pounds of cheese, a suit of clothes and a silver beaker.

From this I learned a valuable lesson: sometimes what we all know just isn't so. ■

One thing I learned in Turkey, and had it confirmed in Colombia, Honduras, Ghana, Sierra Leone and other places, any time I had a problem, way out in the countryside, I could get help from the local forest service office. Wherever I found foresters, I found friends. We are a community.

We are not, however, a very powerful community, which is a major part of the reason why forests are abused and ill used in so many parts of the world. I've dedicated part of my life and career to trying to do something about that problem. As far back as my years in Turkey, having seen the way the UN seeks to make a better world, I have believed that there ought to be an international convention on protecting and developing the world forest; until that happens, forestry will always be secondary to other concerns. Today, I am one of many foresters around the world who are working to bring that convention into existence.

But as a Canadian who has seen much of the world as well as my own country's ways of doing things, I won't point an accusatory finger at people in the developing world. I've been in countries governed by truly corrupt politicians, the kind who didn't quibble about telling me what they are doing and why they do it.

But, as one of them said to me, "Where did we learn this, Apsey? We had teachers. We learned it from the British, the French, the Belgians, even the Japanese – all those foreigners who came to colonize my country, who hacked the hell out of our forests and shipped the profits home."

A hundred years ago, we Canadians liquidated the forest of the Maritimes. Who taught us how to do that? It was the Europeans – inhabitants of the world's largest clearcut who, having achieved enlightenment, are now trying to get the rest of the world to change its practices.

After two years in Turkey, I felt I had accomplished what I had come to do. As well, concerns outside of work were beginning to press

Sharon and me. She had had gall bladder surgery in a Turkish hospital, and it had been a fascinating experience. Susan and Jill were coming up to school age and it seemed a good idea to bring them back to Canada. My parents were aging and, with my dad's bad leg, they could not travel to see us and the girls.

We made a leisurely trip home, seeing Paris and London and Amsterdam, where Sharon received a diamond that she considered suitable for a man to give a wife whom he has taken away for two years in a foreign country. We took the kids on long walks through the European capitals, window shopping and buying them the kind of things that young girls love. We also thought the excursions would educate them in cultured European ways, which led to Susan asking as we wandered down a certain street in Amsterdam, "Why are all those ladies sitting in the windows?" I don't recall how I answered that one.

Then we flew home to Vancouver, rented an apartment, and I began to nose about to see who might have a use for a young forest economist just back from the wide world.

Sharon's mother, a former nurse, came to visit us. We thought it would be a meaningful experience for her if we took her to the place where Florence Nightingale had inaugurated the profession of nursing during the Crimean War.

We jumped into the car and drove to the site. Suddenly we were surrounded by people with pointed questions and, more alarming, pointed guns. We had not realized that the buildings in which Nurse Nightingale had worked were now the western headquarters of the Turkish military.

Sharon's mother wanted us to leave, but once we had explained who we were and why we were there an officer escorted us to see a display of artifacts that had belonged to the mother of all nurses. ▪

CHAPTER SIX

A Failure to Communicate

In late 1970, we arrived home from Turkey and settled in a rented apartment in North Vancouver. I was in no great hurry to find a new job because I wanted to find the *right* one. A number of people had contacted me with offers when I'd still been overseas and more calls came once it was learned that I was back. It's not that I was now some kind of rising star in the forest sector's firmament, but I had gained a broader background than many other forest economists at my relatively young age and there were people who thought my experience might make me helpful to their aims.

I spent several weeks visiting people in both government and the industry, and received a number of interesting offers. But most of them did not make a good fit with how I was trying to shape my career. I wanted that bigger picture and, although there were companies that were willing to take me on and let me invent a niche within the corporate structure, I decided in the end that the Council of Forest Industries of British Columbia was where I would find the wider scope I was looking for.

I met with the Council's vice president, Norm Dusting, and with economist Joe Miyazawa, who was leaving COFI to become secretary manager of the Cariboo Lumber Manufacturers' Association. I was very much intrigued by the idea of working with a broadly based association, developing and refining overall forest sector policy rather than following the more narrowly focused work that I would have found in the corporate world, and to a lesser extent in government. I signed on as COFI's new economist, just in time for years of major and rapid change.

COFI was then in its tenth year of existence. It had been formed in 1960 in an amalgamation of several prior organizations that represented different sectors of the BC forest industry – lumber, red cedar shakes and shingles, plywood, pulp and paper, forestry and logging – along with regionally based associations.

Its senior people were pillars of the British Columbia establishment. When I joined, Bob Rogers was chairman of the Council; he was also a senior executive of Crown Zellerbach and a future Lieutenant-Governor. The board included Poldi Bentley from Canfor, Jack Christensen of Tahsis Company, Tom Rust from Crown Zellerbach and my old mentor Ray Smith from MacMillan Bloedel.

The Council's president when I joined was Gordon Draeseke, a former executive at Alaska Pine. Before him, COFI had been headed by: Major General Bert Hoffmeister, an Officer of the Order of Canada and our most decorated soldier of World War II before becoming Chairman of MacMillan Bloedel; and by the Honourable Jack Nicholson, O.B.E., formerly the senior federal cabinet minister from British Columbia who in 1970 was BC's Lieutenant-Governor.

The Council's role was to represent the BC forest industry to the world. We lobbied governments and we mounted cooperative efforts to make offshore customers aware of BC's products. As the Council's in-house economist, I was responsible for advising on all aspects of the forest sector, from forestry to manufacturing to the marketplace.

I soon found that I had joined COFI in what the old Chinese curse calls "interesting times." The United Kingdom, long an important market for BC plywood, had just joined the European Economic Community. Plywood imports into the EEC faced a 13 per cent tariff. Immediately, COFI's major priority was to convince the Europeans to allow as much plywood as possible to continue flowing into the British market and into Europe, without the tariff.

COFI Presidents: (a) Hon. Jack Nicholson, O.B.E., 1960. (b) Bert Hoffmeister, O.C., 1961–67. (c) Gordon Draeseke, 1968–75. (d) Don Lanskail, 1976–83.

A small team of us – Peter Drake of Seaboard Lumber, Charlie Allen from MacMillan Bloedel and me – stormed through Europe, splitting up to cover nine or ten countries in about as many days. We met with importers, users, government and non-government agencies. We had a lot of help from Canadian trade officials as well as from the British who wanted to keep our plywood coming in almost as much as we did.

This was my first major trade mission. It was exhausting work, but wonderful fun. And we got a good, high quota that kept BC plywood shipping into the UK duty free, and a sizeable duty-free volume into continental Europe.

The world was becoming a more complex place in the seventies. In BC, we were feeling the first stirrings of US protectionism that was to cause our industry so much trouble in the decades to come. In August 1971, the Nixon administration, responding to a rising wave of protectionist sentiment, imposed a surcharge on all dutiable imports, which included Canadian lumber.

Near the end of the mission we were in Amsterdam, meeting with some of the Netherlands' key decision-makers. The Dutch have a well-earned reputation for being tough, canny traders and they had been very hard-nosed about the negotiations.

At a big luncheon hosted by COFI one of the Dutch asked me directly, "Just how much of your plywood do you think you ought to be able to ship duty free into Holland?"

"How about a million square feet for every dollar this luncheon is costing us?" I answered.

The man looked at me closely. "Is Apsey a Dutch name?" he said. "Suddenly you're sounding very Dutch."

"I'll do whatever it takes to get us a big number," I said. But I took it as a compliment. ■

The Canadian government launched an intense effort to have all Canadian products exempted from the surcharge, but without success. COFI went south to meet with our customers, urging them to acquaint their friends in Washington with the importance of BC lumber to the US housing industry. Their representations, coupled with the more sensible attitudes that emerged from the Kennedy Round of international trade negotiations, led to the surcharge being lifted in January 1972.

But another Nixon initiative showed how the US system of government can have America patting Canadians on the back with one hand while punching us in the face with another. By 1972, the first wave of environmental activism was being felt in Washington. In 1970 the National Timber Supply Act, which would have allowed more logging in US old-growth forests, was defeated by a coalition of environmental groups. The administration became concerned about possible future shortages of wood products. President Nixon convened a blue ribbon Advisory Panel on Timber and the Environment, packed with heavyweight industry figures and academics and a former Secretary of the Interior.

The panel asked Canada if it would care to make a presentation on our ability to supply US needs.

Canada's External Affairs department did not feel comfortable sending its people to testify before a US panel about a provincial responsibility and it seemed impractical to ask the different producing provinces to submit individual briefs. So someone in Ottawa had the bright idea of leaving it to the Canadian industry to put together a paper, and since BC was the major exporting province, the request came to Gordon Draeseke. He turned it over to Bob Wood, one of COFI's top men, and Bob decided it was just the kind of thing they had me around for and said, "Apsey, you do it."

So I did, and gladly. It was an opportunity to do a major study that had never been done before. It meant breaking new ground, statistically speaking, which for an economist is like being an astronomer discovering a new planet. I hasten to add that I did not do it all by myself; I was aided by Bob Wood and by Csaba Hajdu, an economist at Macmillan Bloedel.

We sent out a request for figures to governments and forest industries across the country. What came back showed what a peculiar country our Confederation could be. Forest products were in those days Canada's number one export commodity, but no one had ever pulled together a proper national survey of our capacity. There were great gaps in the available information, some of which was suspect as to its accuracy, and no consistency to the data. Some provinces were twenty years behind in their inventory work.

I made two cross-country trips. First I went and met with the people who were supplying me with numbers so that I could get the context behind the data and be sure they were accurate. Then, when I had assembled the information into a comprehensive picture, I went back to the same people to make sure that I had got it right and, more important, to make sure that they all bought into the conclusions I had drawn.

One of those conclusions raised some eyebrows among people who considered themselves knowledgeable on the shape and future direction of the Canadian lumber sector. I had prepared a chart that predicted softwood lumber production from east of the Rockies would show a significant increase in the 1980s and onward.

"Madness!" cried more than a few of the experts, especially in BC where we had led in lumber production for half a century. "The easterners haven't got the logs!"

But I argued that they did. Their forest had smaller logs, but with the limits on harvestable stands on the Pacific coast and the industry's expansion into the BC Interior, new technologies had been and were being developed that allowed our mills to make lumber from smaller and smaller logs. It was only a matter of time before somebody applied those newly developed systems to the forest of eastern Canada.

Fifteen years later, I compared my 1972 prediction to what had actually happened to Canadian lumber production. My projections for growth west of the Rockies were quite close to the eventual reality. But my "mad" predictions for lumber production east of the continental divide turned out to be a huge understatement. The eastern mills not only learned how to make marketable lumber from logs that had formerly gone to the pulp mills, but they had gone berserk. That trend, coupled with rising production from BC's timber industry, would bring us onto a collision course with the American lumber lobby.

But nobody was predicting that back in 1972, when Gordon Draeseke, Bob Wood and I flew down to Washington to appear before the President's panel. Through our paper, *Canada's Forest Resource and Forest Products Potentials*, we were able to assure the Americans that Canada could supply their lumber needs and that our timber resources were more than sufficient to provide for expanded production and increased shipment to US markets. The Americans were much relieved at the time. As the years rolled on, Canada would honourably keep all the promises we made in that presentation, and as a result we have ever since found ourselves in "deep shit."

Lumber production soared, mostly in the BC Interior where the new technology more than repaid our industry's massive investments. The American lumber industry, meanwhile, was experiencing changes that led to higher costs. So Canadian imports rose dramatically and steadily until we were supplying almost a third of the US market with a product that was better than what many American mills could produce.

> We were on the plane flying to Washington, DC, one of the few times to that date that I had flown first class. It was a relaxing trip and we were perhaps halfway there when Gordon Draeseke said, "By the way, do we have some sort of presentation to give?"
>
> I produced the document and he read it as we flew on. But bless the man, he did a fine job of making the opening statement then left it to me to give the technical responses to the panel's questions. ■

Under those circumstances, faced with competition it could not beat, the US lumber lobby cried foul and ran to the Congress and the various administrations to seek protection. US politicians, knowing to the last red cent where their campaign funds come from, readily gave it. Dealing with that situation was to occupy a great deal of my time and energy for the next twenty-five years.

But I am grateful to Richard Nixon for having convened that panel. The report I prepared was unique. It was neither a purely federal nor provincial nor private-sector viewpoint. It was not regional or parochial in scope. And it allowed me to learn a great deal about the Canadian forest industry that I would otherwise probably never have had occasion to discover. And the issues it dealt with – supply, changing products, access – were to become the main themes of the rest of my career.

In June 1972, I was made the Council's vice president of forestry and logging, replacing my friend Bob Wood who had gone back to his consulting business. One of my first jobs was to hire my replacement as the Council's economist. I followed the usual procedures to attract candidates and interviewed those whose qualifications put them on the short list. When I had made my selection, I went to Gordon Draeseke's office and said, "Gordon, I've hired an economist."

"Great," he said. "What's his name?"

"Sally," I said. "Sally Pipes."

He looked at me in silence for the longest time, then said, "Are you sure?"

"I'm very sure."

"Carry on."

I was glad he didn't make a fuss. Not only was she clearly the best person for the job, but the next two economists on my short list were also women. Sally Pipes did an excellent job at COFI. She later went on to the Fraser Institute and is now president and chief executive officer of the Pacific Research Institute for Public Policy, a think-tank headquartered in San Francisco.

As a vice president, I was drawn deeper into the essential role of COFI, which was to attempt to achieve and put forward a consensus position of its members on issues that were important – sometimes

Everything is connected to everything else, Lenin said, and my pro-motion to vice president at COFI was connected to my grandmother Apsey. The link was a fine fellow by the name of Mike Painter, a forester who worked under Bob Wood. He had graduated some ten years before me and came from Kelowna, where my grandmother knew his family. After I went into forestry, my grandmother would often talk to me about Mike Painter and his career. He became in her mind a kind of benchmark for a successful forester and an ideal to which I should aspire.

When I phoned her to tell her that I'd been promoted to a vice presidency at COFI, she said, "Isn't that where Mike Painter works?"

"Yes, it is."

"Will you be working under him?"

"Actually, he works for me now."

It was the first time I'd known my grandmother to be speechless. ■

Throughout all of my years at COFI I was excellently assisted by a female version of Radar O'Reilly, the MASH Army clerk who would magically provide the file, make the appointment, organize the meet-ing, even before his boss asked for it.

Her name is Maryann Costa. She came to work for me as a young woman and was soon indispensable. She remained at COFI after I left and was still there, to my great relief, when I returned years later as the Council's president. She retired in 2003 after a distinguished career.

Let it now be known that when I might have appeared to be effort-lessly on top of some crisis, there was real effort behind the appear-ance and the credit for it should go to Maryann Costa. ■

even vital – to the BC forest sector. I say "attempt" because a consensus was often a most elusive beast.

The Council's membership was highly diverse and still growing and, as the world became more complex, it was more and more difficult to get everybody singing from the same song sheet. The expression, "more difficult than herding cats" didn't do the situation justice; at least cats have certain things in common. This was like trying to herd several different species – elephants, mice, frogs and (given the idiosyncrasies and temperaments of some of the key figures), the occasional Tasmanian Devil.

The Council had very competent professional staff – I had been one of their number for two years – but COFI had not been conceived as a staff-run association. Its members were to be the core of its operations, through their participation in a series of committees. But the committee structure was unwieldy at the best of times; when there was a divisive issue on the table, it was impossible to make any meaningful headway.

My attitude was that we were there to serve the member companies, to deal with the issues that confronted them. Ultimately, there was no point in mounting staff-led initiatives, no matter how worthy, and then looking to the members for buy-in. Their involvement had to be the core of any exercise, and the committee structure I was trying to deal with worked against that principle. After a year as vice president of forestry I went to the chair of the Council, John Hemmingson from MacMillan Bloedel, and told him that either the committee structure had to go or I would.

A task force of senior company representatives was put together and a new structure emerged which enabled the industry to meet quickly and efficiently and also to initiate major efforts relating to emerging or future issues.

But even when its committees were functioning well, COFI's heterogeneous nature made it hard to steer a single course. The membership was drawn from different companies, of different sizes, making different products, serving different markets, operating in different regions, and having different corporate cultures. It was simply not possible to get a unified position on some issues at some times. The more general (or the more costly), the issue, the more likely there would be a meeting of minds, but it could be short lived; often, I would find in my later years, a unified COFI position presented to the Minister of Forests by a group of forest company CEOs would last only as long as it took the executives to get back to their offices and get on the phone for a private chat with the Minister. On some issues, such as log exports, there was never a true consensus.

Years later, during the "War in the Woods" over clearcutting and other forest management issues, the environmentalists would try to portray the BC forest industry as a monolithic force. It never was and I strongly doubt it ever could be. The closest I ever saw the industry come to a unified frame of mind was in late August 1972, when the unthinkable happened: W.A.C. Bennett's Social Credit government was defeated after twenty years in power and Dave Barrett's New Democratic Party was swept into office. The barbarians were no longer at the gates; they were all the way inside, redesigning the throne room and taking stock of the counting house.

In this age of overnight tracking polls that allow political campaigns to be covered as if they were horse races, it might seem strange that a government defeat would take many of BC's captains of industry by surprise. But it must be remembered that in those days public opinion polls were not allowed during election campaigns. It might also seem odd that key decision makers in the province's most important industry had no clear understanding of who the people in the new government were nor what they would do. But BC politics were intensely polarized back then and the two solitudes of left and right – "free enterprisers" and "socialists" in the jargon of the day – had little contact with each other. No senior person in the industry knew the senior people in the Barrett administration, knew how they thought or what their motivations might be.

In fairness, it must also be said that, even if there had been regular contact between them, it would have been difficult for the forest industry CEOs to know what the Barrett government intended to do, because it soon became clear that the NDP didn't know either. As the COFI annual report for the year delicately phrased it, "These elections have left the industry with uncertainties."

There had been a lot of loose talk about nationalizing or expropriating private corporations, especially in the forest sector. Dave Barrett was a flamboyant populist, always playing to the crowd. His background was in social work; how much did he know about the BC forest economy, the complexities of tenure systems, the business cycles in lumber, plywood and pulp and paper? Would he be content to tinker around the edges, or would he fancy himself an Alexander the Great with a legislative sword?

As the main lobbying entity for the industry in BC, it was COFI's job to find out who was now making forest policy and to do our best to influence it. It soon became apparent that Barrett was not the man we had to deal with; the key player was Bob Williams, Minister of Lands, Forests and Water Resources.

In their own way, the members of the NDP cabinet were as diverse as the members of COFI. They ranged from know-nothing, knee-jerk socialists to thoughtful social democrats with a good grasp of how the business world really worked. Bob Williams was in the latter category, having made a very good living as a successful entrepreneur. I once took Noranda's Adam Zimmerman to meet him and the two got along so well that Zimmerman let Williams know that he had a private island retreat back in Ontario that the minister was welcome to use any time he felt the inclination. Williams thanked him politely and said the offer wasn't necessary; he already owned his own island in BC.

I got to know Bob Williams on a professional basis, though I don't think I ever truly got to know what made him tick. He wanted more out of the forest industry and could make cohesive economic arguments for his strategies. Dave Barrett, on the other hand, seemed only to want to milk the industry for revenues to fund his social programs.

But as we had more contact with the Barrett administration, it became more and more apparent that either they did not know what to do with the forest sector or that they could not agree among themselves what their policy ought to be. They had never been anything but an opposition party, and the challenges of governing turned out to be a lot more difficult than they had appeared from the other side of the legislative chamber.

Although Bob Williams was the key man in NDP resource policy, Premier Barrett could never be discounted.

One day, several of us from COFI were in a meeting in the Legislature buildings discussing stumpage. The government was looking at a range of proposals, one of which was to increase the minimum stumpage rate.

The discussion was polite and understandably complex, since changes in stumpage had different implications for the balance sheets and competitive positions of different companies.

Then the Premier came into the room and joined the discussion. It immediately became heated.

"What do you mean, minimum stumpage?" he asked.

Someone gave him an explanation.

"How much is it?"

"Fifty-five cents."

"We should double it to $1.10," Barrett said, and with that he got up and left.

Not long after, the minimum stumpage rate was raised to $1.10. An accompanying rationale for the decision explained that the figure had been established through deep research, profound analysis and calm consideration of all the options. But all of us who had been in that room recognized that we had witnessed an example of the seat-of-the-pants governing style for which Dave Barrett was famous. ■

In regard to a lot of the NDP's forest policies the question we were often left pondering was: who is making policy, Bob Williams or the cabinet as a whole? Williams came across as smart and savvy, but some of the forest-related bills that appeared on the Legislature's order paper smacked of ideology run rampant.

A case in point was the Timber Products Stabilization Act, which the government said was intended to regulate the prices that pulp mills were paying independent sawmills for the chips that the latter provided. The legislation dealt with a serious point of contention within the industry and there was a lot of support from the sawmillers for what the law said it would do.

But the way that bill was written made it an example of the Barrett government's tendency to use a cannon when a slingshot would have done the job. The Act allowed for the establishment of a Forest Products Board that had the power to control the prices of every forest product sold in BC. The Minister of Forests would have had almost unlimited discretionary power over the province's number-one industry. The people running forest products operations in BC, from small sawmillers to CEOs of major integrated corporations, generally did not trust the government and feared that Premier Barrett's real goal was to bring the industry under tight political control. The fact that the government was buying up failing or marginal forest operations, like Crown Zellerbach's money losing Ocean Falls mill, only deepened the industry's suspicions.

In reality, I later came to understand, there was no game plan. For all of their rhetoric and bluster, Barrett and his cabinet didn't understand the forest sector. Worse, a lot of what they thought they knew wasn't true, such as the idea that the industry was a monolithic entity. But as they came to grips with real-world problems, and understood just how much risk to the provincial economy was inherent in this or that decision, they backed off from their grand illusions. Ultimately, they fiddled here and fiddled there, but they didn't fiddle greatly.

They also realized the complexity of the many interest groups that intersect in the forest sector. In those days there were probably as many interest groups with axes to grind or oxen to be gored as there are today. The environmental lobby was not as sophisticated as it has since become, but it was just as fervent. And there were many more communities that depended on small mills.

I sometimes think Dave Barrett must have found himself in the position of the sorcerer's apprentice. It turned out that governing, like casting magic spells (which governing sometimes resembles), was a lot trickier than he had thought. So he began to look for some expert help. At first, the focus was narrow: he asked UBC's Dr. Peter Pearse, the Forest Service's Ted Young, and the industry's Arvid Backman to report on some specific aspects of the forest sector.

But the answers the Premier got back only served to show him that the issues facing the BC forest sector were too complicated to be addressed one at a time. What was needed was the big picture, the wide scope. So, as the Barrett administration lumbered toward its eventual demise, the government appointed Peter Pearse as a Royal Commissioner and empowered him to undertake a full-scale examination of the way things were and the way they ought to be.

The Pearse Commission's report would not come in until 1976, when my encounter with its exhaustive analysis and, in part, radical recommendations would become a turning point of my later career.

Meanwhile, the times were a-changing in more ways than just in terms of politics with a capital P. A social revolution was underway in the western world. Greenpeace had come into existence in 1971, first emerging as a protest against US nuclear bomb tests in the Aleutians then quickly metamorphosing into environmental activism. But their radical antics were just the sharp end of a societal trend that was increasingly catching the attention of mainstream British Columbians. Even before the end of the W.A.C. Bennett administration, BC had passed the 1971 Ecological Reserves Act, a law that set aside numerous unique sites across the province. COFI took part in the selection process and supported the concept even though it meant removing productive forest from the land base.

But for the general public, especially in a province whose population was becoming increasingly concentrated in urban areas, environmentalism in the early seventies was mostly about how things looked – and often about how things smelled. Prince Philip, when his patrician nose first encountered the rotten egg odour that surrounded an old-fashioned kraft pulp mill, spoke for many British Columbians when he said, "Put a sock in it."

But the burning environmental issue as the seventies wore on was the pall of smoke that accompanied many forest industry operations. Throughout the province, bark and wood waste were incinerated in beehive burners and it was routine to pile the slash on logging sites and set fire to it. Slash burning offered two benefits: it quickly returned nutrients to the soil as rain caused the ash to soak into the ground, and it prevented the build-up on the forest floor of fuel that a lightning strike or a careless cigarette could turn into the kind of raging conflagrations that devastated Barriere and Kelowna's suburbs in 2003.

In 1973, a Vancouver radio hotliner decided that taking on the forest industry over slash burning would please his listeners. Other media took up the campaign and suddenly, it was a hot topic. As COFI's vice president of forestry and logging, I thought we should meet the issue head on. I went to the Council's Forestry and Logging committee and suggested we take some members of the big-city press out to Tofino and show them how things really worked in the woods.

I didn't go alone. I rounded up some chief foresters, including Gerry Burch from BC Forest Products. We took along BC's most prominent journalist, Jack Webster, as well as a pride of reporters, columnists, photographers and television cameramen. We didn't take many industry public relations types. Out on the west coast of

Vancouver Island, we showed the media a decadent area full of dead and dying timber. Then we showed them a logging site where all the dead trees had produced a lot of snags and broken branches which had been burned to refortify the soil and reduce the danger of wild-fire.

Near the end of the tour, we took them to one of the ugliest sites in the area. It looked awful, like Berlin after the air raids of World War II – devastation as far as the untutored eye could see. Of course, we were trying to tutor the media eyes we had brought along: the forest-ers were carefully explaining about how the new forest would grow out of this charred landscape, while the media lenses ate up every ugly image.

One of the photographers said to Gerry Burch, "Would you mind standing on that stump while I take your picture?"

So Gerry dutifully climbed the blackened stump and the shutters clicked and clicked. Jack Webster leaned over to me and said, "Front page of the Vancouver Sun tomorrow, Mike."

Walking back to the cars, Jack Webster needed to relieve a full bladder. We stopped on a bridge and Webster added some volume to the water flowing beneath it.

As he was doing so he called over his shoulder to me, "Mike, wasn't there some controversy out this way involving the Indian River?"

The river had been logged in places to its banks and the contro-versy was over the effects on salmon stocks. "Yes," I said, "and now there may be even more."

"Why do you say that?" "Because you're peeing in it," I said. He scoffed. "That's not a river. It's just a wee stream." I told him his contribution had probably done more damage to the river than the logging had. I think he may have taken my remark as a compliment. ■

And of course he was right. The caption read, "Black snags beauti-ful – to a forester."

I called Gerry and asked him, "How's your day going?"

He told me he had just come back from being called up to the office of Ken Benson, president of BCFP, who had gone up one side of him and down the other. The only thing that had saved Gerry's job was being able to explain to his boss, while he was still being yelled at, that he'd been standing on a MacMillan Bloedel stump on an MB site.

I began to receive calls myself, as did Gordon Draeseke. MacMil-lan Bloedel was calling for my head to roll, as well as Gerry Burch's and anybody else who had been part of taking the media out to see what clearcutting and slash burning really looked like. Other voices on the COFI board were equally strident, but eventually the media moved on to other issues, the fuss died down and Gerry Burch and I continued to do our jobs.

Was it a mistake to show journalists the reality of logging? I think not. The mistake was to not have done it often enough. Here we were in a province that effectively made its living from forest products, and a growing majority of our increasingly city dwelling citizens knew next to nothing about where so much of their bread and butter came from.

If there is one consistent failure that I have witnessed through all my years in the BC forest sector it is best expressed in the words of the prison camp warden in the movie, Cool Hand Luke: "What we have here is a failure to communicate." And especially to communi-cate consistently over a long, long time.

In the nineties, when our industry's European customers were targeted by environmental organizations trying to force BC out of all old-growth forests, a prominent forest company CEO once said to me, "Mike, how about we give you three million and you fix this European thing once and for all?"

"You mean three million a year? For how many years?"

No, no, no. He meant three million once, as if the problem were a single fire that could be put out and forgotten. As if the environmental organizations and the marketplace would thereby be convinced to stop hammering away at us, year after year.

Time and again, the industry has mounted short-lived initiatives like Forests Forever and the Forest Alliance, in the hope that they could solve perennial problems. But ignoring problems does not make them go away; usually, it makes them worse. British Columbia may have learned that lesson when three decades of restricting slash burning and prescribed burns built up a massive quantity of fuel for the fires of 2003 that effectively destroyed one small town and devoured hundreds of peoples' homes. Whether the forest industry can apply that wisdom to the challenge of educating the public remains to be seen.

In today's hypercompetitive, market-driven, globalized world economy of the twenty-first century, it's hard to recapture the atmosphere of the BC lumber industry in the post-war boom years. In the fifties, there were no marketing departments at wood products companies; there were sales people, to be sure, but their primary task was to "allocate production." Demand was so great, and supply so comparatively limited, in those days that the problem was to see that customers got their share of two-by-fours, floor joists, and pulp and paper.

By the 1970s, other producers had come into the field and the superheated markets were fading to moderately warm. Sales departments had to get out and *sell*. And long-sighted people in the industry were peering ahead and foreseeing a future when marketing would become the major preoccupation it is today.

COFI and its predecessors had always been involved in promoting the use of BC wood products. In 1930, for example, the BC Lumber Manufacturers' Association had worked with lumber companies, shingle makers, export firms and the provincial government to promote the use of our lumber for housing construction in Europe, especially in our traditional market, Britain.

In the seventies, the Trudeau government was concerned about Canada's increasing reliance on the US as the prime market for our exports. For the BC forest industry, the prospect of broadening our customer base was attractive; we experienced the chill of US protectionism with President Nixon's surcharge on imports and were concerned that America might not always be a safe basket in which to place so many of our eggs.

In 1970, discussions among the federal and provincial governments and COFI led to the creation of the Cooperative Overseas Market Development Program (COMDP). This was an idea that began with the Council and, as the resident economist, I was involved in providing the figures and projections on which the business case was built. I worked with Gene Smith, a very able federal public servant. The idea was that the three partners – Canada, BC and COFI – would each provide one third of the funding for a major program to increase lumber, plywood and shake and shingle sales to Europe and Asia.

This was a major program for the Council, representing spending of $10 million (more like $40 million in today's dollars) over five years. Both the federal trade minister, Jean Luc Pepin, and the BC forest minister, Ray Williston, viewed it as a significant initiative.

Of course, COMDP was happening in British Columbia when the province had in W.A.C. Bennett a premier who regarded federal ministers with the same squint that a farmer with a fair daughter might apply to travelling salesmen. Bennett was also his own finance minister, so the likelihood of prying loose the provincial funding was doubly diminished. However, this being BC, a way was found around the immovable object: Williston arranged for individual forest companies to pay the provincial portion and be reimbursed through deductions from the stumpage they owed to Victoria.

I have never known for sure whether this stratagem was a face-saving measure for the benefit of Premier Bennett or a cunning plan devised and conducted *sub rosa* by his Minister of Forests. It would not have been wise to ask at the time, and so the early years of COMDP involved a certain air of the cloak and dagger.

Not long after the program was up and running, however, Bennett was gone and Barrett was in his place. It was with some trepidation that Gordon Draeseke asked for a meeting with Barrett and Williams. He was relieved to find that the NDP thought COMDP was a fine idea, or perhaps it was just that Dave Barrett knew that the Old Man hadn't cared for the program and that was enough to make him favour it. In either case, COMDP was brought out of the shadows and funded by an open annual provincial payment.

COMDP is a classic example of successful cooperation among governments and private industry for long-term gain. It began in 1971 and ran for twenty-five years, ending in the mid-nineties. In its latter years, the program's membership broadened to include the government and forest industry of Alberta, after BC companies with operations east of the Rockies pushed for their inclusion. In total, the program focused a total of $112 million on expansion of markets in Europe, Japan, China and elsewhere.

My years at COFI were a happy time for me. I was engaged in issues and processes that I found intellectually challenging and I was satisfied with the results of my work. It was a time when everyone sensed that the world was changing; not everyone thought it was for the better, but there was no question that the pace of change was accelerating and that its scope was constantly widening. I've sometimes thought that the best slogan for the time was inadvertently created by John Cleese of the Monty Python troupe: *and now for something completely different.*

I wanted my issues bigger and broader. I wanted to understand the whole business of the forest, from the forest itself all the way to the marketplace. And I wanted to know what was going on in that wider context in which the forest sector was set: the growing interconnectivity of international trade, the redefinition of forest values beyond timber resources that was coming out of both scientific research and a social revolution that was redefining the ethics of resource management. COFI also taught me an advanced course in the art of consensus building that was to come in handy as the years rolled on.

I did not see myself in those days as a prospective future president of the Council. There were many other people who had more qualifications to be seeking that office. If I had any concern about the course of my career it was that the COFI vice presidency kept me focused mostly on matters related to logging and forestry. It was clear to anyone who was reading the newspapers and watching the six o'clock news that forest management was becoming part of an emerging public agenda, so there would be no end of issues and crises for me to get involved in as the years came and went. But as I did so, I would have become more and more a specialist and I had spent my whole career trying to avoid taking up residence in a professional silo.

Yet I was not particularly restless. My life was well balanced: interesting work, success in the projects I undertook, a happy family life as Sharon and I were raising two girls who promised to be interesting and capable women – a promise that they both made good on.

Still, letters and telexes would arrive, the phone would ring and people would want to take me to lunch and talk about this or that opportunity. One of the people who called was an old friend, Les Reed, who had worked for COFI. He had a consulting firm now and he was getting into a consortium with another, bigger consulting outfit, Reid Collins, and with the engineering firm, H.A. Simons. There was a project on the near horizon: Les Reed wanted a partner with my set of skills to join a CIDA-sponsored team that would help plan the development of the forest sector in Colombia. There would also be other interesting assignments during the Colombian project and down the road.

It was an attractive prospect from the beginning. I would be a partner in a small consultancy, but allied with other firms whose aggregate size made us competitive for world-class international projects. I would be working with some very talented people, and that's always the best way to learn and improve your own skills.

Colombia also offered a wider scope than what I was handling at COFI: although I would be mainly concerned with pulp and paper, I would nevertheless be involved in studies that would delineate a whole country's forest-related industrial potential; I would be examining issues of financing and investment in an international financial context; I would be dealing with reforestation and afforestation, wild trees and plantation trees; I would have to understand labour force issues in a markedly different society with a history much unlike Canada's; I'd be mapping out directions and spotting downstream bottlenecks – all the kinds of things I loved grappling with.

Once again, there was much talking it over with people whose opinions I valued – Harry Smith, Bob Wood, Ian Chenoweth, as well as Mrs. Apsey. They all encouraged me to make the leap. I talked to each of the COFI board members, to make sure I was leaving on good terms, with no bridges smouldering in ruins behind me.

In the end, it was the prospect of going to a place I had never been, walking a kind of forest I had never seen, meeting new people with new problems and potentials, encompassing a whole new array of facts and issues, challenges and opportunities. I was not yet forty and I wanted some more adventure. I became a partner in FLC Reed and Associates and started packing for South America.

And, no, it had nothing to do with Dave Barrett having become Premier of British Columbia.

CHAPTER SEVEN

A Stranger in a Strange Land

Many Colombians speak English, but it is impolite, at the least, to go to work in someone else's country without taking the time to learn the language. Before I could pitch up in Cali, Colombia, therefore, I would spend seven weeks in Antigua, the old capital of Guatemala, in a Spanish immersion school. They were to be seven of the most enjoyable weeks of my life.

Antigua then was a relic of old-time Spanish colonial rule, set high in the mountains and overlooked by volcanoes. It was laid out in classic style, with a grid of straight streets that met at right angles, and full of crumbling eighteenth-century churches and the ruins of imposing buildings that had been destroyed in an earthquake over two hundred years before.

Some members of the team stayed in small hotels or *pensiones* but I wanted the full experience and boarded with a Guatemalan family. I do not know if aboriginal Guatemalans now use an equivalent to our term "First Nations," but in those days my hosts were called *indios*, and they all lived together, grandparents, parents, children and various kinds of livestock, in a compound that included the family business, a small general store. Out back were two rows of some small concrete-and-brick chambers in which I and some Guatemalan students lived. Mine had a cot and a chair and I shared it with the family's pet duck that was called Pijije (Pee-hee-hay), a

"Pijije," my Guatemalan friend and roommate, 1974.

name that must have come from a local aboriginal language. I am guessing at the spelling; I never saw it written down and no speaker of Spanish I have encountered knows what it means. Still, Pijije was a civilized being for a duck and we got along quite well.

The nearby school was a delightful experience. A number of teachers worked one-on-one with us; I particularly remember a stern young woman named Gladys who would drill me hard all day in the tenses of Spanish verbs then send me off with two or three hours of homework that she would strictly check in the morning. She spoke very little English and intended to use none of it if she could help it. I was there to learn Spanish and she meant to see that I did.

I came home to my host family who spoke no English at all so I quickly began to pick up the words and expressions that are necessary if one does not want to go hungry. I also practised a lot on the children who always seemed to be swarming about the place. Kids are kids, wherever in the world you go, playing the same kinds of games and always curious about strangers.

The seven weeks weren't all work. As usual, I took every opportunity to get out and about and to see the sights. Again, I saw a forest that was unlike any other, clinging to the slopes of cloud-wreathed volcanoes. I drove around the back roads and explored little villages. Everywhere the people were friendly and open, and each village had its stalls hung with woven fabrics, clothes and blankets dyed in fantastic colours, or roadside stands with animals carved from wood or ingeniously fashioned from gourds, again painted in the brightest pigments. It seemed as if the Guatemalans could never get enough colour in their lives; even the sides of their little two-wheeled donkey carts were decorated with great big mandalas, intricately detailed.

I was fortunate to have arrived in Antigua just before Easter. The Guatemalans' way of celebrating Holy Week – Semana Santa in Spanish – made my high-church Anglican observances look like a pale and bloodless imitation. Days before Good Friday, volunteers from all walks of life come to the streets with sacks of sawdust dyed yellow, red, green, and blue. Using pre-cut patterns, they cover the pavement with brightly coloured sawdust "carpets" decorated with flowers and crosses and religious phrases. The carpets are hundreds of metres long, wonderful examples of folk art.

But the artwork is doomed to destruction. On Easter Sunday, religious celebrants dressed in colourful capes and hats gather at one end of the carpet. Scores of men, carefully chosen to be of equal height, hoist onto their shoulders enormous "floats" of polished wood on which stand life-sized carved figures illustrating the Passion of Jesus. A special float bearing an image of the Virgin Mary is carried by women. Crowds line both sides of the streets as the sacred statues are paraded along the processional way, the footsteps of the float-bearers obliterating the intricate designs of the sawdust carpets as they go.

I saw the process from first preparation through to the last image in the procession. It was an amazing spectacle, solemn and joyous

Guatemala: Semana Santa – Sawdust "carpet," 1974.

Guatemala: Semana Santa – Ladies carrying float of the Virgin Mary, 1974.

at the same time. The dignity of the people carrying the images was profound, the strength of their belief was humbling. We who live in a society that focuses so much on the marketplace should be reminded by those devout Guatemalans, some of them the poorest of the poor, that there is more to human existence than mere getting and spending. I felt privileged to have witnessed it.

When the seven weeks were up, the family with whom I had been staying threw a small farewell party. We had not had many conversations – I had started out with no Spanish and ended up with the rudiments of grammar and a basic vocabulary – but it was an emotional event for all of us. It doesn't take long to come to love people, and I am not ashamed to say that I loved these people with whom I had lived for seven weeks, and that the sentiment was mutual. Two years later, driving back from Panama to BC, I dropped in on the family again. On their living room wall were a few photographs of

On a street in Chichicastenango I saw a man crawling on hands and knees. He was leaving streaks of blood on the pavement. I thought he must have been in an accident, perhaps knocked down by a car. I couldn't understand why I was the only one going to his aid.

But he waved me away, almost angrily. I had acquired enough Spanish to understand that he did not want my help. He was crawling to the church up the street, had already come a long way on his hands and knees, wearing his best suit. His trousers were ripped and the skin of his palms and knees had been worn away, exposing the raw flesh beneath.

As I watched, fascinated and at the same time sickened, the man crawled up the steps of the church and went inside. He was performing a penance for a sin he had committed, or perhaps fulfilling a vow in return for a blessing received.

For a moment, I was reminded that I was a stranger in a strange land. ■

saints and family members – and a photo of me. Tears came to my eyes.

What has all of this got to do with the price of two-by-fours? Not a lot, I'll admit. I was in Guatemala for only a short time, and all I had to do was learn enough Spanish to get along in Colombia. In writing this book I could have skipped over those seven weeks with a single sentence and gone on to the forest of Colombia, but this is not just a book about my work – it's about my life.

The time that I have spent in foreign countries, among people with different cultures and different histories, especially indigenous peoples, has meant a great deal to me. Just as I could never be content to sit behind a desk and accept that reality could be contained in lists of facts and columns of numbers, I would not have missed the chance to see other worlds. To any young forester who is sitting in a comfortable chair reading these words I offer this advice: go and see the world; the wider your scope, the richer your understanding of who you are, where you came from and where you are going.

With just enough Spanish to be dangerous, I flew to Panama City, stayed overnight then caught a flight to Cali, Colombia. I would have liked to have seen the Panama Canal – now there's a project with scope! – but there wasn't time, though I promised myself to come back and examine this engineering marvel when I could.

CIDA's Colombian forestry project was already underway. I was assigned a Colombian government counterpart to work with, Alvaros Vasquez, but not long after I arrived he went to work for the *Cafeteros*, the coffee growers who created Juan Valdez. I saw him later in Bogotá; he always had the best coffee for me.

My next Colombian partner was Francisco Flores from the National Institute of Natural Resources, which was always referred to as Inderena. The project mandate was to work with Inderena to conduct a thorough analysis of Colombia's forest resources and industrial infrastructure, then come up with workable plans for future development and make recommendations on how to get from here to there. Another feature of the project was to facilitate knowledge transfer, including the granting of scholarships for Colombian foresters to come to Canada and study.

I threw myself into the work. It was a dual-track assignment for me: on the one hand, I was the team member with expertise on the industrial side, especially in pulp and paper, and I was giving advice on financing mills and marketing products; on the other hand, I was still learning the territory. I prepared a number of studies on raw materials, markets, availability of capital, size and quality of the labour force and so on.

Naturally, I did not do this work sitting in the project office in Cali. The original focus of my portion of the project was Colombia's Pacific coastal region, although it later expanded to cover every forested region of that country's extremely diverse geography. So as soon as I could I got down to the coast – literally; Cali is on a high plateau about one thousand metres above sea level – and took a look at the reality.

Travel from Cali to the coast was often by plane. In Colombia in the 1970s, "plane" usually meant a dilapidated DC-3. I was advised early on always to ask the pilot of such a plane two questions: "Do you own this plane?" and "Do you have a family?" If the answer to either question was, "No," it was not a good idea to board.

Here is an entry from my diary regarding one memorable plane trip back from the coast:

August 15, Friday
Up very early to get to airport at 8 a.m. as requested by the "Captain of the Airport." It, the airport, is about a 25 minute walk in the humid heat.

We were there at 8, 9, 10, 11, 12, 1, 2 and 3 when we gave up and went back to town, not expecting the flight.

I was thirty-six years old, a forester who had seen the varied forest zones of British Columbia, the forest of many other parts of Canada, the forest of Turkey, even some of the forest of Central America – but I was not prepared for the overwhelming richness of the Colombian coastal forest. This was 1974 and I'd yet to hear the word "biodiversity," though I probably could have come up with a definition if anyone had sprung the term on me. But that definition would have failed by orders of magnitude to capture the reality of Colombia.

Consider the British Columbia coastal forest: vast stands of Sitka spruce, Douglas fir and hemlock and a handful of other species, with a dense undergrowth of salal and ferns and some fast-growing deciduous opportunists wherever a big tree has fallen and opened the canopy to sunlight. Then look at the coastal forest some six thousand kilometres to the south: up to two hundred different tree species or more in a single hectare, and a riot of undergrowth so thick and prolific that a trail chopped through it by machete will disappear within days. Through it all there ran, flew, leapt, wriggled, crawled, slithered and oozed an incredible variety of critters – many of which were eager to bite, suck or bore into tender Apsey flesh, with results ranging from maddening irritation to sudden death.

Just walked back when we heard it come in so ran back to find it taking off for Tumaco. Another hour delay.

They shoved us into the plane at 5 p.m. The other passengers were well oiled by then – 9 hours of drinking. The plane was the oldest DC-3 I have seen – no pressure, wooden floors, etc. Vomit all over the front, dead fish in back, therefore it was an odourous flight.

A weird flight pattern through the Andes and it, the pattern, got weirder as we got closer to Cali. After we landed we learned we had no flaps!

Got home to find Sharon very worried – I guess with good reason as Colombia did lose quite a few DC-3s. ▪

No picture or description does justice to the richness and diversity of Colombia's forest. Part of my assignment was to concentrate on the development potential of the coast, but in order to understand the region I had to know about the whole country. I paddled through mangrove swamps at the ocean's edge, followed rivers into the coastal jungle. From there the land climbs sharply toward the mountains, and soon the ground is covered by higher-elevation rain forest, which gives way to a more dry upland forest farther up-slope. Then the terrain becomes too dry for trees and there is a belt of high-altitude desert. Once over the heights of the mountains, the land descends through more varieties of forest down into the headwaters of the Amazon and a different kind of jungle. In the high country, there were plantations of pines and other softwoods, including non-indigenous exotic species imported from all over the world. And they grew faster than a BC forester would ever have expected – as little as fifteen years from seedling to harvestable size.

There were few roads through the coastal forest; people travelled from port to port along the coast in motor boats; to go inland, they used smaller craft with outboards to make their way up the muddy, tea-colored waters of the rivers; when they got so far upstream that the water was too shallow for outboards, they switched to dug-out canoes whose design had not changed since the stone age.

And when I say "they," I include Mike Apsey. I could have visited the major port cities and gathered second-hand reports from inland. But having read this far, the reader will know that I did not do so. Several times, eager to take a look at the situation on the ground, I gingerly lowered myself onto the thwarts of a hollowed out half-log and set off up some slow-moving stream with a local boatman as my guide.

I have always been an avid amateur photographer and took many snaps during my Colombian jungle travels. There are no images, however, of Mike Apsey precariously positioned in a dugout canoe. To spare posterity, I have destroyed them all. ∎

Colombia: My coastal riverboat and boatman, 1975.

Colombia: Coastal river village, 1975.

I would arrive at a village of reed-thatched huts built on stilts; the rivers were likely to flood and the elevated accommodations discouraged some (but not all) creepy-crawlies from joining the dwellers. The population might have been transferred directly from Africa, the coastal regions of Colombia and Ecuador having been settled originally by escaped African slaves, some of whom formed their own independent states far back in the colonial era. Some of the men, most of the women and virtually all of the children in these places had never been out of their villages and had never seen a person of my complexion. Nor of my size.

My canoe paddled up to a landing, a flight of stone steps deep in the jungle. Three small black boys were standing at the top of the stairs watching me. As I gingerly lifted myself out of the shallow water craft, the boys' eyes widened and one of them, his voice full of awe, whispered, "*Gordo.*" It is the Spanish word for "fat." The little one next to him said, "*Gordísimo!*" The translation: supremely fat!

Colombia: My coastal river village friend, 1975.

Columbia: Typical coastal sawmill, 1975.

I met with all kinds of people: government officials, exporters and importers, executives of corporations, local entrepreneurs
and foreign expatriates running small sawmills, plantation owners,
dwellers in upstream villages who cut a few logs (to which they may
or may not have a legal claim) and raft them down to mills on the
rivers. Few of the facilities were up-to-date by North American standards. Some of the back-country operations were as primitive as
things could get: a barefoot young woman standing on hardwood

In another village, a group of women came up to me. One of them said
something to the others then she rubbed her fingers up and down my
cheek and examined them.

"What does she want?" I asked my guide.

"She wants to see if the white rubs off," he said.

I thought to myself, "Mike, you're a long way from Vernon." ∎

Colombia: Coastal logger, 1975.

logs floating in shallow streams, hacking away with an axe at the wood between her feet or a man on a floating trunk who swings a sledgehammer to drive in a spike positioned by another man standing neck-deep in the water.

The coast of Colombia in the mid-seventies was a socio-economic transitional zone where the modern cash economy met an ancient

Colombia: Well-dressed young lady bucks logs in the coastal forest, 1975.

Colombia: Preparing coastal logs for river transport to mill or for export, 1975.

subsistence economy. The two did not always evenly match up. A local expatriate, Bob Peck, explained to me that the mills used to pay some people who lived in the back country to cut timber and bring it downstream for twenty pesos a log. The arrangement brought in five logs a day, and after a while the companies decided to offer twenty-five pesos a log, thinking that the extra incentive should get six or seven logs delivered to the mill. Instead, the suppliers took the twenty-five pesos and began bringing in four logs a day.

Harvesting rights in Colombia's state-owned coastal forests were allocated under a concession system, but in practice the rules were abrogated by endemic corruption at all levels. Once, after meetings with government officials in a coastal port, I was having an informal drink with them in a seaside establishment when we saw a large cargo ship heavily laden with first-class logs putting out to sea. I asked one of the Colombians where the ship was headed, and he said it was probably going to the United States where the extreme-value wood would become fine furniture. From what I had learned of the fees and taxes to be paid to the government on such timber, I

The people up those rivers and creeks were living a simple life, getting almost all they needed from the forest or from the crops and livestock they raised themselves. For goods they couldn't produce themselves they would cut a few trees to sell down river – the legal ownership of the timber was entirely an abstract concept.

Their ancestors had fled slavery, gone into the jungle and carved out a way of life for themselves. They seemed to be happy with their lives, doing what their ancestors had done for generations. Yet I was part of a project that was intended to change that way of life, ostensibly for the villagers' own good, or maybe because someone far away wanted to make money.

I would wonder if I was doing the right thing. I still wonder about it today. ■

attempted to calculate the revenue that one shipment should bring to the Colombian treasury. After mentally wrestling for a few moments with the numbers I asked the Colombian civil servant, "How much stumpage do you estimate has been paid on all the magnificent logs on that ship?"

He looked at me without expression and said, "What ship?"

Despite the flaws in the Colombian system – and our project identified many – the foresters there were doing their best for the forest. Their dedication to understanding their country's resources and managing them well was unquestionable. They may not have been able to sway their political and economic masters in every case, but they did the best they could in the situations that they faced.

It's easy to be a visiting foreigner and to criticize the locals for corruption. On the other hand, as I was writing this book, the Legislative Buildings in Victoria were raided by the RCMP investigating alleged influence-peddling and the incoming Prime Minister of Canada had his plans entirely derailed by the scandal over the mishandling of advertising funds in Quebec.

To the Colombians, and to people in other countries where I have sojourned, the offering and accepting of benefits are often not seen as corruption. They are the traditional ways of doing business in that culture. But remember: in my early years at MacMillan Bloedel, I was told that the most important thing in my career was that I came from "good stock." Today we would call that racist or ethnic discrimination; back then it was an acknowledged aspect of Canadian culture, though not one we shouted from the rooftops.

These things are better seen in shades of grey than in black and white. And we Canadians, when we are tempted to feel holier than our neighbours, would do well to remember the Biblical verse about the fellow who could see the speck in another's eye but failed to notice the two-by-four stuck in his own. ∎

Foresters are ethical people. That is a truth I have seen in the more than forty countries on six forested continents where I have worked or at least visited.

Of the many reasons why I have never regretted the snap decision I made outside the Vernon Dairy Drive-In all those years ago, one of the blessings I have known from being a forester is the quality of the people I can call my professional brothers and sisters. We work to understand what role the forest plays in the livelihoods and cultures of the people of the world. We work to ensure that the benefits of the forest are shared and enhanced, and that they will continue to flow. We sometimes do so, like my colleagues in Colombia and West Africa, against huge odds, but that just makes the forester's dedication all the more admirable.

For all the cynicism of the times, the profession of forestry remains a noble calling. And the people who practise it deserve respect.

I was on my own in Cali for a while, staying at a pensión until our goods and chattels, including a Ford Maverick, could be shipped to the Pacific port of Buenaventura and brought up to Cali. Then Sharon and the girls flew down. We set up in a very nice rented house in an upscale neighbourhood, and again we had servants. Susan and Jill settled in well, as they always seemed to do, going to an English-speaking school and making friends. Sharon became involved in a number of good works, including a sideline in distributing locally made peanut butter to the many North American expats; for some reason peanut butter was not easily obtained in Cali. My work was engrossing and kept me busy but at the behest of an Anglican priest named Father Hurley who became a good friend, I grew more involved with the church. I am sure it will surprise a few people to learn that Mike Apsey regularly conducted evening classes in Bible study. I was surprised myself to rediscover how much of my early upbringing had clung to me. It struck me as curious that I had to go so far from home – in Cali and among the holy sites of Asia Minor – to reconnect with my spiritual and cultural roots.

We also had an active social life, getting to know many Colombians and other expatriates. Occasionally, however, we received a jarring reminder that we were moving through a foreign culture. Colombia, much more so than modern Canada, had retained the rigid class structure of the Old World, exacerbated by the fact that the upper reaches of society were entirely occupied by descendants of Spanish colonialists, while the lower rungs of the ladder were crowded with the descendants of those they had conquered. I met no Colombian Len Marchands.

When we were getting ready to leave, Sharon and I threw a party for all the people who had been part of our lives in Cali. We invited senior government officials and the wealthy parents of our children's friends as well as people like the men who had driven us around and the nannies who had helped with our girls. It must have been an odd experience for many of our guests because they had never been in the same room with people of the other classes for a purely social occasion.

Another aspect of life that took some getting used to was crime. Cali was not then the headquarters of the drug trade – it was still centered in Medellin – but crime was an acknowledged reality in Colombia, as were the Marxist guerrillas in the hills. Once again, there were unwritten rules to live by. When driving, one wore one's watch on the right wrist; otherwise, it was likely to be snatched through the car window while stopped in traffic. One day, as I was driving Sharon through town and stopped at an intersection, a man dove head first through my open window to grab her purse which she had thought safe enough on the floor. "Hit him" she said to me, and after a moment's shock I did so; it took several blows to convince the thief that the prize was not worth the punishment and sometimes my knuckles still ache from where my last punch missed and connected instead with the window frame.

Our Ford Maverick afforded me a lesson in the unwritten rules of Cali. Our rented house had a garage but there came a time when the car was once left on the street. Although it was unattended for only a few moments, and despite the presence of private security guards in the neighbourhood, one of its windshield wipers was stolen. Months later, in another part of the city, the second wiper disappeared.

I had a car and driver from the project, but Sharon was dependent on the Maverick to get around. When the rainy season was about to arrive, she made it clear that wipers would have to be obtained. Guided by my driver, I went the rounds of dealerships and found that, as he had prophesied, parts were hard to obtain in Cali.

He then suggested we drive to a certain part of the city that I had been advised to avoid. He said there would be nothing to worry about so I accepted his assurances and off we went. We came to

The guerrilla war was in its early days back then, but it was a common experience to be stopped and searched by armed troops or by agents of the Department of Administrative Security (DAS), the secret police. The first time I encountered the latter, I was bemused by the experience until I noticed how my driver, normally a happy, easygoing fellow, was rigid with fear. It struck me once again that this was a different place where they played by different rules, and that they played for keeps. In my last few days in Cali, having put British Columbia licence plates back on the Maverick in preparation for shipping to Panama so I could drive home, I was pulled over by the DAS and put through a very frightening search and grilling.

On another occasion, I was with my friend John Spears of the World Bank, whom I had known when he was taking a masters degree at UBC. He was interested in seeing some high-country softwood growing areas and plantations, so we made arrangements to visit some of the plantations around Popayan.

a street which was lined with small enterprises bursting with used auto parts.

I wanted to stop and look for wipers but the driver said, "No, no, keep going."

We drove slowly down one block, then another. "Keep going," he said.

In the third block, a man stepped into the street and waved us to stop. "Here we are," my driver said.

The man in the street had our wipers. Not just similar wipers, but the very wipers taken from our car in two separate thefts in two different parts of the city, months apart. He'd been waiting for me to come and get them. I gave him money and he handed them over. It was all very civilized.

When you go to a foreign country, you have to learn the rules. Then you can get along. ▪

We set off in our usual first-world innocence only to come around a corner of a country road and find our way blocked by Colombian Army jeeps with machine guns mounted on the backs and trucks full of armed soldiers. They were our escort, arranged without our knowledge by the local governor. They conducted us on our tour and wherever we went we found more soldiers, guarding intersections along the way and standing at the ready among the plantation trees.

I thought it was all a bit overdone. But years later, chatting with some people during a reception at a conference on the world's tropical forest in The Hague, I fell into conversation with members of the Colombian delegation. When I mentioned my time in Colombia another Colombian man overheard and came over to take a look at me. He examined my face closely for a while then nodded. Of course, I wanted to know the nature of his interest. It turned out he had seen my face before. He had been with the guerrillas and the name and photo of Mike Apsey had been posted on a wall that displayed persons who might be worth kidnapping for ransom. I will admit to feeling a chill.

The CIDA project had some useful results. Some of our recommendations were accepted by the government and put into effect while we were still there. I wrote a couple of final reports – my pulp and paper study became the basis for the development of Colombia's industry – and prepared to leave. We had brought some Canadian expertise and we left it behind, though not all of what we proposed was acceptable to the Colombian authorities. We found flaws in their system and recommended some changes, especially to do with managing the coastal forest, that went against the grain. Government policy would have to change drastically, upsetting a lot of well-connected people.

But even with mixed results, I was glad to have been part of the project. My work in Colombia had attracted attention and I was receiving offers from the World Bank, the Asian Development Bank, the UN and other international agencies. I kept reminding myself that if I let my head swell, I would have to buy several new hats.

I was more than content to stay with Les Reed and Associates. During my Colombian time I had taken a leave from the project and conducted a major study for a Chilean company, INFORSA, on the newsprint industry in Central and South America. I did background research on each country, examining their mills, their levels of production and demand, export and import factors, and the opportunities I could see on the horizon. The work took me to Mexico, Panama, Venezuela, Peru, Bolivia, Argentina and Brazil, then to Chile to discuss my findings and back to Colombia to put the main study together. I was also invited to Puerto Rico to visit a forest research station where I saw a rare event: bamboo in bloom.

I was having a very good time being an international consultant. The work was intellectually challenging, the results satisfying, and the opportunities to see more of the world were glorious. I was tackling economic, environmental, social and cultural issues, coming to understand different government processes in a wide variety of contexts – because no two South or Central American countries are the same, any more than France is Germany. I was seeing problems and opportunities from both the government and industrial sides of the table, because I was advising both. I was getting to see how ideas translate into reality on the ground. Much of it was new territory for me, and I revelled in all that wonderfully wide scope.

I already knew that context was crucial and I was getting all the context I could. I came away from Colombia with an understanding of another part of the world's forest. I was coming to understand

I was out in the jungle when the skin of my right foot came off. I peeled away my sock and saw nothing but raw flesh and blisters. My driver said, "We must find a *farmacia*."

We drove to the nearest village and asked a man if there were any medical facilities nearby. He shook his head and asked what was the problem. I showed him my foot.

"Ah," he said, "*Ningun problemo*. You must go to the end of the road and ask for Juan."

We drove down the dirt track to its end. We found a shack with the rusted, vine wreathed hulks of abandoned cars and trucks. Apparently it was where Colombian vehicles, like African elephants, came to die.

Juan came out of the shack. He was not a figure to inspire medical confidence. Still, I showed him my foot.

"*Venga conmigo*," he said. Come with me.

I limped after him to a ramshackle shed. There was a covered pot on the dirt floor. Juan picked up a rusted coffee can from the ground, knocked some dirt out of it, and lifted the lid of the pot. He dipped the can into the pot and scooped up a quantity of grey goo.

"What is it?" I said.

"I don't know," he said. "But I know that this will fix that." "Where did you get it?" I asked. "*De la selva*," he said. From the forest. I slathered the grey goo on my foot. It got better. The world's forest is full of such wonders, if we are capable of seeing them. And if we see them in time, because the tropical forest is being lost at a horrendous rate. ∎

that what we mean by "the forest" depends so much on the context from which we come. In the dry zones, a forest might be a few trees, metres apart. In Canada, it might be boreal pines or thousand-year-old cedars. In Colombia, it was tropical hardwoods in the jungles and tall softwoods in the high country.

I was understanding how much difference a history makes, how we relate to the forest in so many different ways, how we so often see what we are culturally conditioned to see. Some look at the forest and see an economic resource. Some see a home. Some see a holy place. Some see a future. Some see an ancient relationship. The forest is all of these things and more. We have to stretch our minds, perhaps even open our souls, to see all that there is to see, and perhaps we will never be able to see it all.

We sent our goods and the Maverick down to the port of Buenaventura, the former to be shipped to Vancouver, the latter to Panama from where I intended to drive the car home. I had a once-in-a-lifetime opportunity to see the territory between the Isthmus of Panama and the Strait of Georgia, and I meant to take it.

Sharon and the girls were to fly home. I drove them to the airport and discovered the wisdom of always having money on one's person when trying to leave a foreign country. First, it turned out that if my children were to leave Colombia without their father they would need a notarized letter of permission from me.

Apparently, there had been a persistent problem of young Norteamericana women marrying dashing Colombianos but after relocating to their husbands' homeland the northern-bred wives would decide that Latino machismo got wearisome after a while. They would go home, taking with them their children as is common in North American divorces. Divorce in Colombia was a whole different matter: husbands were raised to believe that everything in a marriage, including offspring, was theirs to retain or dispose of. A law was passed to prevent flibbertigibbet females from absconding with the kids. And we ran right into it, requiring a certain amount of argumentation and a discreet cash contribution – ostensibly to purchase new exit visas – to smooth the way.

I was embarrassed and angry for Sharon's sake. Such laws do not serve to make a woman feel that she is an equal and capable human being, which is a minimum description of Sharon Apsey. In a foreign country, you have to play by the local rules, but you don't always have to like it.

In the end, Sharon and the girls flew home and I caught a plane to Panama where I spent some time being a tourist waiting for the Maverick to arrive. I went to see the Miraflores locks of the Canal and a forest preserve or two, and kept checking with the harbour master to see if the ship carrying the car had come into port. Finally I was assured that its wheels were on dry land and went down with the papers to get it.

I found it in a warehouse, but the customs official I had to see had taken the afternoon off. I went back to my hotel and returned in the morning. The car had been moved. I found an American, an agent of the Drug Enforcement Agency, and asked him if someone had been driving around in my Maverick. He said no, they'd spent the day taking it apart and putting it back together. No car coming from Colombia was going to enter Panama without getting a thorough looking over.

The car had been somewhat loosely reassembled. I had to take it to a mechanic to have everything tightened up before taking it on a continent-spanning road trip. Then I made the round of Central American consulates, gathering the required stamps and official documents – I had to go to the Canadian authorities to get ten more pages added to my passport to hold all the stamps. Then I bought myself a Big Mac to celebrate being back in North America, and set off in the direction of Canada.

My journey, along secondary roads and minor highways, was a kaleidoscope of sights and impressions: in David, Panama, I saw more lizards and snakes in one day than in two years in Colombia;

in Costa Rica, the rain forest was magnificent, the scenery of rivers and mountains spectacular. At one spot along the way it was possible to see both the Atlantic and Pacific Oceans; Nicaragua was volcanoes and lava flows, its capital still largely in ruins from the 1972 earthquake.

Guatemala was like coming home – I paid an emotional return visit to my host family, and now that I could speak more than a few words of Spanish we had a wonderful time. I renewed my acquaintance with Pijije and visited my former teachers. But I was sad to see that much of Antigua had been destroyed in an earthquake.

Wherever I had an opportunity, I visited forest research centres and sawmills. Costa Rica's forest management practices and research facilities were impressive. The mills in Nicaragua were much more sophisticated than on the coast of Colombia. And everywhere the forest was different and the people in and around it had adapted their ways of life to meet the realities of their particular part of the global forest.

There were adventures at border crossings: guns directed my way, extensive searches, full-bore fumigations, suspicious looks and pointed questions. At the bridge between Honduras and El Salvador, I asked the border guards if it would be all right for me to take a cooling swim in the river. They laughed uproariously. "Only if you want both sides shooting at you," they said. It was about seven years since the two countries had gone to war in what came to be known as the "Soccer War," after a hotly contested World Cup elimination match.

I drove through the Guatemalan highlands and over into Mexico. The Maverick was again taken apart and fumigated. Then I was seeing Aztec temples and mariachi bands in town squares, all the vibrant life and colour of Mexico. I stopped in Oaxaca to see the oldest living thing in North America: *el arbol del Tule*, the "Tule Tree," a Montezuma cypress that is ten metres thick, fifty-four metres in circumference and forty-three metres high. It is more than two thousand years old and it is still alive and growing.

I drove up from Nogales across the border to Tucson, Arizona then headed west through the desert to San Diego – accompanied for part of the way on a lonely desert highway by scores of Hell's Angels. Sharon flew down to join me in San Diego and we drove home together by the tourist route – Los Angeles, Las Vegas, Reno.

The trip was a chance to think and unwind after two fairly high-pressure years overseas. I decided that I liked the life I was living. I had worked for a government, a major corporation, an industry association and a consultancy. I had seen several parts of the world and wanted to see more. I had had the opportunity to view the forest sectors of those places from a variety of different angles: forest management, marketing, manufacturing, financing, regulating and from the viewpoints of local and indigenous peoples.

A picture was beginning to form in my head, a big picture of the world's forest and the people who dealt with it. The more I saw of the world, the more complex that picture grew, and the more interrelated its many components revealed themselves to be. I was looking forward to seeing more of that picture. It was like solving an immense jigsaw puzzle, but a puzzle that had not come in a box with a photo on the cover. The picture emerged as I fitted the pieces together. I was fascinated to see what would finally develop.

CHAPTER EIGHT
Big Stuff

It was December 3, 1976. I was at home preparing for a trip to London, Dusseldorf, Hamburg, Stockholm and Rome to investigate the market potential of Honduran pine. FLC Reed and Associates had a major contract to map out a larger future for the Honduran forest sector and I had been having a fine time all through the fall trying to discover how much bigger their picture could be.

Then the phone rang. It was my old COFI colleague, Bob Wood. He was working as an advisor to the forest minister in the Bill Bennett government: Tom Waterland, a mining engineer who had put his career on hold to run for the Socreds after witnessing what a pig's breakfast the NDP had made of the once-booming mining sector in British Columbia. Bennett had made Tom the minister responsible for the forest as well as for many of the province's other natural resources. The comprehensive nature of the portfolio was a measure of the Premier's confidence in Waterland's abilities, a confidence that was well founded.

Although Bob Wood had been a close advisor to Bob Williams during the Barrett years, Waterland knew brains when he saw them and had sensibly kept him on. Now the minister was tasking Wood with overseeing one of the new administration's major initiatives, and my friend was calling me to ask if I would like to be part of his crew.

I knew the background, of course: Peter Pearse, the one-man Royal Commissioner of Inquiry into the Forest Resource appointed by the NDP back in 1975, had tendered his report to the Bennett government in September, 1976. Dr. Pearse had done an insightful and wide-ranging analysis of what was right and what was wrong with the forest sector in BC and had not shied away from recommending fundamental changes. Now the new government was expected to respond. They wanted Bob Wood to put together a review committee of knowledgeable fellows without obvious axes to grind who could advise them on what that response should be.

It was suitable work for a Sancho Panza with a varied background in forest economics and Bob Wood thought I might like to saddle up and come take a look at some windmills. He couldn't give me details at the moment but wanted to know if I was agreeable in principle. I was immensely flattered and said yes right away.

I didn't need details to know that I would be happy working with Bob. There was no one I held in higher esteem. He had long been one of my mentors, and I knew that his knowledge of the BC forest sector was encyclopedic. In his mid-forties, he had brains and experience on all sides of the table. He was also a deeply honourable man. If you asked him a question, you got a direct and well thought out answer. And you'd be smart to put your money on its being the right answer.

The other members of the committee were already chosen: Bob Wood was the chair; John Stokes, who until then had been Deputy Minister of Forests, was being seconded to the committee, while Chief Forester Ted Young stepped in as chief executive officer of the Forest Service; Wes Cheston, resources manager, BC Forest Service; and Dr. Jim Rae, an assistant deputy minister from the Ministry of Economic Development rounded out the complement. There would be government staff and consultants to deepen our backfield on legal, financial and accounting questions. We would be known as the Forest Policy Advisory Committee.

Forest Policy Advisory Committee, 1977. L to R: Mike Apsey, Steve Hollett, Jim Rae, Bob Wood, Wes Cheston, John Stokes, Hon. Tom Waterland, Ken Reid.

I called Les Reed and told him of the offer. Bob Wood had said they would need me for ten days a month to start with but when we got well into the review process there would be full months of work. We would be scoping out the future direction of the entire BC forest sector, to the point of writing major new legislation. Les said, "Wow," which summed up my feelings exactly.

I went off to Europe, where I served the interests of Honduran pine to the best of my ability – it was, in fact, a fascinating assignment – and came back to a series of more detailed discussions with Bob Wood and Les Reed over Christmas and New Year's.

I was familiar with Peter Pearse's report; anybody who was interested in the forest sector had got a copy from the Queen's Printer when it was released to the public. I had gone through it with interest, finding much to agree with and a few things, like the proposal for forest products marketing boards, that caused me to say, "Whoa, I don't think so." But there was a difference between being a professionally interested reader and being asked to turn the Royal Commissioner's work into new law.

This was no ordinary consulting assignment. FPAC would be fundamentally redesigning the legislative underpinnings of the forest sector in British Columbia, writing the laws under which the vast public forest would be managed, the industry would be operated and the futures of dozens of communities and scores of thousands of individual lives would be shaped. But the scope went far beyond forest companies and forest workers. It affected all the people who used the forest, from backpackers to hunters. It affected people who fished for salmon, people who looked after tourists, ranchers who grazed their cattle on public lands. And it went far beyond BC's borders: Bay Street financiers and truck drivers all over the continent would be touched by what FPAC did.

The apartment Bob Wood and I shared had a maid service but we were expected to do our own dishes in the built-in dishwasher. Although I felt quite competent to be shaping forest policies, I would admit that Sharon and I had made an old-fashioned marriage that had left me unskilled in the operation of domestic devices. Still, one evening, when the dirty dishes had built up to an intimidating height, I put them in the machine and filled it with soap.

However, the only soap we had was a laundry detergent. I was familiar with its properties from having washed clothes in cold water while out in the bush so I made sure to use plenty. I switched on the dishwasher then went into the living room to discuss lofty forest issues with Bob.

After a certain amount of pleasant conversation he got up to go to the washroom. He did not come back. Instead, he called from the hallway to say that he had to go over to the legislative buildings, having just remembered that he had a late meeting. I said goodbye

It was big stuff. To be asked to stand at the turning point and guide the forest sector onto a new road was a great honour. It was also a daunting prospect. I phoned my father and asked him what he thought. He grasped the dimensions of the situation right away. In fact, for a long moment, he was speechless. Then he told me he believed I could do it, and that it was up to me to get it right.

I had some qualms about whether I could handle this big a job, but I told myself that even Sancho Panza must have had a few of those butterflies-in-the-stomach moments. In the vernacular of the seventies, I went for it. In January, 1977, I put my shares in FLC Reed in trust, swore an oath of secrecy and pitched up in Victoria ready to go to work. Bob Wood and I shared an apartment in the same James Bay neighbourhood where I had lived fifteen years before. FPAC rented a suite of offices at the Harbour Towers Hotel and we started plotting a course through Peter Pearse's map of the future.

I began with a thorough review of the past. I needed to understand how forest policy in our province had evolved, so I read every study, report, and record of debate I could lay my hands on, including those of the two previous Royal Commissions. I made my way

and remained in the living room, contemplating the future of the forest in British Columbia.

A little while later, I rose from my contemplations and began tidying up. I went out into the hallway, only to be met by a scene from a science fiction movie: a dense, glistening mound was pulsating toward me, its rainbowed surface ripe with bursting bubbles. Undaunted, I forced a way through it to the kitchen and ascertained that that room was as full of soap suds as ever a room could be.

Bob, having seen this event at an earlier stage, had decided that it would be far more satisfying to be over at the buildings, telling everyone he could find about it, than to remain at home and join in the four solid hours of labour that it took me to subdue the products of our dishwasher's enthusiasm. ■

through old newspapers and professional journals, memoirs and books. And I studied Dr. Pearse's report from the table of contents to the last appendix.

Peter Pearse's two-volume, five-hundred-plus page report was a coherent argument for a thorough revamping of BC forest policies. He and his staff had received over two hundred submissions and held weeks of public hearings in six cities, not to mention field trips around the province to examine problems at first hand. His conclusions: the patchwork of forest policies, many of them developed in ad hoc responses to this or that emerging situation, were a significant constraint on the ability of the forest sector to expand, diversify and compete in a changing world.

The government, he said, operated without a clear resource management policy and had no adherence to a specific pattern of industrial development. The forest industry had no guarantee of continued – or, in some cases, equitable – access to the raw materials on which it depended, with serious implications for its present stability and future investment. There was also a lopsided relationship between the big integrated companies and the smaller operators which favoured the former over the latter.

A key focus of the report was on the tenure system by which access to the public forest was allocated to private users. Dr. Pearse declared the system to be "riddled with inappropriate terms, inconsistencies, ambiguities and discretionary elements that threaten the security of licensees' rights and undermine the legal clarity required in contractual undertakings between the Crown and private parties."

Dr. Pearse endorsed the longstanding policy of keeping the forest under public ownership, but recommended that the terms of all licences be made more specific – especially the older tenure arrangements that had granted some companies access to large stretches of forest land in perpetuity. He called for shorter-term licences, renegotiable after set periods, and for opening a larger portion of the annual harvest to smaller operators and to Aboriginal users. He also recommended a more up-to-date methodology for classifying forest lands and more flexibility in the regulations governing utilization and environmental protection.

The report was the most comprehensive set of standards and guidelines that had been offered to the forest sector since the Sloan Commission of the mid-1950s. But it was not a blueprint for action. It pointed out what Dr. Pearse thought ought to be done, but not specifically how to do it. That task required the writing of new laws, specifically a new Forest Act, a new Range Act and a new concept: a Ministry of Forests Act that would allow for the reorganization and redirection of the people whose job it was to manage the public forest.

The provincial government, to its credit, did not want to treat the Pearse Report as so many Royal Commission reports have been treated in our country – as an object to decorate a library shelf. The government recognized that we were in the early stages of a time of great and accelerating change. They wanted the forest sector, then providing the single greatest stream of revenue to the treasury, to be fit to expand and succeed in the coming new era. FPAC was not to tinker with the system; we were to rebuild from scratch.

The government wanted to introduce a new legislative package in the 1978 spring session of the Legislative Assembly. That gave us a little more than a year to consult with the forest sector and create the new draft bills.

We put out requests for briefs from anyone who wished to make comments. We held meetings around the province, most of them one-on-one encounters with representatives of a particular company or association. These sessions were private because we wanted people to tell us what they really thought rather than be constrained by the prospect of having their views overheard by business competitors or those who had conflicting interests. The focus, however, was the Pearse report. We asked: do you agree or disagree with this or that recommendation; if so, why? if not, why not?

Most of what we heard was positive; the industry, as a whole, wanted to get rolling and make gains. There was a fair amount of what could only be called individual special pleading and a substantial portion of what we heard concerned somebody's particular problem with some specific regulation.

I developed some sympathy for those in the political process as I realized that almost every regulation has its detractors but each also has its die-hard defender. Later, when I was drawn more deeply into the coils of government, I would be constantly reminded that just about everybody would like to see the annoying confinements of regulation swept away – except, of course, for their particular subclause. Behind every regulation is an interest.

I also came to realize that democratic government works by responding to all those interests. Government does not sit on Olympian heights and create broad visions of the future for this sector or that industry. Instead, it endeavours to give people what they ask for. Sometimes it delivers in a flood, as British Columbia did with the new Acts we were being tasked to create. Sometimes it delivers by creeping increments, as laws are minutely amended.

One thing I've learned: you can't necessarily judge the importance of an issue by the amount of public attention it attracts. For example, the forest management practices that allowed for the build up of massive amounts of dry fuel on the forest floor, resulting in many of the terrible fires of 2003, were a matter of huge import once their inevitable effects ensued – but for two decades virtually no one paid any attention to the issue.

On the other hand, log exports are a continuing hot-button issue, sometimes flaring up into major disputes, especially when some town's mill is idle for lack of timber. Yet exported logs represent only a small percentage of the annual harvest in BC.

The reason why the two issues get different treatment? Perhaps it is because the fire fuel was not a problem until the fires broke out,

But wherever government acts, you can be sure that it is only after it has heard a chorus of voices saying, "Give us such-and-such," with another chorus singing the counterpoint of, "Hands off!" While I was a member of FPAC, I heard from all of them.

It wasn't all regulation-specific, however. Many groups wanted the Forest Service to be more open to public participation in the management of the forest. Forest-dependent communities recognized where their bread and butter came from, but at the same time they saw the quality of the forest around them as a key part of their quality of life, and they wanted their say. As well, the environmental movement, though still in its fledgling state, was certainly stretching its wings as we moved through the 1970s. We were left in no doubt that a growing proportion of British Columbians valued the forest for more than its timber volumes.

The more I heard, sitting in meeting rooms or reading well-argued briefs, the more it dawned on me that we were embarked upon an enormous task. The issues being put before us went all the way from the ecology of the forest through the complexities of the global marketplace. Nor did forest policy exist in splendid isolation from other governmental, economic and social priorities. Everything was connected to everything else, and our action on a particular subject – timber supply, for example – would have repercussions and ramifications in the realms of taxation, transportation, social programs,

while the log exports question comes to life whenever a forest community mayor sees truckloads of logs rolling through his community, passing the idled mill, on their way to some other mayor's town, whether in a foreign country or some other part of BC. If he goes to the press, his complaint will be seconded by the president of the union local that represents the mill workers who have been laid off or had their hours cut back.

The fire fuel issue would have terrible potential some day, but log exports have people shouting and protesting right this minute. Guess which one attracts more TV cameras and newspaper photographers? ∎

community stability, fish and wildlife, investment patterns, and much more. And the reverberations would travel beyond BC's borders, affecting all of Canada and even the economic matrices of other countries.

As all of that dawned on me, I told myself that the enormity of what I was embarked upon was exceeded only by the excitement I was feeling at being right at the centre of things. But that excitement was tempered by an understanding of the importance of getting the answers right. The secret to getting it right was to bring to the work enough scope – not just an understanding of economics but a grasp of the different, and sometimes competing, values that were inherent in the forest resource and of how those values had changed in the past and would certainly change in the future.

Creating a new legislative and regulatory structure for the BC forest sector was the most complex, most challenging assignment of my career. But I was not intimidated. All those trips into Colombian jungles and down the back roads of Turkey and Central America, all those mill visits at MacMillan Bloedel and all those times spent teasing a consensus out of a COFI committee meeting now paid off. I was still only in my late thirties but I had become an all-rounder in more than just my physique. I had looked at the forest from several different sides of the table, had acquired experience and perspective without also acquiring a lot of baggage. I owed no favours and was owed none in return.

Although I was deep into the midst of the FPAC process, I remained a consultant with FLC Reed and Associates. My old employer, the UN's Food and Agriculture Organization and the World Bank asked me to go to West Africa. Ghana had requested the World Bank's assistance in reviewing its forest sector, which was then operating at about half capacity at best. I was the forest economist on a small team drawn from several countries. We spent three weeks conducting a full study of the Ghanaian resource and infrastructure, getting plenty of good information and cooperation from the Ghanaians. We met with port authorities, chiefs of the Ashanti nation, local people in the forest, the Ghana Timber Marketing Board and other government and non-government agencies. One of the Ghanaians had been taught by Peter Pearse in UBC, though I doubt that the connection was where Dr. Pearse's idea for a BC timber marketing board had come from. All told, the assignment meant three weeks in the field, then more time in Rome as we wrote up our findings.

Once again, I encountered another entirely different forest, with its own ecology and history. The trees were magnificent tropical hardwoods. Even in the rain forests of coastal BC and Colombia I had never seen trees so huge. The wood was richly coloured, nothing short of beautiful. And vast areas of this forest had been over-harvested, often cleared for subsistence agriculture. The Ghanaian farming methods rapidly reduced the fertility of the soil; after a few crop cycles the local people would have to cut more forest or starve. And the forest was their only source of fuel. With Ghana's population of 10.5 million expected to double in twenty-five years, the

Section 6, subsection 1 of the regulations that governed the membership of the (since disbanded and reorganized) Ghana Timber Marketing Board stated that *No person shall be qualified to be a member of this board –*

(a) if he has been sentenced to death or to a term of imprisonment exceeding twelve months without option of a fine or has been convicted of an offence involving dishonesty or moral turpitude...

(b) if he is adjudged to be a person of unsound mind.

I would sometimes quote these regulations to members of boards to which I reported. ■

future of its forest was challenged. On top of the expanding population, the northern part of the country was seeing an encroachment
of the Sahel, the sub-Saharan dry belt, into formerly forested land.

As always, I couldn't just stay in the capital city, interviewing
talking heads and reading tables of numbers. I went out to see the
forest, and to see the life of the people who made their homes there.
I visited forest company operations, most of them owned by large
corporations from Europe. A lot of logs were being exported, being
turned into high-value products in European furniture shops and
panelling plants.

The heat and humidity were amazing, even greater than in Colombia. I was advised by our Ghanaian guides to drink fluids constantly

Context is everything. You can learn that in a meeting room in
Victoria or in the presence of an Ashanti chief in Central Ghana.

While inspecting the Ghanaian forest, our study team was invited
to meet the local royalty. We changed out of our normal bush gear
and put on suits and ties, and travelled through the sweltering heat
to meet the royals.

We were ushered into a small room and told we could sit on the
several low stools while we waited. We waited quite a while in the
airless space, with the sweat running and trickling under our north-
ern-hemisphere clothing. Finally, the chief and his staff came in,
almost in a procession.

Unlike the temperature in the room, their atmosphere was cool.
They spoke to us in Ashanti, a translator relaying the chief's formal
remarks. He nodded distantly as the functionary translated our
responses.

Then one of our party mentioned the World Bank's sponsorship of
our study. I saw the chief blink. He did not wait for the translator to
put the words into Ashanti. Suddenly he was speaking to us directly,
very informally, in perfect Oxford English. ■

or I would become ill. One of the Europeans on our team disregarded the advice and became seriously sick.

Despite the menace I fell in love with the Ghanaian forest. I defy anyone to stand under those trees and not be awed. And all around were the constant sights and sounds of burgeoning life: the twirling vines and the blossoms that filled the air with head-spinning pheromones, the creeping, leaping and flying creatures of all colours and sizes, the cheeps and chirps, whirrs and squawks, as the nonhuman inhabitants defend their territories or attract their mates.

I had got a handle on biodiversity in Colombia, but now Ghana was giving me a post-graduate course. I was gaining a real understanding of just how diverse the world's forest must be, and how we must not make the mistake of seeing the forest as only timber. There was so much more here than commercially useful wood; there were fruits and vegetables, meat and medicine, culture and meaning, and after seeing an expanding desert, I was struck by how great a role the forest plays in sustaining a resource that most British Columbians take for granted: fresh water.

I saw how far the village women had to walk to get water, saw the forest giving way to desert while the population constantly grew. This was 1978 and the world was only just starting to apprehend the issue of deforestation: how, at that time, up to fifteen million hectares of forest were being lost every year. Here we are, twenty-eight years later, and too many of us still think that deforestation is somehow "their" problem – a concern for some obscure people who live far away in tropical countries. But it's not just "their" problem; it's ours. If some part of the world has a problem, then the world has a problem. I was only beginning to see that reality in Ghana, but even then I knew that someday there must come a reckoning. And we will all have to settle up.

There will be some who will read that last assertion and say, "Apsey, you may be a crackerjack forest economist, but you're confused. We must use the forest, and that means international investment. If foreigners don't come in to places like Ghana and harvest the wood, it will still be lost to the indigenous population's need for fuel and agricultural land. Is it not better to get some economic benefit from harvesting and using all that magnificent wood?"

Of course, it is better to make use of the forest. It is best, however, to make wise use of the resource. Bans on harvesting cannot preserve a forest like the one I saw in Africa. But over-harvesting and high-grading – taking the best timber and leaving the rest – are not wise use. They are short-term gain for a distant few at the expense of long-term loss for the many who live with the forest.

I am not naive. I know that many first-world companies go into countries like Ghana and Colombia only to cut down the finest trees

While I was in Ghana, the World Bank and the FAO asked some of us to extend our time and take a look at the forest in another West African country. It was not a full mission, we were assured, just a "low-key pre-mission" glance at the situation; we'd look around, ask a few questions, no big deal.

So, along with John Spears from the World Bank, I flew into the island airport offshore from Freetown, the capital of Sierra Leone, and caught the Second-World-War-vintage landing craft that was the local equivalent of the airport shuttle bus. We were met by Sierra Leonean officials who showed us the trip's itinerary. The next day we were to meet, first, the Deputy Minister in charge of Sierra Leone's forest resources, then his boss, the Minister; finally, we would meet the President of the Republic, Siaka P. Stevens.

"So much for 'low-key,'" I said to John Spears. But it was all part of the international consulting business. It was funny when we filed in to meet the head of state: next to his desk was a stuffed leopard, teeth bared in so lifelike a snarl that John Spears froze in fear, causing a chain reaction collision as each one of us lined up behind him bumped into the man ahead. I'm not sure what we accomplished for the national forest, but we certainly gave the national leader his best laugh of the day. ■

and get them to market. Fortunately, over time, there has been a social evolution. People's ideas about the forest have changed and those changes have made their way through the mechanism of the market to the corporate suites where decisions are made.

Does this mean that Mike Apsey recommends boycotts? Will boycotting Ghanaian wood help Ghanaians or save their forest? In my experience, the answer is no. But the credible threat of boycotts can jar the thinking of those corporate decision makers, can bring social change into the executive suite. That is what happened in Canada and the US. Corporations have learned to see a wider scope. So have governments. Market pressures and international agreements are having an effect, and I believe that the extent and pace of that change can only increase.

These were the kinds of questions that were popping into my head as I saw yet more stretches of the world forest in between helping to shape forest policy in British Columbia. It was useful to see our situation, our challenges and our opportunities from an international context. I could come back to Victoria and look at the task from a wider perspective. What we needed was a set of legislative and regulatory requirements that could give us the best of all possible worlds: economic, environmental, social and cultural.

Seated around the table at the Harbour Towers, we members of FPAC were trying to get a sense of how things would evolve in the future. We didn't have all the modern technical language in which such concerns are expressed today, but we were seeing the outlines of today's issues even back then. Looking forward, as best we could, we knew that things were indeed changing. There were some in the forest industrial community who were leaders and there were others who needed to be pushed along. Was it best to do so with incentives, or should we create a neutral operating environment and let social and market forces act as they would, or should we fashion a hammer to drive the recalcitrant? Our philosophy was consistent with the government's stance: we should find a way to reward good action and not penalize all in an attempt to constrain the few who acted badly.

As we debated and consulted, another thing that became clear about BC's forest policy was that public ownership – and therefore publicly mandated protection – of the resource is crucial. Many of our competitors operate on privately owned lands, plantation forests that need only be farmed for their timber values. In order to be able to compete while maintaining all forest values, BC's government and private capital must form a mutually beneficial partnership. And that partnership must evolve over time as the global economy changes and as the appreciation of the forest by its owners – the people of BC – also undergoes an evolution.

We conducted our review and made our recommendations to the provincial cabinet. They were approved and the experts in the Attorney General's ministry were assigned the technical task of translating policy into legislation. The bills were introduced into the legislature on May 12, 1978.

It was a heady moment for me. I had been part of a major policy exercise that would affect the first forest that I had fallen in love with. The new Forest Act was the first complete revision of the law since 1912. The new Range Act replaced the Grazing Act that had been in place since 1919. And the new Ministry of Forests Act would revamp the BC Forest Service from top to bottom. The process had begun under the NDP then had continued under the Socreds – six years of fact finding, research, study, argument, consultation and consensus seeking, involving thousands of concerned, committed forest people all over the province.

I had been deeply involved only in the latter part of that policy development process, but now I was going to be intimately concerned with the policy's implementation. On March 23, upon my return from overseas, I found waiting for me a letter from Bob Wood, on behalf of Tom Waterland, Minister of Forests, in which he asked me to consider being his Deputy Minister. On my fortieth birthday, while Sharon and the girls and I were vacationing at Disneyland – an appropriate setting for a man born on April Fools Day – I decided to accept.

CHAPTER NINE
Another Side of the Table

The offer of a deputy ministership came as a real surprise. Perhaps it shouldn't have. It was obvious as the committee made its review of the Pearse Report and considered the shape and future of the BC Forest Service that the government was holding the position open. John Stokes, the previous Deputy Minister, had been seconded to FPAC without being replaced; Ted Young, the Chief Forester, had been temporarily put in charge of the service, but with the title of Chief Forester and Chief Executive Officer.

So we all knew that there would be a new DM, and at least one member of FPAC knew that it would likely be me. That member was my friend Bob Wood who, I realized later with the clarity of hindsight, must have promoted me to his Minister as a potential candidate. Hence my appointment to the committee was in the nature of an extended job interview and shakedown cruise. I say he "must have" because we never discussed the matter.

I did ask Tom Waterland at one point and was told that the decision had been his. He had consulted Premier Bill Bennett, however, during a sitting of the Legislative Assembly. Bennett had passed Waterland's desk on the way to his own. Waterland had a note on his desk concerning offering me the post. The Minister passed it to the Premier and said, "I'm thinking of making Mike Apsey my DM."

Bennett took the note to his seat. Later, on the way out of the House, he dropped the paper back on Waterland's desk. A note in one corner read: *Do it.*

After I received the offer I did as I always did and consulted my mentors and friends. They all urged me to take the job, though my partner Les Reed was both elated for me and sad that our partnership would thus end. I must admit I never leaned toward a refusal. My career had been a succession of things done for the first time. I doubt that I could ever have been happy, as my father had been, doing much the same thing in much the same way all of my life. I always wanted to see bigger and bigger pictures, to look at wider and wider issues from an ever higher vantage point. If I have a mortal sin in me, it is the sin that motivated Goethe's Faust: I wanted to know more, see more, understand more. I could never have turned down the chance to know what it was like to reorganize and run a respected forest service.

I met with Bennett and Waterland to discuss the offer. They made it clear that they wanted me to be Deputy Minister of Forests, not Minister of Forests. "We want you to implement policy," Bennett said, "not make it." If I saw a need for new policy, it would be my duty to examine the options, make recommendations to the Minister and go no further.

"You want me to be a chief executive officer," I said, "while you and the cabinet are the board of directors."

"Yes," said Bennett.

"And if you don't like what the CEO is doing, you get another one," I said.

"Bingo."

So that was clear. The demarcation line would grow fuzzy later, but that's another chapter.

I reported for duty as Deputy Minister on June 1, 1978. In those days the Ministry of Forests executive offices were in a wing of the

Harbour Towers Hotel, although the government had acquired and was renovating a building at 1450 Government Street that would become the new hub of Ministry operations. The three bills recommended by FPAC had been in the legislature since May 12 and I had been meeting with Tom Waterland and the senior Ministry staff, getting to know who was who.

The first priorities were to get the legislation passed and then to move rapidly on the reorganization that the new Ministry of Forests Act would ordain. There would be plenty more to do in the coming months: writing and implementing new regulations, preparing new licence documents, redrawing the boundaries of timber supply areas, calculating a new annual allowable cut, and on and on.

There was no time for a soft introduction to my new duties. I had to hit the ground running. Fortunately, there was no great need to learn all the myriad ins and outs of how things were done in the Ministry, since my assignment was to change so many of them. Still, I was undertaking an enormous challenge. Spread across the province was a huge and vital industry and we were redesigning its operating environment. The job was made more delicate by the fact that the entire forest sector had already come through such a long period of uncertainty. For six years, beginning with the initial NDP tinkering, then the whole Pearse Commission process, followed by FPAC, then the writing of new legislation, the industry and the communities that depended on it had been in limbo.

I was determined to minimize the remaining time that all those people and businesses had to remain on tenterhooks. I had been given a mandate and I needed to get on with it. I would do my best to understand the intended consequences of what I was doing and to anticipate the unintended ones. I had no doubt that, once the changes were put into practice, I would hear about any unanticipated side effects in short order.

My team and I began to redesign the Forest Service. We took ideas from the Service itself, from the FPAC review, from the government, and some from my own thinking. There was no doubt that the Service's structure did not meet the requirements of the BC forest sector in the 1970s and it would certainly become even farther out of step in a rapidly changing world.

The Forest Service had become a very centralized agency, run far too much on top-down decision making. The old legislation had contained clauses that stated, "Notwithstanding anything in this Act contained, the Minister may...," so that almost every decision was in the hands of the Minister unless he specifically designated it otherwise. On top of that legal framework, decades of ad hoc responses to situations in the field had created a mishmash of practices. Some decisions could be made by field staff, but most had to be kicked back up the organization chart to some manager in Victoria. It was like an old-time army, where the front-line troops always had to wait for orders from far behind the lines.

To make things even more confusing, the lines of authority between field operations and headquarters managers often crossed and short-circuited each other. Field staff would receive conflicting orders from different managers, so the forest companies whose operations depended on getting a decision out of the Service frequently had to go to Victoria to get answers on the most picayune matters.

The Forest Service dated from the province's frontier days, when much of BC was still a roadless wilderness. Consequently, it owned a sizeable fleet of boats and ships that went here and there along the coast, as well as a large maintenance depot in the Lower Mainland where the ships were serviced. But now there were good roads to places that used to be accessible only by sea, and if there were no roads there were float planes and helicopters. There was a strong attachment within the Service to the old boats but they had to go.

Another holdover from an earlier time was that the province was divided into some one hundred ranger districts, The rangers were the people who had looked after forest protection, especially from fire, and had overseen road building and forest industry operations. As with the fleet, there was a sense of romance about the rangers; like many small-town British Columbians when I was a boy I had seriously entertained the notion of becoming a ranger when I grew up.

But their time was gone. They were left over from a system that had worked well when the public's view of the forest was that it was mainly a remote backdrop to their lives, and that its primary purpose was to provide timber and jobs. But now we were moving rapidly into a new world, with cities and towns growing in the hinterland, genuinely urban places in what used to be the backwoods.

Every year hundreds of thousands of British Columbians left the cities and went into the forest to camp, to hunt, to fish, to backpack. Coupled with what they saw for themselves was a growing awareness of what the environmental movement had to say. The public was developing new values and they wanted to see those values recognized in the management of their forest. They wanted it all – jobs, stable communities and respect for the new ways of seeing the forest.

Meeting those modern expectations required a modern Forest Service, a flexible, responsive agency whose principles and procedures could evolve along with a changing society. And with a changing resource, because British Columbia was entering an unprecedented age in which there would be little if any new timber to be allocated.

By the late 1970s, we were facing the era of tight supply. Anyone who wanted a portion of the annual allowable cut, whether it be for a new small business forest products program or a wilderness preserve, would have to take the trees from somebody else. Thus the word "no" would come to be heard in the land, often spoken to people who were hearing it for the first time.

The new era required new thinking, new understanding, new organization and a new accountability. One thing I had learned from my years abroad and at COFI was that change is most easily effected when those whose lives are being changed are part of the process. I said to the senior Ministry staff, "We've got to reorganize the Forest Service, so we need to find how best we can involve the Service in that re-organization."

We asked for input and we got plenty of it, from general ideas to specific details. There was a great deal of dedication and talent within the Service and, after all the years of top-down decision-making, there were more than a few people who had put their minds to questions of how to make things work better. We were able to draw on a lot of pent-up pondering. We did not take everyone's advice, but any such effort will yield stronger results if you seek a buy-in from those who will be most affected.

Ironically, one of the failings of the old Service was that it was stuffed too full of foresters. Just as not every doctor makes a good hospital chief of staff, not every forester can fill an administrative position. We had too many people who lacked the training or the aptitude to do the changing job that needed to be done. The system had allowed such people to kick a decision upstairs to a headquarters manager. I made a conscious decision to open up the Service to non-foresters who had the talents we needed. The rule was, if we could find a forester who could do the job, that was well and good; if the best candidate was a technician or an engineer or an MBA, we would bring them in. The new policy attracted some very fine non-foresters into the Forest Service, including two assistant deputy ministers: John Johnston, my ADM of finance and administration, who went on to become BC's Deputy Minister of Lands, and his successor, Roy Cullen, who is today a Member of Parliament from Ontario and

Ministry of Forests Management team, 1984. L to R: Ken Reid, Bill Young, Ralph Robbins, Me, Al McPherson, Roy Cullen.

Parliamentary Secretary to the Minister of Public Safety and Emergency Preparedness.

I suppose Premier Bennett and Tom Waterland must have thought that it would be easier to have an outsider direct these changes. And certainly I came into the job without any of the baggage one almost inevitably acquires after several years inside a government structure. But once I got into the Service and came to know the senior people I was deeply impressed by their quality and their understanding of how the world was changing.

I remain proud of my senior management team, and I remain in their debt: Bill Young, Chief Forester, ADM Forestry Division; Bill Bishop, ADM Timber, Range and Recreation Division (succeeded by Al McPherson); Pete Hemphill, ADM Finance and Administration Division (succeeded by John Johnston and Roy Cullen); Ralph

Robbins, ADM Operations Division; Ken Reid, Executive Director Legislation and Policy, an indispensable fount of legal and administrative knowledge.

We went to work and in short order and with a minimum of problems we rebuilt the Forest Service. I have to give full credit to the union leadership, particularly John Fryer, head of the BC Government Employees Union. By the time we met, he had already seen early drafts of the reorganization plans. It's hard to keep secrets from the unions; when you try, it just makes them more determined to know what's going on. The unionization of the Forest Service, done under the Barrett government, had never been a completely comfortable fit – for example, a rigorous eight-to-four working day doesn't always make sense out in the woods.

Fryer was a pragmatic unionist, not a doctrinaire class warrior. He said to me, "Lay it out, what do you want?" I showed him a simple chart, and said, "I want this level out of the union, and this one, and the other." He followed my finger, said, "Yep, yep, yep," then "Let's discuss it." We discussed it and came to an understanding.

I went out of my way to ensure good relationships with the unions. It made things much less difficult when the great provincial restraint program landed on the Ministry in the early 1980s. With the trust of

After I had come to an agreement with John Fryer I received a call from the premier's office. "We've just heard you've had some five hundred Forest Service positions removed from the union."

"Yes," I said, "that's right." "Exactly how did you do that?" "I sat down with Fryer. He thought it made sense, I thought it made sense, so we made a deal." "Where was the government's central agency in all of this?" "What central agency?" I said. If I'd known there was a process-in-place I would have had to go through it, and I doubt we would have been able to get the job done. Knowledge is power, but sometimes ignorance can be almost as powerful. ∎

the union leadership I had the flexibility to be able to downsize the Forest Service in as humane a manner as possible, rather than have to make across-the-board cuts ordained by the powers that were. When the big Solidarity strike came, I could cross picket lines outside the Government Street headquarters without rancour and my striking staff felt comfortable about asking me to water their plants. And water them I did.

In the latter half of June, the three bills were passed by the Legislative Assembly and I entered the busiest summer of my life. The Ministry began a practice of issuing white papers on various issues – woodlot licences, incentives for intensive forest management, alternatives for crown timber pricing, responsibilities for fire control and prevention, and much more – "to obtain the views of all concerned parties before policies and procedures are finalized."

I spent a lot of time meeting with what are today called the forest sector's "stakeholders" – individual companies and industrial associations, the forestry profession, labour unions, government and non-government organizations, and forest-dependent communities. Some of the meetings were behind closed doors, others were come one, come all.

I also began, for the first time in my life, regularly standing up in front of microphones and making speeches to groups of all kinds. No Deputy Minister of Forests had ever had to be out on the speaker's circuit as much as I was and I had never been much of a public speaker. But we were changing the context of so many people's lives and livelihoods and this brave new world needed to be explained.

I also found it was an invaluable way to have other people explain things to me. I would always follow my remarks with question and answer sessions and invariably I would get useful feedback. Besides, getting out of the office and finding out first-hand what's going on in the wider world has always been my way of doing things.

These days, when the trend in the present BC government has been to consolidate more and more responsibility in fewer and fewer hands, public servants need to remember that they can't sit behind their desks in Victoria and understand what the issues are out in the rest of the province. They have to get out to the northern Interior, and the central coast, and the Kootenays, and the Cariboo, and the Okanagan, and all over BC, because that's where the forests are, that's where the fires are, and the insect attacks, and the mills that are opening and closing.

As long as I'm preaching, anyone who is involved in creating legislation to govern as wide and varied a community as BC's forest sector can learn from the three bills that came out of the FPAC process and became the legal framework for that vast enterprise. The new Range and Forest Acts were not arbitrary sets of rules based on ideology or straight-line thinking. They represented a tremendous balancing act among a range of interests that were sometimes competing, sometimes cooperative, sometimes both at the same time. They sought to ensure the public good while giving the widest possible scope to private enterprise. They tried to preserve the best of the past while opening up new directions into the future.

The Ministry of Forests Act contained a provision to chart the shape of that future: the province's first Forest and Range Resource Analysis and Five-Year Forest and Range Resource Program. There had been no such analyses before, only sporadic inventorying to set cut levels. Now BC would have a full description of its forest and range resources, coupled with an analysis of its industrial infrastructure, markets and macroeconomic trends, from which five-year programs could be made.

At FPAC we had seen the five-year analysis as a useful tool for policy makers on both the private and public sides of the resource table. The plan had been to conduct the first one in 1979, then repeat the exercise five years later in 1984, after which new iterations would come every decade. The last analysis was performed on schedule in 1994, but as I write this in 2005 no new analysis is underway.

BC's first Forest and Range Resource Analysis and Five-Year Program, 1979.
Presentation to cabinet, Hon. Evan Wolfe and Hon. Bob McClelland.

Although the world has become far more complex, competitive and interconnected than it was in the 1970s, the present government in Victoria has decided to forego this essential element of policy making. It has dropped the requirement from the legislation.

When the first resource analysis and five-year program were conducted, British Columbia regularly recorded surpluses in the public treasury. It was decided to devote some of that financial overage to a special fund which would finance the five-year plans. It turned out, however, that that decision only stood until the recession and restraint years of the early 1980s, when the Bill Bennett administration drained all the dedicated funds. Since then, we have seen much greater flexibility in the ways that public moneys are handled in BC. Governments of all persuasions prefer having as much leeway as possible to reconfigure their priorities. It is a sad fact of political life, here and in other places I've visited, that "income generators" like resource sectors are never as high on the governmental priority scale as "income absorbers" like health, education and security where spending earns headlines – and votes – for politicians.

In my deputy minister days the old phrase "new world order" had yet to regain the currency it acquired after the fall of communism, but among those of us who did a lot of looking out at the world – and especially forward in time – there was a definite beginning of a shift in our thinking. Perhaps in the past we could develop our legislation and policy structures as British Columbians, without much reference to the rest of the world, but by 1978 it was becoming clear that, especially for an export-dependent industry, the world was changing. The resource analyses and programs were one way of starting to cope with that change, a way of understanding just what was changing and how. Traditional markets were no longer ours to count on. New markets were appearing, but so too were new producers. Technological change was opening new doors and windows every day, revealing intriguing new opportunities for our forest industries even as it offered threats to traditional products.

And society was changing. The environment was at first mostly a domestic issue – most people were mainly concerned about their own back yards – but all of those back yards were now connecting across the globe; we were clearly entering an era when new international norms would be set and when they would be enforced by new international agreements.

Over the first six decades of the twentieth century change had come at a steady but generally comfortable pace. In the 1970s, the pace picked up, then picked up again. It was a cliche that change was the only constant; now it was becoming clear that the real constant was acceleration. When I had conducted that 1972 study for our presentation to Richard Nixon's Advisory Panel on Timber and the Environment I had predicted that forest companies east of the Rockies would eventually use new technology to process smaller logs into lumber. I'd been laughed at then, but by 1978 my forecast had come true. But it had done so much sooner than I had expected. The future kept arriving ahead of expectations.

As government employees we had realized that we had to build more flexibility into our policy and management systems, because whatever we were used to was always in danger of becoming obsolete. We had to look at an increasingly fluid, shifting world and ask ourselves, "How does this or that change affect the industry we have to deal with? Does corporate integration, vertical or horizontal, lead to a greater concentration of timber rights? If so, is that good or bad? And if it's good in the short term, is it bad over the long run?"

I was a deputy minister for six years. In that time, I dealt with issues large and small, too many to crowd into one chapter of a memoir. But here are a few of the major matters that came across my desk.

THE RESTRAINT PROGRAM

When I rejoined the public service, it was still the age of budget surpluses and economic boom. Then in the early 1980s came the sudden crash. Academic economists might argue that the term "crash" is technically inaccurate; from the standpoint of the BC Forest Service the early eighties brought a sudden collision with an unyielding wall. The cabinet said we were going to cut back by some 20 per cent.

It must be borne in mind that the Service had barely come through a full-scale reorganization; in fact, we were still in the tweaking and settling-out phase. I went to the minister and the powers in the premier's office and said, in effect, "I will give you 20 per cent, but it will be my 20 per cent. It will not be 20 per cent across the board, because all that does is cause inefficiencies.

"The five-year program is already showing us where we need to shift emphasis and we can combine some of that effort with the cutbacks. But you need to understand that while we are closing some offices, you might also see ads in the paper saying that the Service is looking for people in other areas."

I was resolved to involve the Forest Service in its own downsizing. Like every other part of the BC forest sector we had enjoyed the upper reaches of the long post-war economic expansion, and now we would share the difficulties experienced when the cycle turned. But we were not going to be silly about it. We would decide what needed doing and what didn't, and we would determine what things we could best do as a Service, what things were better done by industry and what might be more efficiently contracted out.

One example of where I believed we could make a contribution was in what we then called research and development – today, the phrase is "science and technology" – and I maintained our research efforts. An area where it made sense to cut the strings was in the nurseries

I was in a cabinet meeting, discussing options for restraint when a Minister said, "Mike, I notice that there's this money here for nurseries."

"Yes, Minister." "I also understand we have a research program that can result in growing trees faster." "Yes, we do, Minister." "Well, what if we make you a little deal?" I said, "I didn't know deputy ministers could make deals, Minister."

There was brief, general laughter, then the Minister continued, "What if we shut down the nurseries but gave you more money for research into speeding up growth? Then when the recession is over you could start up the nurseries, and with your faster growing trees, nothing would be lost."

"An interesting approach, Minister," I said. "Perhaps I could ask you to be part of it?"

"What have you in mind, Mike?"

"That it be your signature on the press release that announces that the Forest Service will destroy millions and millions of baby trees."

where we grew seedlings for replanting. We began by capping capacity and leaving it to the private sector to add any new facilities; later the government nurseries were sold to private operators. Ironically, Charlie Johnson, Director of the Silviculture Branch, who fought the privatization, went on to own a number of the private operations and ended his career as the operator of a very successful company, and we have since become good friends.

One thing I would not abide in the downsizing of the Forest Service was the classification of people as "redundant." I loathed the word and all that it implied: that someone who had joined the Service, had spent a life in devotion to the forest and colleagues and had been an exceptional worker, would now near the end of a career be labelled redundant. The word added insult to injury, and neither I nor any of my staff would apply it to our colleagues. I saw in other departments, as I have seen in the federal public service and in industry, cases where people who had dedicated their lives to their

"How's that, Mike?"

"Well, Minister, the nursery business cannot be just turned on and turned off. After you put the seeds to work there's a lead time of a year or two before the new trees can go out into the field. If we shut down we would have to clean out millions and millions of seedlings. There would be photographs in the newspapers."

"No, Mike," said the Minister, "that's not an option." ▪

There were no "Dear Sir," letters in my Ministry. I could not have sent such letters to those who were losing their jobs, some of them people I had known for years. When the time came for the inevitable bloodletting, I sat at my desk through a full day and personalized and signed each and every one of the more than five hundred letters. On some of them I added a personal note. Each and every one of those letters hurt. ▪

work were treated in such a shoddy fashion. I was not going to have any of that. We did our best to help our people find other jobs. It was the right thing to do, although it seems that it was not the normal practice, then or now.

SYMPATHETIC ADMINISTRATION

I coined the phrase "sympathetic administration" in an October, 1981, memo to Forest Service staff instructing them to give all legally possible leeway to the industry during the recession. The phrase came back to haunt me when critics of the government's policies called it shorthand for "pandering to the butchers of the forests." But in those days many forest companies were in genuinely dire straits, under threat from their bankers of having their loans called. Some longstanding corporate names in the BC forest sector almost didn't make it through the early eighties.

When people criticize the era of sympathetic administration – and some still do – it should be remembered that the Forest Service itself was being downsized, and every group in and around the BC forest sector – companies, unions, lenders, communities – was looking closely at how every dollar was earned and spent. We all had to look for the flexibility that would get the province through those unprecedented lean times so that we could all enjoy the upside of the economic cycle.

Faced with the situation again, would I do what was done? Yes. I would. Would I use such a potentially loaded phrase again? Definitely not.

BOWRON CLEARCUT

During the "War in the Woods" between the forest industry and some of the more radical environmentalists, the world was informed that the two man-made things that could be seen from space were the Great Wall of China and the Bowron clearcut. To this day, I still

Me and the
Great Wall of
China.

sometimes encounter Europeans who upon hearing my name say,
"Ah, Herr Apsey (or Monsieur Apsey, or Mijnheer Apsey), you are
the man who clearcut the Bowron."

Whenever it happens I reach for my maps and explain. In the late
1970s, following a major blow-down, there was a serious outbreak
of spruce bark beetle near Prince George. The bugs spread fast and
furious, attacking vast tracts of forest and showing no signs of ever
moderating their appetites. So, working with some thirteen companies, the BC Forest Service dealt with the infestation by the only
practical method: we allowed the industry to cut the trees in which

Part of the Bowron Clearcut.

the beetles were established and the trees into which they would have moved next.

We cut and cut and cut, some four hundred truckloads of logs per day. Altogether we cleared some fifty thousand hectares. We saved a great deal of wood from those beetles, saved it to be usable in the area's mills. Then nature gave us a break, primarily in the form of a sharp drop in winter temperatures. The weather stayed cold long enough to hammer the infestation. We went back to a normal harvesting regime.

And the Bowron was replanted. Today, it is visible from space as a plantation, because it is completely grown in with healthy young trees. Not for a nanosecond do I regret ordering that rescue effort. Now we are facing an even worse infestation of pine beetles in the

Interior. Every British Columbian should be praying for an early onslaught of a truly mean and nasty winter over very large stretches of the province, with sharp temperature drops and long, long cold spells to knock that menace down.

Purists may say such events are just nature's way, but to a forester there is no sadder sight than a dead or dying forest. We will be facing more of these kinds of issues – insect infestations, disease and fire – and I believe the people of BC will have to do some very serious thinking over the next few years. Our relationship with the forest is changing, in part because more and more of us are living closer to the natural world – the so-called interface zone – but also because the forest itself is changing.

The present pine beetle infestation could well be a side effect of global warming. Do we have to accept that, in a post-glacial world, the forest we've grown accustomed to will disappear and something new will take its place? Or do we make changes to our management regimes, and if so what kinds of changes? Do we go back to controlled burning of forest-floor fuels to keep fires to a minimum, or do we accept that fires are part of the forest's natural life cycle? As more and more of us live closer and closer to the forest, these issues grow in importance.

SHOAL ISLAND

I would be remiss if I did not mention one of the most controversial issues during my tenure as deputy minister. In 1978, BC Forest Products began setting up dryland sorts – i.e., places where logs are sorted by size and species and scaled to determine their commercial timber content. One of them was at Shoal Island near Crofton on Vancouver Island. Theoretically, a dryland sort offers advantages over the traditional water sort – less likelihood of logs escaping from booms and being lost – but the process that BCFP put in place was complex. Logs were not scaled in the bundles in which they arrived, but only after they had been sorted and relocated around the site.

There were different codes for some twenty different types of log on the sort, and logs were continually coming in and going out.

The result was that the scaling was thought to be inaccurate. Logging contractors who had supplied the timber were arguing that they had not been paid for all they had delivered. The government, too, may not have received all the stumpage it should have. Some contractors quietly brought in their own scalers to check the BCFP figures and found discrepancies – one report said that 11 per cent of logs were not being accounted for.

Eleven per cent represented serious money; legal action was launched. And as with any contentious issue touching the forest industry in British Columbia, questions were soon being asked in the legislature and allegations of canoodling between the government and BCFP flew thick and fast.

Despite in-house investigations by the Ministry and a review by the Ombudsman, I don't think anyone ever knew exactly what went wrong on Shoal Island. Certainly, the scaling was inaccurate, and the resulting political and legal fuss revealed that the Ministry's checks and balances needed to be strengthened, and they were. There were also changes made on the corporate side. But to this day, I am still not sure if there was a problem. If indeed there was a problem, I do not know if it was a case of deliberate chiselling on the part of BCFP or if Shoal Island was just one of those incidences of people turning what should have been a simple system into a labyrinth of complexities in which we all stumbled around looking for an exit.

FIRE PROTECTION GROUP

My diaries for my early days as deputy minister show that on August 5, 1978, I awoke to the news that the province was beginning the day with more than 350 new forest fires started overnight by lightning. I spent most of the day with the Protection Branch staff and the next day I flew to Kamloops, Williams Lake and Prince George to make

The Conair Fleet as I knew it, 1983–84.

sure the field crews had sufficient people and equipment to do the job. Firefighting is hot, dirty and dangerous work. I had seen, as a young forestry student helping with fire research, how a fire can turn on a sudden shift of wind and blow up into a deadly inferno in minutes. The men – and these days, women – who fight forest fires in BC have always been among my personal heroes. On the fire lines and in the air above the fire fronts, they put their lives at risk to save people and communities, provincial assets like power transmission lines and bridges, and the forest itself.

I am immensely proud to have had such people working with me, both the Forest Service staff and the flyers from Conair, the company with which the Service contracted to get crews and supplies to the fire zones and to suppress blazes from the air. I was also determined that I would never have to write a letter of condolence to the family of one of those brave people – or to any of the thousands of

Premier Bill Bennett presenting Premier's Safety Achievement Award to the Ministry of Forests, 1982.

The Rappattack Crew, 1981.

Ministry personnel who went out into the often dangerous woods to do their jobs. One of my first acts as deputy minister was to institute a rigorous safety awareness policy. During my watch we minimized accidents within the Ministry of Forests, and we consistently won the Premier's Safety Achievement Award. And I am glad to say that I never had to write one of those sad letters.

Because of companies like Conair and the BC and Canadian Forest Services, our province leads the world in fire-fighting technology and expertise. The Rapattack training school near Salmon Arm is world class, and with no separate qualification standard for female fire-fighters – because that's the way those tough, proud women wanted it. I honour the quiet heroism of all the firefighters, and the no less essential contributions of those who fly the planes and helicopters, and those who keep the equipment in constant readiness.

To all those who have fought fires, are fighting fires and will fight fires, I say: thank you!

FORINTEK

The Canadian Forest Service had long maintained two laboratories that did first-rate research. In August 1978, the Trudeau government announced that, as part of its restraint program, the labs would be privatized. Crown Zellerbach CEO – and later BC Lieutenant-Governor – Bob Rogers was asked to set up a new corporation to operate the labs. He put together a board of directors with representation from the major forest companies and governments, as well as the UBC forestry school. The feds were willing to contribute $4.6 million per year for five years and asked BC to contribute.

It was clear that the labs had been doing good work. If they ceased to do so we would have to invent something to replace them, because there was a growing need for forest product research. The deadline for the closing of the labs was coming. Philosophically, the BC government agreed that the industry should be responsible for such

Presentation of BC government's first contribution to Forintek, 1979. L to R: Peter Macfarlane, Bob Rogers, Hon. Tom Waterland, Bob Kennedy.

research. Practically, we needed to do something to secure the labs before some of the best minds in the field dispersed to new jobs. I went to cabinet and argued that BC should take a leadership role: $1.5 million for the first year while we worked out a long-term federal-provincial-industry deal. The government said yes and Forintek was created. I was on the first board. As I was writing this in 2004, Forintek celebrated twenty-five years of success and looks forward to the next quarter century of contributing to the Canadian forest sector. If I may quote my remarks from the celebration: "I believe the role for research in the future will be pivotal. I expect research, plus the use of new technology, will be as important as – if not more important than – the resource itself. I expect to see the Forintek partnership, any challenges or obstacles notwithstanding, strengthen, flourish and play an essential role."

Forintek Canada Corp.

KALAMALKA RESEARCH STATION

In 1981, I was able to come home to Vernon in my official capacity, bringing with me the opening of a new research station at the south end of the city. There was pressure from local governments to name the station for Vernon or Coldstream; I resisted and named it for Kalamalka Lake. Today it plays an important part in tree improvement and gene conservation programs in the Interior and has numerous ongoing research projects in other fields.

THE VALHALLA WILDERNESS

A group of residents of the Slocan Valley and surrounding area formed the Valhalla Wilderness Society in 1975. They had grown concerned about the future of the land base and decided they wanted to see the slopes of the Valhalla mountain range along the western shore of Slocan Lake protected as a wilderness area. There were a number of groups in the region, both industrial and non-industrial, who thought differently. It became one of those issues that frequently ornament the BC political process. Tensions heightened, people appeared on the streets bearing placards, the local press ran editorials and letters to the editor, politicians and pressure groups weighed in.

The Forest Service was by law and custom the custodian of the land and thus we would be an integral part of the process that decided the future of the Valhallas. As the debate heated to a boil, I decided I would go out and meet with the Valhalla Wilderness Society, look the situation over and find out about the issues. This caused some consternation, within the Ministry and without; deputy ministers were not usually seen in such circumstances. But my Minister, realizing that I couldn't properly advise him without a fuller understanding of the issues, supported me.

I went out to New Denver, accompanied by Bruce Fraser, a special consultant to the Ministry on public involvement who had been seconded from the Ministry of Education. We met with all the conflicting interests, including Colleen McCrory of the VWS, for whom I have much respect. There was a large and somewhat raucous public meeting. The next day, Bruce and I went out and took a look at the land. We helicoptered over the whole area, and also travelled a lot of it by boat and on foot.

I went back to Victoria and recommended to the government that, considering all of the arguments pro and con, and having met with the people who advanced those arguments, and having had a close look at the land, the wilderness area should be established. The ultimate shape of the set-aside area was modified, mostly at the north and south ends, but the decision went in favour of the Valhalla Wilderness Society.

The economics of the Valhalla have been questioned, whether tourism dollars and their multipliers outweigh the wealth that might have been generated by logging those slopes. Well, I am a forest economist but I know that there are some things that you can't boil down to mere dollars and cents. Sometimes decisions have to be made that override pure economics.

The Valhalla decision came as a surprise to those who saw the BC Forest Service as handmaidens to timber barons. We were and are anything but. We realized that the world was evolving rapidly and that the owners of the forest resource, the people of BC, were developing new values, new desires. We were recognizing those values – given the times we were living in – and we were making appropriate decisions. I am proud that we preserved the Valhalla wilderness as a provincial park.

We were a forest service, not a timber service, after all. Our concern was for the land base. We could not look after the trees and forget about the rivers, the lakes, the non-forested areas. We were concerned about it all, had to understand interactions with other elements, and jurisdiction be damned.

Since my days at FPAC I, along with many others, was trying to move the Service towards being a holistic manager. But so many interests impinge on the land base that we faced continuing, immense challenges. As well, we live in a world that operates on cycles – the business cycle and the political cycle are just the two most obvious. But the forest doesn't work to our timetable; its cycles can absorb whole human lifetimes.

Even back then I was asking myself, what are the options we could look at? What about the rest of the world, how do they do things and are they better off? What could we learn from other models and how could we perhaps fit those lessons to our circumstances?

Funding was often the big obstacle. The Ministry of Forests was a line ministry like any other, although often with less attractiveness than the "spending" ministries like education and health that provided programs and services prized by the voters. It was hard to argue at the cabinet table that some revenues gathered by the Forest Service should stay with the Service rather than be poured into the general revenue stream. Besides, with the advent of the restraint program I saw what happened with "dedicated" and "perpetual" funds once the tide of red ink began to rise.

I did some outside-the-box thinking. Perhaps we would have a better chance of managing the Crown forest for the long term if we privatized some of the Crown lands, putting the ownership into the hands of pension funds or other broadly based groups. If a large number of voters knew that their future income directly depended on how much was invested in the forest, they might generate the political will among their elected representatives to manage the forest properly.

I also examined the feasibility of turning over ownership and management of the forest to a Crown corporation. BC Hydro had been effective in channelling serious and sustained investment into the province's hydro-electric resource, while remaining relatively immune from year-to-year machinations; might a similar entity in charge of forest resources achieve an equivalent result?

I engaged consultants to investigate these ideas as well as having people look at what other forest nations – such as Sweden, Britain, New Zealand, Finland, Norway – were doing. This was on my own initiative, though Tom Waterland was interested in what we might learn and would have pushed any good ideas onto the cabinet agenda. But by then we were well into the 1980s, the very definition of "interesting times," and BC was headed into a period of political upheaval that, as I write this, has yet to subside. So the research was done, but nothing came of it.

In any case, the idea of privatizing part of the British Columbia forest or putting it in the hands of a semi-independent Crown corporation may never appeal to its owners or to the people we elect to manage our province. One of the overlooked political advantages to Crown ownership of most of British Columbia is that, when the Crown wishes to do something on the land – such as flooding a river valley for a hydro dam or cutting a highway right-of-way – it's a lot easier than if Victoria had to get the land back from a couple of hundred private owners. Even the most privatization-friendly politicians of the past twenty years have recognized that inherent appeal of Crown land.

The other constraint on long-term management of the forest is the change in corporate culture that began in the 1980s and shows no sign of abating. Corporations now operate on much shorter time horizons, with senior managers who seem too often driven by the concept of "shareholder value" as expressed by the daily quote of the company's share price on the stock exchange. Again, the forest knows nothing of day trades and stock options, and I sympathize with corporate foresters who must argue for long-term strategies in an increasingly short-term business environment. I believe it is doable, but I know it is not easy.

TANIZUL

As we moved into the 1980s, there were many demands from the industrial side for expanding the timber harvest. In some parts of the province there was still some room for expansion, for granting new tenures, but in most areas the timber supply was tight and promised only to get tighter. We were entering an era where more of the annual allowable cut would be coming from second-growth stands and less from old growth. It was a simple mathematical fact that old growth trees were bigger than second growth – no one wanted to wait a couple of hundred years for the new trees to thicken up – so the total volume of available wood was heading for an inevitable fall-down. Inevitable, that is, unless we did something to improve forest renewal, to introduce more intensive silvicultural practices, and to make more efficient use of the existing wood.

But even though we were close to a full allocation of the existing harvest, having made room for a small-business program and some Aboriginal forest operations, the line-up of those who wanted cutting rights was always at the Ministry's door. It was always, "Apsey, get me some timber."

"From where?"

"From him," was the usual answer, accompanied by a judgmentally pointed finger. "He's making a product that's not as good as the one I'll make. So crimp his supply and shoot it over to me."

Having gone through a complete reorganization of the tenure system, I didn't believe that the whole province should be covered by area-based tenures, but where they would fit without disruption I was and remain a strong supporter of Tree Farm Licences. In 1981/82, I saw such an opportunity in a proposal presented by Grand Chief

Ed John, representing the Stuart-Trembleur Lakes Band (now the Tl'azt'en First Nation). We wanted to combine some reserve lands with adjacent Crown land into a TFL that would allow the operation of Tanizul Timber Ltd.

The problem was that the reserve lands were under federal administrative jurisdiction, while the TFL Crown lands were under provincial administrative jurisdiction, and federal lands were not supposed to be managed under provincial laws and regulation. So we were setting out to do something for the first time, which is always a tricky business with just one bureaucracy and becomes the equivalent of walking the high wire while juggling cats when both the federal and provincial establishments are involved. There were many meetings with the Department of Indian Affairs and Northern Development with all the usual blind alleys and crossed signals. Near the end of the process I was sitting in the Chateau Laurier in Ottawa taking a phone call from BC's then Attorney General and future Lieutenant-Governor Garde Gardom who had called to express his sympathy that the proposal had run aground on some federal regulatory sandbar. Fortunately, I was holding in my hands the DIAND documents that authorized us to go ahead. Note to students of government: a signed document usually trumps a phone call. Tanizul continues to hold and manage the TFL.

There was a growing rapport between the Forest Service and BC's Aboriginal communities and a fair amount of goodwill on both sides. But the old ways were also still around. I recall one day when there was a sudden blow-up in the Cariboo. A forest road had clipped the edge of a reserve and the band council was justifiably upset. I called in my staff and when I'd been briefed, I asked them, "Has this sort of thing happened often? "

"Mike," they said, "you don't want to know."

I didn't have to think about it long. I said I did want to know because I ought to want to know. And hence forward I wanted us to build roads only where we had a right to, and to take care that we observed the rights of the people whose land we encroached upon.

The Forest Service planted its first reforestation seedling in 1930. At a ceremony in Duncan in 1981, we planted our billionth tree. By 1989, we were planting our second billionth seedling. That was fifty-one years to reach the first billion and eight years to reach the second.

Ceremonial planting of seedling Number 1,000,000,000 at the Forest Museum, Duncan, BC, 1981. L to R: Alf Bamford, Me, Hon. Tom Waterland, Silvicultural Contractor Representative

The third billionth tree came only four years later, in 1993, and the fourth billion followed in 1997. By 2002, we had planted five billion trees and now we are working our way steadily toward six billion. We hit 5.5 billion as I was writing this book, a record we can all be proud of.

And that's not counting natural regeneration. BC is never going to be devoid of trees, short of another ice age, or unless global warming lets bugs and fires get them all.

An incident from the 1997 planting of seedling number four billion, at which I was merely an interested observer; actually, a number of seedlings were being planted by several provincial premiers, including then Premier Glen Clark, at a ceremony in Campbell River.

The seedlings were small trees with their roots encased in cylindrical containers. The holes had been dug for them to be planted in. Each dignitary advanced in turn to the holes, inserted the seedling and tampled it gently down.

All went well until Premier Clark's turn. He stepped up, cylinder in hand. Then he saw that his hole, unlike those of the other three planters, was not round but square.

A round shape in a square hole: there may have been a message there. From the way the crowd laughed, apparently everyone got it. As did Mr. Clark, who gamely laughed along and somehow got the seedling into the hole. ▪

HARDWOOD TFL

Another proposed TFL came from Scott Paper. They wanted a licence to cover a number of islands in the Fraser River between Hope and Chilliwack and on some lands in the Homathko and Kingcome areas up the coast. I went and had a look, and said, let's move forward. But when we held public hearings in Vancouver, we received a fair amount of critical comment – the "don't do it" kind of comment – from other forest companies.

The reason for the opposition was that Scott was proposing a TFL to grow cottonwood, a hardwood species, and the industry reps were arguing that the land was better suited for softwoods. Some environmental groups were worried about the stability of the river islands if there were plantations and harvesting operations.

The arguments went back and forth, the correct official process was followed and we were moving toward granting the licence. At the same time, the unofficial process of phone calls to ministers, MLAs and civil servants was proceeding on a parallel track. So all hell broke loose, as it often does when someone's ox is anticipating a goring.

I was called to cabinet to hear familiar words: "Mike, we're getting a lot of criticism and comment. Why is this a useful project? Can you explain?"

I was delighted to explain, and went through all the details. There were a couple of pointed questions regarding softwood versus hardwood. I said, "Let me put it very simply. This province covers ninety-five million hectares, a huge proportion of which is forest, and if within that whole area we can't find ten thousand hectares on which to plant a fast-growing tree species for a high-value product that each of you uses every day, then we really don't have an open mind." The Tree Farm Licence was granted on its merits.

There is room for hardwood in BC – personally, I like red alder, the subject of my undergraduate thesis. And I hope we will see more of it. The fact that we can find room for hardwood and for Aboriginal forest operations, that we can reclaim marginal lands for forestry, indicates that our thinking about the resource has evolved and continues to do so.

Our thinking changes, our perspective widens, our understanding deepens. We are a dynamic species. We learn. That's why I have optimism for our future and the future of the forest.

I left the public service in 1984. I felt that I had done what I came to do and had left a good legacy in the shape of a more effective, modernized Forest Service and a more up-to-date regulatory environment for the forest sector. I had been approached by the BC Council of Forest Industries to become their president after Don Lanskail retired. Short of being named to head a UN agency for all the world's forest – that is not a gentle hint; I am now too old to accept – the COFI job offered as wide a scope as I could imagine.

Once I decided to take the offer, I tendered my resignation to my Minister and the government with only two days' notice. It would have been inappropriate to remain in the position once I had decided to return to the private sector. Indeed, in order to show respect for the proprieties, I took a hiatus of four months before assuming my new duties at the Council.

My resignation was greeted almost entirely without controversy by the legislative assembly's press gallery. One commentator did opine that I had been an industry plant all along, but the rest of the

There was one other job offer I want to mention, though it came in 1988. The phone rang and it was my old schoolmate Len Marchand, now elevated to the Senate.

"Apsey, we want you to run," he said.

I was not designed for running, though I could manage a brisk walk. It turned out that the Senator had another kind of race in mind. "We want you to run for Parliament in Okanagan North."

I was surprised. No one had ever asked me to commit candidacy before. I said, "Who is we?"

"John Turner and I," he said.

John Turner was Leader of the Opposition. He was about to take on Brian Mulroney in a rematch of the 1984 election that had seen the Conservatives sweep the country.

The Senator sensed that I was not enthusiastic. "You'll be a cabinet minister," he said, "after we win the election."

I hemmed and hawed. "I have to discuss it with Sharon," I said.

That discussion was short. Her initial response was four short but well chosen words. The rationale behind those words was also briefly expressed: winning election would have meant moving to Ottawa. I discovered that we were never, under any circumstances, going to move to Ottawa. Apparently the place has far too much climate.

I reported this news to Senator Marchand. "You'd be a great cabinet minister," he said.

The truth of that prediction would never be tested. ∎

scribes said they were sorry to see me go. I had apparently been easy to work with.

There will always be dissenters, I suppose, and it is easy enough to make insinuations about an individual who holds influential positions in both the public and private sides of the BC forest sector. But I wish that there was more exchange of senior people between government and industry. It would lead to a better public service and a better industry. I would also like to see people from other forest jurisdictions brought in to cross-fertilize our views. As I believe my career attests, the more sides of the table you've sat on, the better you understand what gets brought to that table.

Although here in BC our concentration is on our own forest, we need to know about all the things that touch upon it: industry considerations, political considerations (and not just provincial and federal politics but international as well), community considerations and environmental considerations (again, local, regional and international).

There is only one world and we are open to the forces that affect it, environmentally, economically, culturally, politically, scientifically. If we "stick to our knitting," as a recent corporate buzzword advocated, we put our forest sector at a competitive disadvantage. If all we know is our own forest, then we are managing it without a full understanding of how unique it is. It's hard to see a picture when you're standing in the frame.

CHAPTER TEN

Once and For All

My time as president and chief executive officer of the Council of Forest Industries was the most productive and happiest stage in my career as a Sancho Panza of the forest. But before I talk about the joys and otherwise of those years, there is one thing I'd like to bring up: a recurring four-word phrase that I have heard time and again in my career, and never more often than when I was at COFI – "once and for all."

I'd hear, "Mike, here's three million dollars. Get on over to Europe and straighten out those people about our forest management practices, once and for all."

Or, "Mike, get on down to Washington, work with our lawyers and let's get this [expletive deleted] countervail business settled, once and for all."

Or, "Mike, we want you to put together a public relations program that will put an end to all these blockades and people living in and spiking our trees, once and for all."

Maybe, way back in a simpler time when nothing much changed and sons followed fathers into the family trade, maybe then it was possible to think we could fix problems once and for all. But not in our time. Today, there are no solutions, only evolutions.

Take one of the great concepts that made its way into public discourse during my years at COFI: sustainable forest management. It

was, and is today, too often held out as a goal to be reached – adopt these policies, enforce these standards, and voila, we'll have achieved sustainable forest management.

But that's an illusion brought about by semantics. SFM is not a state; it's an evolving process. It's not a destination, but a continuous journey. And so were most of the issues confronting the BC forest sector in the 1980s and 1990s, just as the issues facing the sector today are constantly evolving – most of them, of course, having evolved out of what we were dealing with, for better or worse, twenty-odd years ago.

Somebody once said, there's no such thing as a thing; there are only events, some of them very fast, others very slow. Einstein proved that the apparent dichotomy between matter and energy is merely an illusion created by the fact that we measure our lifetimes in decades while the universe measures its existence in billions of years. Everything around us, from the mountains to the moss on my garden walk, is an event; whatever it is today, it used to be something else and it is always in the process of becoming something completely different.

A tree is a process that turns air, water, minerals and the decayed matter of bygone plants and animals into a temporary shape. Although, like the Tule Tree, it may hold that shape for thousands of years, eventually it must become something else, even if it's just more detritus to be reused by its seedlings.

A forest is also an event. Indeed, it is billions and billions of con-current events: the myriad of plants and animals, each evolving through their own cycles, all connected to each other, all interacting with each other and with chemistry and the weather, on and on, world without end. Can we summarize all of that in the three syllables *a forest*? No! Yet we act as if we can, telling each other, "The forest is this, the forest is that."

When the Europeans first came to British Columbia, the forest was nothing more than a nuisance that had to be cleared to make farm land, because the civilization then growing in Canada was an agricultural one, in which half the labour force lived and worked on farms. Within a couple of generations, the forest had become merchantable timber; when people spoke of "the forest," the image that came to their minds was logs on skids and stacks of timber loaded onto ships.

A generation or two further down the time line and the forest was still timber, but now it was also where we went for recreation and to escape our increasingly hectic and unnatural urban lives. Another generation and it had also become a place to re-establish a spiritual bond with Mother Earth and all her wondrous works. A few years later, it added a new identity as the lungs of the biosphere, as a carbon sink to offset the effects of greenhouse gases, as an endangered, dwindling treasure. Who knows what the words "the forest" will convey a hundred years hence? One thing we do know: the forest will neither know nor care what we think about it; it will be what it is and what it has always been.

The words that make thinking possible also limit our thinking. In BC, people effortlessly throw around the words, "the forest industry" as if all of the industry's multitude of pieces could fit into one easy-tote container. Yet when I took over the reins of COFI, its membership was highly diverse. There were lumber companies, there were pulp and paper companies, there were integrated companies that produced both. There were companies that were publicly traded and there were privately held, family firms. There were big companies and small, and plenty of mid-sized outfits. Some companies operated only on the coast, others operated only in the Interior. Some were BC headquartered, others were foreign-owned branch plants, and a few were based in BC but – like my old employer MacMillan Bloedel – had out-of-province and out-of-country divisions. Some made generic commodity products for international markets, others made specialty goods for local builders, some provided services or products or equipment to other forest companies. Throughout the time I worked there, the event we call the BC forest industry acted like every other process in modern life: it grew yet more diverse and complex.

Often, in the public mind, "the forest industry" equals the big corporations. Certainly, that seemed to be the definition favoured by the growing environmental movement as we headed toward the eventual "War in the Woods" that enlivened many a court and logging road in the mid-1990s. But though the major companies saw eye-to-eye on many issues, there was no monolithic "corporate forestry" in BC. I had learned that as a deputy minister receiving delegations of chief executive officers come to present a unified position to the Minister of Forests.

They would troop in, sit down, drink coffee and lay out the "industry's" position on the issues of the day. There would be handshakes all around and off they would go. The first time this happened, the Minister said, "They seem to have made up their minds."

I said, "Wait until they get back to their hotel rooms or their offices – any place with a private phone." Sure enough, it was not long before the phone would ring and one of the CEOs from the meeting would say, "Listen, I know that I went along with what was expressed when we were in your office, but I want you to be aware that – although I support the position in principle – in my company's case there are certain exceptional circumstances that apply."

The minister and I would listen politely, take notes and hang up. A few minutes later, the phone would ring and we'd hear from another CEO about another set of exceptional circumstances.

Nothing gratifies political decision-makers more than a divided constituency. It means they can do what they want to do without fear of a unified opposition. In my experience, this was as true of Social

Credit politicians as it was of the NDP ministers. With the NDP, in fact, the ministers I dealt with on behalf of COFI were always urging me to shepherd the corporate top brass into their offices. "Mike," they would say, "we love to see you and it's good of you to bring us these memos and materials, but when can we sit down with your CEOs?"

Given that almost every senior officer of the big corporations was loath to meet with the NDP – not out of ideological disdain, but because they feared being singled out for punitive measures – my answers were always bland explanations of the difficulty in coordinating so many busy schedules, how it would be wrong to bring some but not all, and other evasions worthy of Sir Humphrey Appleby, the ever-so-smooth functionary of the television series, *Yes, Minister*, on one of his best days.

When the mercurial Glen Clark was premier, and the Machiavellian Doug MacArthur was his deputy, the industry faced a number of top-level financial and resource management issues. I believed that it was important that we pull the CEOs together and have a meeting with MacArthur and the Forest Service senior staff. I put the meeting together, enlisted a sizeable number of chief executives and off we went to Victoria.

I had arranged for a pre-meeting at the Swans Hotel, on Pandora Street just down the block from the Forest Service. We had a good discussion of the issues and built on the consensus that we had brought to Victoria. Then one of the CEOs asked me how far the Forest Service offices were from the hotel, would we walk or take a cab? Others had the same query. The question took me a little aback because it meant that these people had never been to visit the Service. That was a change from my day when I would frequently see senior figures from the industry in my office.

I assured them that it was a half a block's walk and we were about to leave when one of the CEOs volunteered an opinion on one item on the meeting's agenda and suddenly the hard-won consensus fell apart. Arguments broke out, got heated, became a general back-and-forth.

We were expected in the Deputy Minister's office at the top of the hour. It was now ten minutes to, and the room was a babble of cross-talk and accusations. Suddenly the CEOs heard a sound that none of them had ever heard before; Mike Apsey, that cool, collected man, was standing up and shouting at them in a surprisingly loud voice.

The room quickly became quiet. I was surrounded by looks of astonishment. These were corporate titans, used to telling other people how things were going to be. It was a long time since anyone had shouted at them and a hell of a long time since the shouting had come from an association staffer.

I said, "Gentlemen, we had a strong consensus. I don't know why it fell apart. I do know that in five minutes we go to the Forest Service. That means you've got five minutes to get it back. We will go, and we will all speak to the same consensus, with no sidetracks, no arguments in front of Doug MacArthur. When we leave MacArthur will know that he's met a real consensus."

I couldn't leave it there. I went on, "And gentlemen, there will be no follow-up phone calls to explain to the DM or to MacArthur that, oh by the way, yes I was at the meeting, but I want you to understand that our circumstances are exceptional. If any one of you does that, MacArthur goes and tells Clark that there is no consensus and then they get to do whatever they want."

We walked to the meeting, all strung out in twos and threes along the sidewalk. Some of the CEOs came up to me as we went along and said that it was a good thing I had yelled at them.

In fact, some that I ran into after leaving COFI expressed regret that they haven't had anyone yell at them since.

To my association colleagues, this advice: choose your moment carefully, then let your CEOs hear something they are not accustomed to hear. It does them and the industry a great deal of good.

I was often taken aback to discover how many senior business people in the forest sector believed that governments, federal and provincial, were working to long-term, detailed, even Machiavellian plans. As if everything was worked out and provided for years in advance. I would explain to them, "That's not how government works. Government wants to be pro-active but is almost always forced to be reactive. Someone is always on their doorstep screaming, and they have to deal with his issue right now. No sooner have they dealt with today's screamer than another one steps up tomorrow, opens his mouth and it all begins again."

It's always about someone pushing and someone else pulling, and government is strung somewhere in between. That's why it is crucial to have a consensus when you go to government. If they sense that you'd rather be screaming at each other instead of at them, they'll let you go at each other for as long as you want while they do what they want. ▪

In truth, the NDP would not have done such singling out. Politicians simply do not operate that way in our system. But I could never reassure some of the CEOs of that benign reality. Their image of "the government" was of this monolithic entity, operating on simple mechanics that were just as illusory as the ideas that many people entertained about "the industry."

Between these two solitudes I stood in a role that Sancho Panza would never have accepted, with not only a whole slew of windmill-giants before me on the horizon, but with a multitude of Don Quixotes, each different from his fellows, at my back.

Looking back over my diaries and through the annual reports for those thirteen-plus years I was the Council's chief executive officer I can see the trends that became the main currents through which I swam. Before those years, back in the 1960s and 1970s, COFI was like most industrial trade associations: it concerned itself primarily with economic issues like markets, trade, and ways to improve the business climate. With the arrival of the 1980s, the issues began to change. Slowly, at first, then with increasing momentum our society entered into a revolution. New values emerged. The public moved rapidly toward new standards and expectations about how human beings ought to relate towards what earlier generations used to call "nature," but which would soon become "the environment," "the biosphere," even "Gaiea, the earth as goddess."

The people of British Columbia, owners of the forest, had always expected their asset to be managed properly; in the 1980s, properly became a synonym for sustainably. But exactly what "sustainable forest management" meant was one of the issues on the table, and around the table was a spectrum of strongly held opinion.

For those at one end of the spectrum – we might call them the least evolved segment of the industry's leadership – sustainable forest management meant replacing today's timber harvest with new trees that could be harvested a few decades from now. At the other end of the opinion rainbow, where gathered the most extreme proponents of environmental activism, sustainable forest management meant leaving the forest absolutely untouched – even backpackers should stay out. Between these two poles of black-and-white thinking was a spectrum with several distinct shades of grey.

Because it was the public's forest, and the province was the public's appointed steward, the provincial government grew steadily more active on sustainability issues. Many people's memories might offer up recollections of initiatives taken by the NDP administrations as the focus of all this activity, but in truth the currents of social change first coursed through the Social Credit cabinets of Bill Bennett and Bill Vander Zalm.

By the mid-1980s mainstream British Columbians were forming very firm expectations of how they wanted their forests managed. To basic requirements like clean air and water, they were now adding protection of fish and wildlife habitat, and even aesthetics. They didn't want to see the denuded hillsides that their parents or grandparents had once considered signs of "progress" – they wanted a more natural appearance to what had heretofore been an industrial zone. Individual companies within the industry responded as their corporate cultures dictated, some more readily than others, but the overall effect was to bring harvesting operations more in line with the new values.

The public also expected to be participants in setting these evolving new standards and seeing that they were met. They wanted opportunities to speak to the managers and they wanted evidence that their views were being heard. The result was process, process, process: a stream of forums, commissions, committees, round tables, action groups and task forces that grew into a flood.

The Council, as the eyes, ears and voice of most of the BC forest industry – disparate and even fragmented as it sometimes was – was increasingly drawn into that flood of meetings, hearings, studies, reports, town hall meetings and feedback sessions. Government relations and public affairs became a major thrust of COFI's day to day work, even more than it had always been back in less interesting times. But as the 1980s moved toward the 1990s, the Council could no longer connect to the owners of the resource through their elected and public service stewards. We had to go public.

THE WAR IN THE WOODS

To my mind, it never was a war. It was a disagreement between those who wanted to move slowly and those who wanted to move faster. The extremes on either end of the spectrum noted above never had much lasting effect on the process that was unwinding from the mid-1980s to the mid-1990s, though their stunts and rhetoric commanded a lot of media attention.

Although some of COFI's members fumed and swore at the greens, I couldn't find too much fault with people who were willing to go to jail for blockading a logging road or tying themselves to a piece of equipment. I had been raised on my grandmother's stories of women who chained themselves to railings of gentlemen's clubs and endured harsh treatment in jail to get the vote. What made me furious were the extremists who cold-bloodedly drove spikes into standing timber and harvested logs in the hope that a faller or a mill worker would unknowingly cut into one of those hidden hunks of metal and shatter his saw into lethal flying shrapnel.

But that period did see a real evolution in the ways that British Columbians were thinking about their forest and the values they saw in it. And, this being an increasingly interconnected world, it was also a time when the feelings of groups far outside our province had an effect on us. The demonstrations, the blockades, people tying themselves to trees and logging trucks, storming the opening of the legislative session in Victoria and breaking an old man's hip – all that that accomplished in the end was to focus the minds of those involved and perhaps to move events forward a little faster than they would have otherwise proceeded. I can see the activists' point of view: they had to push the envelope wherever they could, force a change in thinking among decision makers in government and industry, before time moved on and foreclosed some of the options the activist groups favoured.

In some respects, the strategy worked: new forest practices codes were written and rewritten; experiments in new techniques were tried, evaluated, kept or discarded; new harvesting styles were adopted; new methods of road construction and slope stabilization and a multitude of other practices were designed in accordance with the emerging new forest management philosophies that had grown out of the evolving new values.

COFI's role in all of this was to monitor events to identify trends, develop positions, promote understanding and education among the members and the public, and assist the member companies that found themselves targeted for "direct action" by the greens. The first targets were companies operating on the BC coast. It was a natural place for the environmentalists to pitch up and start drawing global attention because the forest there is unique in all the world, with magnificent ancient trees offering awe inspiring visuals that could be contrasted with the unpleasant image of a recent large clearcut. It was also a place where there were still many options as to how those unique stands of timber would be managed. Most of the original, pre-settlement forest was still standing, whereas the old growth of the US Pacific Northwest was largely gone to the mills.

It was an irony that when the operations of coastal companies came under attack from people who insisted that the BC forest industry was a monolithic force, some of the Interior companies saw no reason for COFI to get involved. "Mike," their executives would say, "that's a coastal issue."

And I would say, "Yes, but one of these days you'll wake up and find that the 'coastal issues' have been dealt with and then who's going to be the next target?" Of course it would be the Interior forest, and after that the boreal forest. It took no brilliance to predict what has in fact come to pass. Obviously, the professional protest organizations would move their targets. They have to have targets in order to keep fundraising and going about their work of saving the world from the windmills they feel impelled to tilt at.

I give the environmental groups full marks on their abilities to play the game they exist to play. I sometimes even envied them: it would have been fun to have been on their side of the table, beholden to nobody, completely unaccountable for whatever they did or said. They didn't have to worry about keeping communities alive, making jobs for people who had families to support, bringing in the Crown revenues that paid for health care and schools. All they had to do was push and push and push to shut it all down. They were like bargainers in a labour-management negotiation, shooting high, going for all they could get, although they were never at risk of having to give anything of theirs to get what they were shooting for. They were a little like a python strangling its prey; whenever the victim exhales, the snake constricts, but it never loosens its grip to let its dinner take a breath. The direction of force is all one way.

They also knew how to attract the media and hold the media's attention with language and provocations. We on the other side, whether we were companies, associations, or governments, were restricted by our accountabilities. We couldn't call the extreme greens members of a terrorist conspiracy or pour instant glue into their fax machines. We just had to grin and get on with it.

But though they were able propagandists the greens were not much when it came to science. You didn't see many of them offering to debate a professional forester, and certainly they wouldn't do that twice. They weren't arguing the science of the forest; all they were saying was that we had to protect large tracts of forest land, and the larger the better. I never saw any lengthy list of sound reasons why we should shut down logging, nor any thought being given to the effects of the extremist green agenda on the economy and society. The great missing point in what little real debate took place was the fact that the forest was being re-established through replanting

One of the most effective countermeasures against green propaganda was to bring the targets of their lobbying efforts – European and American buyers of BC forest products – to see the reality. I was standing one day with a group of Europeans in the middle of a vast tract that had been clearcut then replanted. They had seen carefully selected pictures taken just after the harvest. Now a few years had gone by and the new trees were about waist high. I asked a German what he thought about the clearcut.

He said, "Where is it?"

I said, "You're standing in it."

He looked around and I saw that he understood. I said, "What would you have done with this land?"

He said they would have clearcut it and replanted, the same as us.

The truth is, we are doing an admirable job of looking after our natural forest. Canadians need not take second billing to anyone, although we started late. Today we are world leaders in the management of the natural forest – literally the best on Earth – and we will be better still tomorrow. ■

or would re-establish itself naturally. Their most effective argument was aesthetics: clearcut logging looked awful.

COFI, both in its collective activities as an association and through the individual actions of its members, did not shy away from the fight. We went out and established a strong dialogue with the three levels of government, with the unions and where possible with the environmental groups, then we continued to keep the lines of communication open. But where we always seemed to fall down, as an industry and as a sector, was in public relations follow-through.

There were our opponents, with their wonderfully evocative language – Brazil of the North, the Great Bear Rain Forest, the Lungs of the Planet – and their full-time focus on the war. I was often the target of particular pieces of propaganda because I led much of the industry's efforts, and my magnificent shape lent itself to the kinds of cartoons that are popular with protest movements. The eco-groups consistently beat us in sloganeering and stuntsmanship. Even so, we were evolving new ways of thinking and devising better practices in response to society's changing values; unfortunately, we never seemed to remember to tell the people out there about all the good things we were doing.

There would be efforts at public relations, like Forests Forever, with its newspaper and television ads. It would run for a few months or a year or so, then the program would wind up and any gains that had been made would be lost in the continual din from the activists whose mantra never changed: shut it down, shut it all down. I would always argue that we had to do more, had to think of the long term. But the forest sector seems to attract many short-term thinkers. Perhaps it's because the sector is governed by several distinct cycles: the fifty- to one-hundred-year growing cycle; the formerly seven-year but now completely irregular business cycle; the five-year political cycle; the one-year or shorter corporate financial cycle; and lately the seemingly endless US protectionist cycle. Whatever the cause, I have long been aware that when sales turn down, the mood in the forest sector is that they'll always be down; when sales go up, then they'll always stay up.

The problem has not been helped by the current corporate culture that concentrates so tightly on the day-to-day share price. We need to be keeping people continuously in touch with how the sector is changing, how we are meeting our domestic and international obligations to the forest. And we need to let our ways of reaching people evolve, with new messages through innovative and still evolving communications channels. There is no "once and for all."

One thing that bothered me about the "War" was that the provincial government, be it Social Credit or NDP, always left the industry hanging out to dry. We were harvesting and reforesting on public land, with full government sanction and under rules set by the government through a process of public involvement. A constant torrent of money poured from our operations into the public treasury

I was involved in Globe 90, the Vancouver conference that brought together the capable and the illustrious to discuss sustainable development. At one of the receptions, I met Madame Gro Harlem Brundtland, who was then between terms as Prime Minister of Norway. She was Chair of the World Commission on Environment and Development. I had read the Commission's groundbreaking report, *Our Common Future* and had listened attentively to the speech she had just given to the Globe 90 delegates.

We chatted amiably for a while, then I noted to her that her speech had not touched on the issue of world population. Her expression turned serious and she looked around to see who was listening before she answered, "Mike, if I had used the word 'population' in my speech today, I would have had to speak for forty minutes instead of twenty, to put my remarks into the full religious and ethnic contexts. It is one of the most sensitive topics on the agenda."

I said, "But the world's population is still expanding at a rapid rate, and that affects everything. What is the solution?"

She said that her studies indicated that as the rate of industrial development increases, the rate of population growth declines. So, as the world develops sustainably then population growth rates will drop.

I thought about it and I believe I can buy that theory. It has happened that way in most parts of the developed world. But even in the developed countries, where populations are static or even shrinking, we still foresee heavy environmental impacts from continued development. What will happen in the developing world – China, Africa, India – with all of those billions of people and their numbers still rising, if we superimpose a rapidly expanding industrial sector? What will be the trade off between population and environmental degradation?

Long before the Brundtland Commission, I talked about this issue with Mike Pearson when I met him in Turkey. He told me that most people, even those in positions of responsibility, tend to discount the future. We think of the world in static, not dynamic, terms. We draw a line around a part of the earth and say, henceforward this will be a protected area. It's as if we're taking a snapshot and, like the contents of a photographic image, nothing's going to change. But everything changes, and managing anything is managing change.

Here in BC, we tend to think about land-use issues in static terms. But there are more than four million of us now, and soon it will be five million, then six. We can't put up a firewall and tell the rest of Canada or the world, "Don't come here, we're full."

Yet we don't ask ourselves often enough what it will mean to have millions more living here. Exactly where will they live? In ever larger urban centres? But near those burgeoning spreading cities will be a lot of very sensitive fish and wildlife habitats, the sources of our fresh water supplies, areas known to be the best growing sites for commercial timber. That means there will be conflicts.

Are we ready for those conflicts? I don't think so. Will we plan ahead and solve the problems before they become critical, or will we take the Royal Commission approach: wait until everyone is screaming and then try to patch together some kind of compromise – which will last only long enough for the next round of conflicts to develop? ■

and every penny of that revenue was spent. Yet when bridges burned and truck tires were slashed, the government was always a politely interested bystander.

These days, most of the activist groups have changed their approaches. The chant is no longer "Shut it all down." Today, the target has shifted and the groups are saying, "Shut some of it down, but not all," while the industry has moved away from wanting to keep the woods wide open. We've met in a middle where everyone accepts that we have to protect biodiversity and make room for species that are at risk. Of course, there are still some extremists at either end of the spectrum, and I suppose they will always be there, but the industry, governments and the local and international environmental groups somehow managed to find at least enough common ground to work together. It was not achieved without pain – people lost jobs, communities were hurt – but somehow we managed to move things forward.

We all learned that the adversarial approach – the "War" – was a great way to get people focused on the problem but it did not lead to any solutions. Ultimately, it was only when the adversaries agreed to a collaborative model, when they sat down around a table and starting looking for compromise and consensus, that we really got anything accomplished.

The extremists walked away from the collaborative process. In the long run, their inability to cooperate did not help their cause. The more moderate groups stopped listening to them and so did the general public.

The most effective strategy used by the environmental groups was not mass civil disobedience but the threatened consumer boycott of companies like the large home renovation supply chains in the US and in Europe. The marketplace was the ideal means by which to get the industry's attention and redirect corporate thinking into new channels. Out of the boycott threat came the movement toward being able to certify that the products being offered to consumers came from sustainably managed forests. The question then became, and remains today: whose certification process should the consumer trust? We still have these competing "brands" – the Canadian Standards Association, the Forest Stewardship Council, the different US and European systems – and it will take another evolutionary stage before I see the realization of my dream of bringing them all together in one common voice.

The continuing struggle of competing certification "brands" underscores one of the lessons learned over the past twenty years: we can't say that we've had our war in the woods and now things are solved "once and for all." Today evolves into tomorrow. After the certification debate ends, there will probably be new areas of contention. The debate over setting aside great tracts of land is largely over in BC. We have set aside 12.5 per cent or more of the province's land mass, and British Columbians can be justly proud of having achieved a higher standard than the global target of 12 per cent. Some may argue that too much of that one eighth of our province is rock and gravel, but the fact remains that there are whole countries smaller than the aggregate of preserved and protected land in our province.

Now we may expect the focus to shift to how the "working" forest is being managed. And the pressure in that regard will not come just from activist groups. We live in an increasingly interconnected world, and we are entering a time of more and more international agreements, of global conventions on matters that affect all of humanity. Issues like climate change, fresh water, biodiversity and global deforestation are everyone's business and British Columbians, as good citizens of the world, should expect to find the world taking more of an interest in what we do and how we do it, just as we take an interest in what the rest of the world is doing.

I believe in the certification approach, though I would like to see some coming together of the various brands at least on some basic understandings, albeit we might have different standards of measurement for boreal forest versus coastal temperate versus tropical. I know that many people are confused by the competing certification systems, and the confusion is not good for the forest nor for the different groups trying to protect it. I am hopeful that the certification movement will evolve and mature, but I doubt it will ever become as simple as I would like to see. Still, it has been encouraging to see, even among the Forest Stewardship Council's proponents, signs of practical adjustments to their thinking as time has gone by. And the emergence of competing certification regimes, in response to the extremist brands, is also a sign that the evolution of ideas is underway.

THE FOREST ALLIANCE

As the War in the Woods heated up, opinion polls that had always shown that the forest industry was accepted as the economic lifeblood of the province began to show a growing distrust of the big companies over issues like clearcutting and pollution from pulp mills. Several of the major companies hired an international public relations firm to create a grassroots organization to deal with the problem. There was scuttlebutt around the industry that the firm had thought up the idea on its own and sold it to the CEOs as one of those "once and for all" solutions. If so, I wasn't invited to that meeting.

Opinion among the members of COFI was divided but I thought the idea for a citizens' group to represent the forest-dependent communities was timely. I participated in a number of meetings, as did people like Jack Munro, president of the IWA. But then people with our kinds of affiliations – COFI, unions – were asked to step off the bus because they were building a citizens' participation vehicle, although of course it had corporate members.

The Forest Alliance might have worked. A more aggressive approach to taking on the well-financed green groups was a relevant idea for its time, and there were certainly plenty of communities being hurt by the growing boycott movement. But it was always haunted by the suspicion, almost as strong in some parts of the forest sector as among the greens, that it had been conceived as a means for a perhaps too-clever public relations outfit to make some money out of a troubled industry. The Alliance was not much use in helping to develop markets for BC forest products. COMDP and other programs were much more effective.

ABORIGINAL AFFAIRS

For the first 119 years of British Columbia's existence as a province of Canada, BC provincial governments of every stripe had maintained that Aboriginal title was extinguished when the former colony joined the Canadian confederation, after which all Aboriginal issues came under federal jurisdiction. Then in 1990 Premier Bill Vander Zalm overturned tradition by agreeing to discuss the Nisga'a nation's land claims. In 1993, Mike Harcourt's NDP government established the BC Treaty Commission and the process of negotiating new treaties began. The issue soon grew into a major feature of the BC political and economic landscape and has remained so ever since.

Back in my days with FPAC, it had become clear during our review of forest and range regulations that a large number of treaty issues remained outstanding. I had some grounding in the issue because I had kept in touch with my old schoolmate, Len Marchand, for whom the land claims question was a central theme of his career. We had talked about it a number of times over the years. Later, as

Len Marchand made a point of keeping me abreast of how his people were faring. A recurring event was his habit of bringing me up to date on the correct nomenclature as it evolved over time.

The phone would ring. "Apsey," Len would say, "you've got to stop calling us Indians." "All right," I would say. "What shall I call you?" "We're natives." "Right you are." Time would go by. The phone would ring again. "Apsey?" "Yes, Len?" "Apsey, you've got to stop calling us natives. Hell, you were born here, weren't you?"

"Yes, I was. Not far from where you were born." "Then that means you're a native, too. So you can't call us natives." "What shall I call you?" "Call us Aboriginal peoples." "Right you are." More time would pass. The phone would ring. "Apsey?" "Yes, Len?" "Apsey, you've got to stop calling us Aboriginals. That lumps us in with the Métis and the Inuit." "What shall I call you?"

"Call us First Nations. And remember, Apsey, it's nations, plural. We are distinct peoples."

"Right you are."

I await with interest Len's next phone call. ■

Deputy Minister of Forests, I kept a close eye on the progress of First Nations court actions. Land claims were – and remain – the great unfinished business of British Columbia. The people who were here first did not get a fair shake, and we who came after must find some way to square things. It was with that thought in mind that I pushed the legal envelope to create the Tanizul Tree Farm Licence.

During my years at COFI keeping on top of the developing land claims process became one of our core functions. We were learning as we went, as were the governments and the First Nations themselves. Cases were moving through the courts. The political process was finally engaging the issues. We could sense the direction of events.

The key question was going to be certainty. Who would control the land base? If we were moving toward treaties and settlements, would it be a transfer of land or of money, or of both? If it was to be forest land, then how much land and under what terms? My staff and I felt that the industry had to be forward-thinking on the issues; it would not have done to have fallen behind the curve on a question that could so profoundly affect the land base. We made a point of going out to visit with chiefs and councils. We wanted to hear directly what the issues were from their perspectives, to get the facts and figures on First Nations employment in forest operations, to discuss existing and proposed joint ventures, to find out what worked and what didn't, and why and why not?

I believe the industry has done a good job of evolving its thinking on this great issue. No one disagrees that there must be a fair and just settlement. And the settlement must be negotiated, not litigated. We have to resolve this matter through collaboration and consensus so we can move on together. I firmly believe we can do it. I have met a lot of Aboriginal leaders – First Nations and Métis – over my career;

When the Nisga'a Treaty was under negotiation, my staff and I invited Chief Joe Gosnell, the Nisga'a's lead negotiator, to meet with the COFI board. He came to the Council's offices and we had a short discussion before I took him in to meet the board.

"What would you like me to say?" he asked me.

"Whatever you want," I said. "The floor's open. Help us to understand."

The boardroom was packed. Joe Gosnell stood at one end of the table, an impressive man, full of the knowledge of his people's history. He let a silence grow for a few seconds then he said, "Many of you in this room today think that we're after a lot of land."

He paused and looked around, then he said, "You're right."

When that had sunk in, he said, "Many of you think that in addition to a lot of land, we're after a lot of money." Another pause, then, "You're right."

He looked the industry in the eye again and said, "And many of you think that in addition to a lot of land and a lot of money, we will want a lot of access to additional resources."

He paused, then he said, "And you're right, again."

There then ensued a full-tilt, in-depth discussion of the issues – one of the best meetings we ever had. There was not a question Joe Gosnell wouldn't or couldn't answer. It was a genuine education for the COFI board; Some of the directors were CEOs of multibillion-dollar corporations, but they realized that they were talking with a man who was a match for any of them in intelligence and strength. He told them, "If you are going to operate in our traditional territory, you are going to come and talk to us first," and they knew that he meant it. When it was over, they crowded in to shake his hand and thank him for coming.

I have witnessed a number of events in my life that I recognized as watershed moments. That was one of them. ■

Here is a partial list of the processes that came and went during the 1990s:

Task Force on Environment and Economy;
The Commission of Inquiry into Compensation for the Taking of
    Resource Interests;
Commission of Inquiry into the Public Service;
Forest Resources Commission;
Commission on Resources and Environment;
The Task Force on Employment and Training;
B.C. Round Table on the Environment and the Economy.

The Round Table was one of several in which I was involved. Created by the Social Credit administration and carried on by the NDP, it brought together a group of people representing disparate interests and backgrounds. We were asked to conduct a public discussion on the major issues and try to find some common ground. We issued papers, held meetings all over the province, and listened to a great variety of views from experts and non-experts alike. Then we talked it over amongst ourselves and, lo and behold, came to a consensus. We gave our recommendations to the Mike Harcourt government, and awaited their response.

In my darker moments, I suspect that the government hoped we would simply go on talking forever. Instead we presented them with something they might have had to respond to. Perhaps a small panic ensued. In any case, they promptly shut us down. ■

I haven't met a stupid one yet. I might argue with some of them over their bargaining tactics, but I don't question their sincerity. It is my fervent desire that British Columbia and Canada will work with the Aboriginal peoples so that we can complete the treaty process in the shortest time possible.

That will be better for them, and it will be better for the rest of us.

FOREST PRACTICES CODE

The 1990s were carried along on a flood of processes intended to resolve the conflicts over land and resource use in British Columbia. COFI couldn't afford not to be involved in them, and a great deal of my time and that of my staff and the member committees was devoted to researching, discussing, presenting and rebutting. Similar movements were going on nationally and internationally and I was involved in many of them.

Was all this effort well coordinated? No. But to me the more important question was: to what purpose are we engaging in all this process? Is it merely process for process's sake, to satisfy a necessity to say, yes, we engaged in a process? Where does the process lead? What is the vision we are trying to achieve? I have not yet had an answer. We always seem to be able to develop great vision statements – we had a good one at COFI – but we don't grab them and move forward. What use is vision without action?

One process that clearly began with a vision and went on to action – though not the kind that I or the BC forest industry greatly appreciated – was the immense Forest Practices Code brought in by the NDP in 1995. It was not a revolutionary code – it wrapped up a lot of existing rules and standards in one grand, encyclopedic format – and it did add to that mix some important new ideas as to how the forest should be managed, ideas that came out of the ferment of changing knowledge, values and philosophies regarding the forest.

For the most part, the industry agreed with the objectives of the code; as I've said here before, no forester wants to see any forest destroyed or even hurt. Where we came unglued was in the decidedly prescriptive nature of the FPC. It was a mountain of detailed manuals of procedures that covered every phase of forest management down to the micro level. So detailed were the rules and procedures that they effectively did away with the need for foresters; all that was required was someone who could read and had the strength to carry the armloads of instructions.

Like many government approaches, the FPC was well intentioned but overdone. The province needs a code based on objectives. Instead of arbitrarily saying, thou shalt not log within x-distance of a creek, a code should pragmatically set out the goal to be achieved: protecting fish habitat, conserving fresh water resources, creating wildlife corridors. The 1995 code was based on a "do as nanny says" philosophy that did not trust the industry to live up to the objectives that the government and the public wanted met. To be more precise, the government believed that some elements of the industry would not measure up, consequently it imposed a blanket prescription on the whole industry. In essence the FPC punished all for the expected transgressions of a few. Back when I was a schoolboy I never liked it when some overly strict teacher would make the whole class stay late because one malefactor had shot a spit ball. I didn't like it when the NDP applied the same technique to an entire industry.

Of course, the government was also hearing from critics who said the FPC didn't go far enough – "Shut it down, shut it all down," was the constant subtext behind those criticisms. At COFI we were worried about the code's impact on the allowable cut, and especially on the extra expense it added to the cost of harvesting operations during a time when the Americans were playing protectionist hardball. As the code was being phased in we developed our case for modifications and took it to government. We didn't get very far.

The basic question in any management systems is: what are we managing for? In managing a forest, are we managing for timber supply? Or for wildlife, for fresh water, for aesthetics, for fish, for recreation? If we're managing for all of these goals, how do they interconnect with each other and which has priority over the others and under what conditions? It can be difficult to set those objectives, and judging whether or not they have been met on a case-by-case basis can lead to ambiguous results. A prescriptive approach lends itself to easier auditing; you can go down a check list and see if the mandatory procedures were followed. Of course, that approach makes the outcome, good or bad, irrelevant. Is that really the philosophy we want to take into the forest?

Sir Humphrey Appleby would have loved the Forest Practices Code. I did not love it. I have always been more interested in consequences than in processes. Whenever I have considered a course of action, whether as a consultant or as a manager, my first analysis is directed to scoping out the intended consequences of the plan. Once those are known, it is time to consider the unintended consequences that might flow from what we are about to start. The unintended consequences of the Forest Practices Code strained the BC forest industry, unnecessarily in my view, at a time when it was under attack from many quarters.

FUTURE HISTORY

I have said that in Turkey I discovered the past. At COFI I discovered the future. One process that I was proud of was one I initiated: COFI's Future History Project.

As the 1980s edged toward the nineties, it was evident that we were in for an unprecedented degree of change in the new decade. Sitting in my office, I could not be entirely confident that the Council would be in a position to deal on behalf of our members with the new kinds of issues that would be coming at us. I decided we should go out and take a look at the future.

For several weeks, the staff and I regularly turned ourselves into think tanks, read all that we could find, brought in consultants and futurists to jolt and enlighten us. We discussed, argued, ran scenarios and then discussed and argued some more, and finally we put together our best projections in a series of snapshots of the future. From the rapidly accelerating events of the eighties we extrapolated into the nineties: economic trends, the dynamics of our major markets, the outlook for forest products, political trends both locally, globally and in the US. We made predictions on the changing roles of governments in Canada and British Columbia, on where we expected government-business relations to go, on social trends, demographics and employment as they would impact on the BC forest sector.

When we were satisfied that we'd taken the best look at the future that we could get, we put the results before the COFI board in a series of detailed presentations. We also generated plenty of copies of our findings to circulate among the members to encourage them to examine their own corporate thinking.

COFI's Future History paper filtered throughout the industry and I still get questions on it, with people asking if we had ever taken a similar look into the 2000s. Regrettably, there was no second act. COFI changed as the industry and the world in which it operated became increasingly different from the past. But the project was the kind of useful exercise that all organizations, private or public sector,

We were convened in the COFI boardroom. The staff and I had just concluded a full presentation of the Future History Project's findings to a group of chief executive officers. There had been charts and slides, individual presentations on where we saw the global economy going, on changing modes of government regulation, on the rapidly – even radically – evolving social values related to the management of the public forest.

When we concluded, there was a thoughtful silence around the big table. Then one of the CEOs, the head of a northern lumber firm, scratched his head and said, "Mike, what's all this got to do with the price of two-by-fours?"

I said, "Everything." ■

need to do in this new world we now inhabit. We all have to ask ourselves the pressing question: are we set up to deal with the future?

In the BC forest sector, the practice has been to establish a system that meets the economic and political priorities of the day then to operate under that system until a changing world reveals it to be no longer functional. At that point, we engage a Royal Commissioner to study everything and propose a new system which, after some to-ing and fro-ing, becomes the new regime. Until it no longer works and we repeat the process.

That "steps on a ladder" approach may have been appropriate when change proceeded at the more leisurely pace that we were used to in the first three-quarters of the twentieth century. I'm not sure it remains a useful strategy. Today change is so constant, so pervasive and so increasingly fast that, instead of periodic re-examinations, we may need a process of continuous review – A Ministry of Change, or at least a Directorate of the Future in every government department and every industry, if not every company that is serious about still being in business five or ten years from now.

REORGANIZATIONS OF COFI

With every aspect of the BC forest industry's operating environment constantly evolving, it had to be expected that the industry's major association would also come under pressure to change. During the seventies, there had been two full reviews of COFI's structure and goals. As the eighties advanced into the nineties, we went through another.

An association is only as good as its members want it to be. The members' commitment to being involved is the key. COFI's strengths were in its board, whose members were CEOs – people who expected to make decisions – and in its committees, where staff from the member companies worked with each other and with outside decision-makers in government and other entities whose actions had direct and indirect effects on the industry .

The process of working toward consensus on a large and complex set of issues – forest management, trade, public perceptions of the industry – lent COFI its strength. The higher the level of participation by member-company staff, and the more senior the staff who were involved, the better a job we could do for the members. Given the wide variance between COFI's different categories of members, the worst approach we could have taken would have been to become a staff-driven association, whose members contributed little more than their annual dues.

I devoted a great deal of my time to keeping the big collective ball rolling. My diaries are page after page of meetings, phone calls, visits to and by members of the COFI. The objective was always to keep them involved, to ensure that COFI did not become an afterthought to be looked at only after they had put out today's or this week's or this month's fires.

It was, of course, a fluidly evolving relationship. There were always changes going on in the higher echelons and at the operational levels of companies big or small. People moved around, among companies and within individual firms. They retired or got transferred or quit to form consultancies. Downsizing during recessions made borrowed staff hard to get. Increasingly, as the ownership structure of many firms changed, there would be wholesale dislocations of corporate teams and the sudden appearance of major new players who were moved in from out of the province. Keeping it all in play was sometimes like juggling a slew of random objects, then having someone arbitrarily yank one of the plates out of the collection and replace it with a burning torch.

Playing Sancho Panza to this shifting crowd of distractible Don Quixotes was always a fascinating task, sometimes a frustrating one. Their bottom line was always, "How will my participation help my corporation?" Sometimes the answer was obvious, sometimes obscure. But I enjoyed coming up with it. Often the ultimate answer, when we faced a less than sympathetic government or a growing public concern about our stewardship of the forests, was Benjamin Franklin's observation that those who do not hang together are at risk of being hanged one by one.

In the early nineties, COFI underwent a major reorganization of its committee structures and developed a new mission statement. Its governance structure was also radically changed, so that the Council ceased to be an association of member companies with a board of decision-making CEOs and became instead an "association of associations," whose directors were the representatives of regional and sectoral industry groups. I argued against the change but other views prevailed. It may have looked good on paper, but the result of the reorganization was that COFI was now governed by people who could not make a decision without going back to the bodies they represented and working out a consensus among each governing board.

The new governance structure made for more complexity and slower decision making at a time when every aspect of the industry's operating environment was not only changing but constantly accelerating. After a few years the inherent dysfunctionality of the "association of associations" approach led to a review of COFI's governance. We went back to a board whose members could make decisions at the table. I also argued that there should be no provision for the CEOs to be represented by alternates – if we were to have a board of CEOs then only they should sit there and they should be prepared to spend some serious time at the table.

By the time I was preparing to retire, in 1998, the ongoing rush of change had again caught up with us. The different issues affecting the coast versus the Interior, for example, caused me to put before COFI's board, along with a number of other options to consider, a question I had raised eight years before: whether the Council should continue to represent both regions. The answer, which came within six years of my retirement, was in the negative. Today, there is a separate Coast Forest Products Association, and COFI represents the

Interior forest sector. Ten years from now, I would not be surprised to see further fragmentation or recombination of the industry's elements. Everything changes, all the time.

For that reason, especially in light of recent consolidations, my recommendation to the industry today is much the same as it was when I retired: instead of full-scale periodic reviews – our own equivalent of the Royal Commission – undertake a continuous process of re-evaluation of what must be done and who should do it.

Life no longer resembles a game of American football, with set plays and regular stops and starts; it's more like the soccer I played as a boy, with continuous, shifting action all over the field and very few time-outs to comfort the wounded.

TRADE

COFI was conceived in the early sixties as primarily a trade development organization and although government relations grew more and more important through the eighties and nineties, the role of developing, securing and expanding markets was never far from my mind. Of course, the single largest trade challenge of my time at COFI was the sequential "lumber wars" brought on by US protectionism – in fact, the first American countervailing duty (CVD) offensive came during my term as Deputy Minister of Forests – but that is so large and tasty a subject that I will devote all of the next chapter to it.

In the early days of COFI, demand for BC forest products was so ripe and continual that companies "allocated" production to their customers. By the time we had weathered the recession of the early eighties, things had changed markedly. Everything was new: new producers, new products (including once-derided competitors like eucalyptus pulp), new international trade regimes, new regional trading blocs, and – thank goodness – newly developing markets like China.

The Council's continuing concerns were to secure access to existing and new markets and to diversify the products the industry was selling to a world that was growing increasingly choosy as to what and from whom it would buy. When I'd been a vice president at COFI, back in the seventies, we had had a very large market development program for commodity products like lumber. Some aspects of it were financed on our own as an industry; other efforts, like COMDP, were jointly funded with the federal and provincial governments.

By the mid-eighties, we were creating more specialized market development programs for more advanced forest products. We asked ourselves, after looking at our opportunities in the familiar stomping grounds of Europe and the US, what might be out there in the way of non-traditional markets for BC wood products? What about China? India? Taiwan? South America? We did make some sporadic shipments to the Latin American countries, to North Africa and the Middle East, but the new initiatives were aimed at China. I had been there a number of times as deputy minister with Tom Waterland and delegations of CEOs and other people from the BC forest sector. China had come through its Cultural Revolution and the internal coup that removed Mao Zedong's ideologically driven

In 1988, COFI moved from its West Hastings office to new space in the Bentall Centre on Burrard. I took a look at the new space while it was still empty and it struck me that, on the topic of value-added wood products, here was a chance to put the Council's money where its rhetoric was. "Why," I asked, "would we want COFI's offices to be an advertisement for the plasterboard manufacturers?"

The new offices were panelled and furnished entirely with value-added wood products from the BC forest. It was a beautiful space in which to work. ▪

China–Canada Shanghai Friendship Farm House, 1987.

remnants from power. There was a new pragmatism in Beijing and a new openness to the western world.

We made a serious attempt at opening the Chinese mind to the advantages of wood frame construction. Together with the federal or provincial governments, and sometimes with both, COFI built demonstration buildings in places like Shanghai and Beijing where today's booming Chinese economy was then emerging from the shell of Maoist restraint. We used some imagination and found ways to marry traditional Chinese construction methods and materials with our products, creating combination stone, concrete and wood frame buildings.

We knew that at some point China was going to get its act together. COFI's idea was, let us develop a relationship. Forget the politics, even though they're authoritarian communists, can we not still have a relationship? Today, everyone knows China is an emerging industrial superpower. Back in the eighties, people said "Where's the market? The average Chinese income is peanuts." But we looked at the strip of coastline, places like Guangzhou (formerly Canton)

In the spring of 1989, we had completed construction of three demonstration buildings in downtown Beijing. By the time they were ready to be officially opened, in May, the city was in a turmoil over

China–Canada
Building
Demonstration
Project, Beijing,
1989.

the mass pro-democracy demonstrations by students in Tiananmen Square. I went with a COFI delegation to speak at the ceremony. It was a very strange time to be there. Every intersection was thronged with thousands of people demonstrating, debating. When they would see our convoy of vehicles full of western faces, they would crowd around the windows making "vee" signs and calling to us, "Tell our story!"

The Canadian ambassador, Earl Drake, was anxious to see us leave the country. But we had come to open our buildings and we were determined to do the job. It was not an auspicious event, however: as the speeches proceeded toward the ribbon cutting, I looked down the wide Beijing avenue on which we had built the model buildings and saw a great yellowy billow – at first I thought it was smoke – rolling toward us. It turned out to be one of the choking sandstorms that occasionally sweep across northern China. As we went through our official motions, the yellow cloud came inexorably on until we were all caught up in swirling grit.

To be in Beijing in late May, 1989, was an eerie experience: trucks and jeeps packed with unsmiling soldiers roaming through the streets, students riding on the fenders, arguing with the troops. I remember seeing what must have been a surface-to-air missile mounted on a truck launcher going by, a few students straddling the rocket as if it were a horse. I walked through Tiananmen Square, one of a vast crowd that numbered some 1.2 million, the mood almost like that of a carnival.

Earl Drake told us we were the last mission out of China. A few days after we left, it got very ugly. ■

and Shanghai, a piece of China with some 300 million people. The per capita income there was a lot higher and it was growing faster. That was going to be the heart of a new China, and its people would follow the Asian practice of doing business with people they knew, people with whom they had developed a long-term relationship.

Today's business strategies, it seems to me, are often geared more to the shorter term – today's share price, next quarter's earnings. But I would like to hear that we are building on that old strategy of the long-term relationship with China. We need to be engaged with China because China's burgeoning demand for all kinds of commodities, from concrete to fuel oil, is already having an effect on everybody's costs. We also need to be able to influence China's development in ways that will let the Chinese minimize their environmental impacts, because there is only one biosphere and what one quarter of the world's people do affects all of us. And it's not just about helping China get to more advanced production methods without taking a long sojourn through an age of smoke-belching industries. China should also be a major market for recycled materials and the technologies that process them.

Before the great financial meltdown of 1997, Japan was a significant market for BC forest products. The Japanese had tended to like our raw logs and squared timbers best, which they cut according to their own precise – some would call them finicky – standards. Getting into the Japanese lumber market meant overcoming a host of non-tariff restrictions, such as their labyrinthine building code and standards. COFI played a continuing role in working with Canadian trade officials to show that homes made with our products met Japanese standards for fire safety and strength of construction; in fact, Canadian-style timber frame homes survive Japan's frequent earthquakes better than their traditional post-and-beam construction.

Again, we built demonstration houses and brought over people from the Japanese construction industry to train them in how to use our lumber.

I was at the Canada-Japan Business Conference in Fukuoka, Japan, in May 1996. At the opening ceremonies I was seated at the back of the vast meeting hall. After the keynote speaker was finished I began to make a few notes. Then I sensed a presence beside me. I looked up and saw the man who had just been speaking. He was the chairman and CEO of a very major Japanese corporation and he was standing there looking at me.

He bowed and said, "Excuse me."

I rose, bowed and said, "Yes, sir?"

He said, "If I may, I must say that you are rather large."

I said, "Yes, sir." It seemed appropriate to add, "Thank you."

"Do you know sumo?" he asked.

"Yes, I do."

"Do you think you could win?"

I spoke the truth. "With training, yes!"

He said, "I think so, too!"

We bowed again and said goodbye.

Unfortunately, the hypothesis was never put to a test.

On a Saturday morning in May 1994, I was at my hotel preparing to catch a flight home from Tokyo, when I got a call from former US Vice President Walter Mondale. He was then Bill Clinton's ambassador to Japan and he invited me over to the embassy for a cup of coffee and a chat about trade. I got into a suit and tie – I'd been casually dressed for the long plane flight – and went over to the US Embassy, where I found my host dressed in clothes just as casual as the outfit I'd left at the hotel.

He went down the hall and got the coffee himself, then he asked me to tell him all about what COFI had been doing in Japan over the years. I obliged and gave him chapter and verse, answering all of his questions. By the time I was finished, it was getting late and I had a plane to catch.

As I was leaving, he gave me a big smile and said, "Mike, what you've been telling me is so much in keeping with the Canadian way of doing things. Let's make a deal: you keep on being Canadian, pursuing the long-term, low-key approach. And every now and then, if Japan needs a kick in the ass, we'll handle that."

I don't think I've ever heard anyone give a better summing up of the Canadian and US approaches to trade negotiations. ■

INTERNATIONAL ACTIVITIES

For much of my time at COFI, I had two full-time jobs: head of the Council and staff head of CFIC, the Canadian Forest Industries Council, which was fighting the US protectionist lumber lobby. CFIC was the brain child of Adam Zimmerman, CEO of Noranda, which for a time was the controlling shareholder of MacMillan Bloedel. He realized that although there were the various provincial associations and sector-specific bodies like the Canadian Pulp and Paper Association, there was no single national entity that brought together all the different elements of what was for decades Canada's number one provider of jobs and earner of export dollars.

Yet we had national issues to concern us: forest management, social and technological change, land use conflicts, and especially trade. Unfortunately, the latter concern became so paramount during the successive waves of protectionism in our major market, that the other issues slid off the CFIC table. Then CFIC itself fell into fatal internal divisions as the Americans used their traditional divide-and-conquer approach to unpick any unified Canadian response to their trade war. But now the Forest Products Association of Canada has moved from Montreal to Ottawa and seems to be providing the point of cohesion that Zimmerman rightly saw a need for.

Despite being doubly in the service of COFI and CFIC, I often found it hard to resist when someone would ask me if I could fit a study of some aspect of the world forest into my schedule. In late 1984 and early 1985, I served on an International Task Force convened by the World Bank, the UN Development Programme and the World Resources Institute to study a whole raft of issues affecting the world's tropical forest, including destruction of woodlands, desertification, floods, soil degradation, lack of fuel wood among local populations, governance structures and financing constraints.

It was a review of what had worked and what hadn't, of success stories and failures, across the whole of the developing world. We developed an agenda for action, trying to cross-fertilize examples that might work in one place because they'd worked somewhere else. We offered general strategies for a five-year program: strengthening institutions, slowing down illegal logging, building up local communities. It was frustrating to go through all of that process but not to see enough follow-up. The UN does what it can, and so do other international institutions, but we always run up against that bland question in the developed world: the developing world causes its own problems through corruption, inefficiency, whatever; so why should we care? But we don't hear the answer: because many of the southern hemisphere's problems have been caused by people from the northern half of the globe. That boatload of magnificent timber I saw leaving the port in Colombia, illegally cut and without a penny going to the government, was leaving the third world and heading for a first world buyer, to be turned into high-value products for first world homes.

In 1995 the Canadian and Dutch governments thought it would be fruitful to pull together the forest nations of the developing world in an International Workshop on Forestry at The Hague to see what action had been taken on our study of ten years before. I was invited to chair a week of meetings at which some thirty-five developing countries were represented. We reviewed what had happened since our study, identified the issues and problems, and made some projections as to what would happen next. It turned out that the work we'd done in 1984–85 had been useful, there had even been some movement on actions we had recommended, but nowhere near enough even to keep up with the problems. We left the Netherlands with a set of recommendations the delegates could take back to their countries, the donor agencies and the UN bodies in the hope that further actions might be taken. Were they taken? Probably some were. Would that be enough? No.

I would have loved to attend the 1992 UN Conference on Environment and Development (UNCED), the World Summit, as it was called, in Rio de Janeiro. It was chaired by Maurice Strong, for whom I have the highest regard, and I was invited by Canada to go but couldn't because I was buried in the trenches of the lumber wars. However, I helped develop Canada's positions.

With the assistance of Linda Coady, an exceptional COFI staffer who is today Vice-President, Sustainability – Vancouver 2010 Olympic and Paralympic Winter Games, I prepared a paper – *Timber, A*

Raw Material – that I delivered to the World Forestry Congress in Paris in 1991 but then there was yet another crisis in the lumber wars and I had to hurry over to Washington, DC. It turned out I missed being kissed on the cheeks by French President François Mitterand who was there to name me a *Chevalier de l'Ordre du Mérite Agricole*.

The International Institute for Applied Systems Analysis, located in a former royal summer home in the town of Laxenburgh just south of Vienna, asked me to chair a study team that was looking at the Siberian forest. The opportunity to see yet another part of the

I regretted not being decorated by the President of France but I did wonder if the award was something that they gave to many people, like a good conduct medal. Then, a few years later, I was at the Normandy horse farm which was the family home of my friend Pierre Desclos, who represented COFI in France and Italy. Pierre's father had been involved in the Résistance, saving Allied pilots who were shot down in their part of France.

We were at the breakfast table in the big house and Pierre was telling his father and mother that I had been given the medal. The old man's face grew grave and he got up and left the table without a word. I wondered if we had committed some *faux pas*, but a few minutes later Pierre's father returned, came to my side of the table, shook my hand and showed me his own *Ordre du Mérite Agricole*. I realized that to be in such company was an honour indeed. Later, the old man produced a very, very old bottle of champagne – Pierre said he kept them hidden in various places around the estate, and no one else knew where – and I was privileged to see a grand old custom of the French: disdaining to let him squeeze out the cork, the father bade the son open the bottle in keeping with ancient tradition: Pierre did so – holding the bottle out at arm's length, he sliced through its neck with one swift stroke of the family sabre.

It was very fine champagne. ■

University of
Forestry and
Wood Sciences,
Sopron, Hungary,
1990.

world, even if it was only to fly over it, was irresistible. I found the
time, telling myself it would be useful to know about the world's
other great boreal forest.

While working with IIASA we took a bus ride across the border
into Hungary for a couple of days to attend a meeting in Sopron.
Our Hungarian hosts were interested to know if I had been to school
with the Sopron foresters, and when I said I had they took me to see
the forestry school from which the Soproners had fled. We entered

by the back door and went through the facility, ending at an alcove near the front where there was a display of framed photographs of each year's class. Four frames contained no pictures – the years of the emigrants. The Hungarians told me that they would like some day to see those frames filled. Today, I believe they have been.

After NAFTA was signed and in effect, the three signatory states created a North American Commission for Environmental Cooperation, including a Joint Public Advisory Committee of Canadians, Mexicans and Americans. I sat on the JPAC until I retired and found it an instructive experience. In those years the linkages between environmental issues and trade were being made, the green boycott campaigns only the most obvious example. It was clear to me that the time when different issues could be stored in convenient silos, never touching each other, was coming to an end. We were into an age of velcro, where anything could hook onto anything else. I learned a lot that was useful to bring back for discussion around the Council's board and committee tables.

In 1994–96, Les Reed and I worked up a report called *World Timber Resources Outlook: Current Perceptions*, a comprehensive discussion paper that I commissioned on current perceptions of the state of the resource, the extent of infrastructure and the shape of the future. Les and I read everything we could get our hands on and consulted around the world with experts of all stripes. We got a full briefing on all that was known. But then we asked "What about the things we don't know?"

There were great gaps in our understanding of the global forest. We had scarcely begun to consider the question of biodiversity, the interlinked needs of forest species. Even in the world's plantation forests, of which there are more and more, we didn't have a full understanding of what was going on.

The more we looked at the world forest as a single entity – and the idea that it had to be seen as one mega-organism was beginning to come to me – the more it became clear that we knew much less than we ought to. On issue after issue, whether it was the accelerating loss of forest lands, or illegal logging, or the rising demand for fuel wood (which exceeds the global harvest of commercial timber), it was clear that neither national nor international mechanisms were keeping pace. It was also clear that the problems were not just for the developing world to solve, with whatever help well-meaning governments and groups in the developed world might care to give. If there is only one world forest, then its problems are our problems.

I was preparing a report on timber but I knew that the world forest is so much more than timber. I pulled together vast amounts of information but even as I was doing it I was constantly reminded of all the information we didn't have but should have had. I realized that in all the world, there is no single source of information on the world forest – no encyclopaedia of the forest. We don't even have common definition of what a forest is. I have seen forests in Turkey or West Africa that Canadians would call a pasture with a few trees scattered through it. Canada's definition of the extent of our own forest yields a total land base that is about twice what the FAO says it is. No one today could tell you, even approximately, how many trees there are in the world.

After a lifetime of studying the forest, I was approaching retirement age but only just coming to understand that what I and all the foresters of the world collectively knew about the forest was no more than a good start. The gaps far outnumbered the knowledge.

EXITING COFI

As my sixtieth birthday approached, I decided it was time to retire. Not really, completely retire, to putter around the house and pursue hobbies. As Sharon told me when I broached the subject, "I married you for life, not for lunch. Find things to do."

I believed I had found something to do. Going through the eighties and nineties as the head of an association of companies operating in a small open economy and selling to an increasingly globalized marketplace, I had discovered that the world was a hell of a lot smaller than I had thought. Along the way, I had also discovered that it only had one forest, and that forest was in peril. And if the forest was in peril so were we. I thought I would try to do something about it.

I let my employers know that I was going as of April 1, 1998, and offered some food for thought about how COFI might like to evolve in the coming years. There were some simply wonderful retirement parties, people said kind things and we promised to meet regularly. I am pleased to say that those promises were not empty: I was privileged to work with many exceptional people and we do get together for historical lunches and dinners. I am always moved by their affection and they know that they will always have mine.

From my retirement dinner remarks, the history of the BC forest industry during my career, encapsulated in a few seconds:

"We have experienced evolution, devolution, revolution, legislation, regulation, deregulation, complication, simplification, certainty, uncertainty, profitability and lossability.

"We have had innovation, computerization, certification, modernization, centralization, decentralization, vertical integration, horizontal integration, globalization and regionalization.

"We have been called sunset and sunrise. We have been exposed to agreements, accords, plans, strategies, missions, visions, MOUs and protocols. We have deforested, reforested, and afforested. We have used hi-tech and low-tech. We have gone from sustained yield to sustainable forest management, We have downsized, upsized, right-sized and dumbsized. We have suffered inflation, deflation and more than a little flatulation,.

"But most memorable of all, we have even experienced some 'sympathetic administration.'" ■

CHAPTER ELEVEN

The Lumber Wars

Canada and the United States have had disagreements over the lumber trade since before there was a Canada. Back in the 1820s, timber lands along the border between Maine and the unconfederated colony of New Brunswick were a festering issue between London and Washington. In the 1850s, eastern US lumber interests manoeuvred in Congress to keep lumber from "the Canadas" out of the American market to keep up the price of Maine's spruce and, according to one Ohio Congressman, its "inferior pine." Thirteen decades later, in the 1980s, the US lumber industry's goal was still the same; only the tactics had changed.

What follows is a precis of the main events of the Lumber Wars. For a more detailed analysis, the reader is referred to a 1997 paper prepared by the author and J.C. Thomas entitled *Lessons of the Softwood Lumber Dispute: Politics, Protectionism and the Panel Process.*

SOFTWOOD LUMBER I

As inflation and an unprecedented housing construction boom raced in harness through an overheated American economy in the 1970s, lumber sales and prices skyrocketed. US lumber producers who got their logs from state and federal timber rights auctions bid up the amounts they were willing to pay for future supplies. When the Federal Reserve Board dramatically raised interest rates at the end of the seventies, causing a severe downturn in the residential construction sector, some of those producers found themselves contracted to buy timber at costs they could not sustain. At the same time, increasing quantities of high-quality lumber from efficient new mills in British Columbia and other parts of Canada were reaching the US market, aided by a low-value Canadian dollar.

A number of major US lumber firms, supported by some smaller outfits, put together a financial war chest and, calling themselves the US Coalition for Fair Canadian Lumber Imports, lobbied several pliant members of the Senate and the House of Representatives to call for restrictions on Canadian softwood lumber imports, as well as shakes and shingles and fence. Specifically, they pressed the US Department of Commerce to levy a countervailing duty on our products, using a provision of US trade law that allows for a duty on a particular commodity from another country if the latter is subsidizing the export of that commodity.

In late 1982, the Coalition filed a petition with the US International Trade Commission and the gears began to turn in Washington. The basis of the complaint was that Canadian stumpage regimes constituted an unfair subsidy. The Commerce Department conducted an investigation, and a coalition of Canadian lumber producers known as the Canadian Softwood Lumber Committee mounted a strong defence of our position that the way we managed our publicly owned forests could not be considered a subsidy.

In the spring of 1983, the Commerce Department concluded its investigation by ruling that we were right. The US investigators looked at a range of Canadian federal and provincial programs and decided that stumpage did not constitute a subsidy. Technically, there were some programs that conferred subsidies but their total effect on the prices of our wood exports was no more than one-half of one per cent. *De minimis non curat lex* was the legal Latin phrase used in the judgement, meaning, "The law does not take note of trifles." We were vindicated.

In a perfect world, that would have been that. But international trade relations are conducted in a decidedly imperfect world, especially when they involve US industries that are old hands when it comes to working the levers and pulleys of the American political system. As far as the Coalition was concerned, our lumber was indeed subsidized and we had been acquitted merely on a few technicalities. The next step was to convince Congress to rewrite US trade laws so that the Coalition could get the finding it wanted. They proceeded to do just that, bringing forward a number of bills intended to make the administration change the rules.

SOFTWOOD LUMBER II

The second round of the dispute over lumber imports was a curious experience for those of us on the Canadian side.

American lumber producers and their friends in Congress and the White House kept insisting that there was a subsidy problem. Canadian producers and our trade officials would point to the Commerce Department ruling and say that there was no problem because there was no subsidy. It was a cultural dislocation: we were playing chess, while the Americans were playing poker; we saw the legal process as a means of determining true from false, right from wrong, while the Americans saw the law as a malleable instrument that could be shaped to give them what they wanted.

In 1985 Canada gave the US the perfect opportunity to solve the "problem" when Brian Mulroney's government told the Ronald Reagan administration that we wanted to negotiate a Free Trade Agreement. President Reagan wanted it too, but there was a high Congressional hurdle to be gotten over: in the past, US presidents had signed trade deals only to find that Congress refused to ratify them without drastic changes to make the agreements more profitable for their constituents. To get the Canada-US FTA, Reagan needed Congress to agree not to amend whatever pact his trade representative negotiated; Congress would only be able to ratify or not ratify. But the Senators and Representatives were not willing to give Reagan a commitment to "fast-track" the FTA unless he first solved a problem or two for them. And one of the biggest problems on their agenda was this business of "subsidized" Canadian lumber.

It did no good to argue that there was no subsidy. The major economic policy of both governments was the FTA. In the mid-1980s, as the FTA was being negotiated, the Coalition filed another case, timed to have maximum effect on certain key Congressional elections where Republican seats were at stake. They called for a countervailing duty of 30 per cent.

Canada's response was to declare the case to be harassment and to take the matter to the dispute-settlement process of the General Agreement on Tariffs and Trade (GATT). The case would also be fought in Washington, but this time the industry would not present the defence while the Canadian government handled international relations; Instead, Ottawa and the producing provinces, working together with the industry, all played leading roles. The industry was represented by the Canadian Forest Industries Council.

The Canadian side did not offer a well-coordinated response to the US harassment. British Columbia's new Premier, Bill Vander Zalm, made some off-the-cuff remarks about reviewing stumpage that played right into the Americans' hands, while his Minister of Forests, Jack Kempf, publicly stated, "I think stumpage rates at present are too low." Canadian Trade Minister Pat Carney, under pressure from British Columbia and Quebec, asked the Americans if a substantial provincial stumpage increase would settle the matter. She then made an offer to have the key provinces increase their stumpage by some $350 million – which would have raised Canadian costs by about 10 per cent – and also made it clear that this was a "one-time offer," not a negotiation. The Americans said, "Oh, it is so a negotiation," rubbed their hands and nicknamed her "One-Time Pat," then the Commerce Department determined a subsidy of 15 per cent.

Some people found Pat Carney very difficult to work with. My feeling was that though she was the minister on whose desk the trade file reposed, behind her was a Prime Minister and a cabinet.

Our political system has changed since the days of powerful, independent ministers like C.D. Howe. When I hear a minister speak, I assume that I am hearing the voice of a government. In 1986, the voice of the Canadian government said, *We want a Free Trade Agreement* and it spoke much more loudly than the voice of the Canadian lumber industry.

In a letter to an influential member of the Senate Finance Committee, US Trade Representative Clayton Yeutter, Reagan's point man on the FTA, added a hand written note: *We'll get lumber fixed*, it said. And they did. ▪

The fix was in on both sides of the border. Canada's free trade negotiators were finding that there would be no FTA unless the Americans got their way on lumber. At the end of 1986, Canada signed a Memorandum of Understanding with the United States, agreeing to impose a 15 per cent export tax on lumber exports. The MOU also required that Canada let the Americans keep an eye on our industry; they were to receive information on any changes that might affect the lumber trade.

The Commerce Department proceedings in Washington thus came to an abrupt end without the industry being able to fight its case. The GATT complaint was also withdrawn. There were not very many happy faces at CFIC. However, the MOU was seen as a temporary expedient – it could be ended on thirty days' notice – while stumpage and other charges were restructured so that the Americans would have no cause for complaint. Such was the degree of innocence on our side of the border.

From our point of view, Canada did learn one lesson from Softwood Lumber II that was applied to the FTA negotiations: the need for a binational process to resolve disputes. The result would be Chapter 19 of the FTA, which allowed for the creation of binational panels of experts to review decisions by either country's trade-dispute tribunals. Again, Canadians thought they had created a set-in-stone process that would bring rational certainty to any future disputes over our lumber. Again, the Americans saw a process that was set in Plasticine, as we would find out in Softwood Lumber III.

Adam Zimmerman had a strained relationship with the trade minister. Thus there was considerable surprise in his voice when he phoned me over the 1986 Christmas holiday season to ask if there was any reason why Pat Carney would have sent him a gift. He had received a very strong letter from her in which she repudiated his uncomplimentary assessment of the Memorandum of Understanding, but the missive was accompanied by a six-foot tall menorah.

"Why does she also seem to think I'm Jewish?" Zimmerman wanted to know.

I made discreet inquiries on his behalf. It turned out that an aide to Carney had left the letter to be picked up by a courier in the lobby of the building that housed her ministerial office. To make sure the courier didn't miss it, the envelope was attached to the box that contained the menorah, which was there to celebrate Hanukkah, along with a Christmas display. Quite reasonably, the courier saw the multi-branched candelabra and the letter affixed to it as a single delivery unit and hauled both away.

A fuss ensued. Zimmerman eventually sent the menorah back, but not before he had a photograph taken of himself standing beside it. ■

SOFTWOOD LUMBER III

After the MOU was in effect, BC and Quebec changed their stumpage regimes, with the effect that new costs were added onto the industry. These new costs affected all forest products, not just lumber and not just the portion of lumber that went south. The industry's balance sheets felt the impact. But with the new regimes in place, the export tax on US-bound lumber from these two provinces was reduced, (in

BC's case to zero), and by the time the eighties were rolling over into the nineties, the industry was seriously pressing Ottawa to end the MOU.

To bolster Canada's case that our lumber was not and never had been subsidized, Canada and the industry spent a fair amount of money to have experts in the accounting system used by the US Forest Service apply that same system to our situation north of the border. For once, we were comparing apples to apples and the subsequent analysis showed that, even by US definitions, there were no subsidies.

Armed with this data, Canada's trade representatives tried to interest the Americans in mutually dissolving the MOU. Their American counterparts declined to cooperate; in fact, they expressed interest in "improving" what to many Canadians was a noxious intrusion into our sovereignty. Finally, in late 1991, after almost five years, Canada gave the US the required one month's notice that the MOU would be terminated.

By then, George Bush had succeeded Ronald Reagan in the presidency. The Bush administration professed to be taken by surprise. Apparently the US trade officials who had been on the receiving end of all of our representatives' approaches toward ending the agreement had never passed the Canadian position up the ladder to their superiors. More than surprised, the Americans were outraged. It seemed that the Reagan administration, while horse trading and log rolling to fast-track the FTA, had told the Coalition and their congressional allies that the MOU was to be a permanent state of affairs.

George Bush had now succeeded Reagan, but the lumber coalition were holding him to Reagan's promise. They mobilized their Congressional allies and sixty-six senators sent Bush a letter urging him to retaliate against Canada for our "breach" of the MOU. The President readily complied. He even spared the Coalition the bother of filing a petition; instead Bush ordered the Commerce Department to self-initiate a case against us. The Americans imposed a bonding requirement on Canadian lumber imports, except those from BC, and began collecting money in expectation that a countervailing duty would be imposed. Once again, Canada was playing Boy Scout while America was playing Cowboys and Indians, and the Indians – us, that is – always had to lose.

This time, the US was attacking on a broader front, not only claiming subsidization but dragging in decades-old BC policies limiting log exports, even though the US had much the same ban on logs from federal lands. But this time the Canadian side responded with better coordination: every interested party – Ottawa, the producing provinces and CFIC – retained expert US counsel. Even better, we all worked together to eliminate duplication of effort and to cover more legal ground.

We went back to GATT. We fought in the US government's own trade law tribunals. However, the American process was now heavily slanted to favour the US complainants. It was a bitter joke amongst our forces that in Softwood Lumber I the quasi-judicial process had been "90 per cent *judicial* and 10 per cent *quasi*," but in Softwood Lumber III the proportions were reversed. The American authorities were starting from the position that Canadian lumber was subsidized, despite the exact opposite having been proved in Softwood Lumber I. The Commerce Department's adjudicators engaged in a lot of careful evidence selection and an equal amount of blind-eye-turning when the facts proved uncooperative.

To no-one's surprise, they found that a lumber subsidy existed. At first it was found to be 14.48 per cent, then a few months later it was adjusted to 2.91 per cent *ad valorem*. That would never have been enough to satisfy the administration's clients in the US lumber industry, so they topped it up with another 3.6 per cent supposedly from the log export restrictions, calling for the imposition of a total duty of 6.51 per cent. The US International Trade Commission then chimed in with a ruling that all this subsidizing had materially injured US lumber producers.

Canada immediately requested that the decisions be reviewed by two binational panels under Chapter 19 of the FTA. Each panel consisted of five trade law experts from both sides of the border. The panel reviewing the Commerce Department's findings unanimously rejected its evidence-paring practices and ordered it to reconsider its decision in light of the Canadian arguments. The panel reviewing the ITC's ruling also unanimously found that its finding was not supported by substantial evidence and told it to rethink the matter.

The Americans' response was the quasi-judicial equivalent of a Bronx cheer. The Commerce Department rejected the panel's rejection and nearly *doubled* the duty to 11.54 per cent. The matters were referred once more to the FTA panels, which made the same determinations as before, although this time the panel reviewing the ITC decision split. The two American representatives decided that a recent US court ruling in an entirely different case involving an entirely different industry somehow affected our situation. They promptly reversed themselves. Their reversal had the distinct odour of politics.

Having lost in the unbiased arena of the FTA panels, the US lumber interests began hurling mud, accusing panel members of conflicts of interest based on the fact that partners of the Canadian panel members had advised the Canadian government on other matters. The claims were farfetched – it would have been difficult to find qualified experts who were not members of firms that had consulted with Ottawa. But the Coalition arrayed their Congressional allies once more and demanded NAFTA's last-ditch mechanism: an extraordinary challenge panel made up of three judges. As luck would have it – and it is luck that determines the make-up of such panels – the panel of jurists included two Canadians and one American. They ruled in favour of Canada, splitting on national lines that reflected the previously noted differences in the way Canadians and Americans view the role of law.

The American judge's dissenting opinion invited the Coalition to challenge the constitutionality of the FTA's Chapter 19 dispute resolution process. Finally, the lumber lobby had gone too far; Bill Clinton was now in the White House and powerful elements of his

Me, Canada's Trade Minister the Hon. Roy MacLaren and Jake Kerr celebrating the return of $800 million from the US, 1995.

Administration – the Justice Department, for example – decided that the law had been bent as far as could be allowed without damaging some of the Administration's other priorities.

Some $800 million collected by the US from Canadian lumber exporters was refunded in 1994/1995, a payout that the Americans considered a bitter aggravation. Various members of Congress immediately began writing new laws that would guarantee a victory in the next round. We Canadians had scarcely finished celebrating our victory before it became plain that this struggle would not end until the US lumber coalition got what it wanted: higher domestic lumber prices achieved by raising the cost of Canadian imports.

So in 1996, we gave them what they wanted: not free trade, but *managed* trade. Canada, with a divided lumber sector, negotiated a

 A 1995 letter from Mack Singleton of the Coalition spilled the beans. It said, "If we reduce artificial price suppression [i.e., if the Coalition's efforts resulted in artificially boosted prices] ... by even 1% for one year, we will pay for a three-year effort four times over." ■

five-year agreement which set quotas for how much of our lumber could be exported to the US. Beyond those quotas a sliding scale of duties would be applied. The effect of the deal was to limit the amount of Canadian lumber entering the US, creating an artificial shortage to drive up prices.

This was, of course, the complete opposite of the free trade that the FTA and NAFTA were supposed to have brought in. Indeed it is ironic that, prior to the great movement to create these trade pacts, the Canadian lumber industry enjoyed free and unfettered trade with their US customers. Coincident with the arrival of bilateral and trilateral free trade regimes, we lost it.

The quota system seemed like the least evil option available to Canada. It bought us "peace" and a "guaranteed" share of the US lumber market that was about 90 per cent of the historic high-tide mark of 1995. The problems began in late 1997 when the Asian financial crisis tore a large hole in what had been a growing stream of lumber exports across the Pacific. The quotas had been set not on a national or regional basis, but company by company and mill by mill. Those companies that lost their Asian customers found they could not increase sales to the US without incurring punitive duties at the border.

Now we are past the era of quotas, Canada having declined to renew when the five years were up. And so now we are once more at war with the US lumber producers, on the battlefields of US trade tribunals and now GATT's successor, the World Trade Organization. Once again, we are winning on the merits of our case – our lumber is, after all, not subsidized – but it is hard to envision any lasting peace with the Americans. When it comes to trade wars, their only definition of peace is victory.

I have no official role in the current lumber war, although I answer the phone when it rings and offer institutional memory pro bono when it is asked for. One piece of advice I offered the industry over the years, and still do, is not to make such a fuss about their poor financial performance. The Americans are always looking for a pretext on which to take trade action to drive up the price of lumber. If our lumber producers keep spouting off about how they're continually operating in the red, it wouldn't be long before the Americans would pitch up with an accusation of dumping. And now they have.

At the fiftieth anniversary of UBC's Forestry School, in 2001, I happened to be stuck in an elevator with Mike DeJong, then the minister responsible for the BC forest. He asked me if I had any advice for Softwood Lumber IV and, as it happened, I did. I said, "Stop throwing things at the table."

Since the Gordon Campbell government took office, there has been paper after paper proposing new policies. Without questioning the merits of any particular policy shift, we have to remember that the US is closely monitoring what we do, and that the Americans have an unquenchable thirst for policy changes up here, if those change will increase our industry's costs.

When we throw new ideas on our table, we are also throwing them on the Canada-US negotiating table. We cannot afford to forget that, with the Americans, *everything* is *always* a negotiation. It makes no sense to change our policies as if they concerned nobody but ourselves. Because if, after making all those changes, we then go to the Americans to talk about trade their response will be, "Well, all those new policies are a good start, but now we need to get serious."

First, let us make sure our proposed policy changes are in the best interests of British Columbians. Then let us use those changes that are in our interest as bargaining tools. It doesn't work to give the Americans what they want then try to get them to give us something in return out of the goodness of their hearts.

In Softwood Lumber I, I played a less prominent part; as BC's Deputy Minister of Forests I advised my Minister and worked closely with the industry as it fought the good fight in Washington.

My participation in Softwood Lumber II and III was much more involved. For the second go-around, the Canadian industry had

Canadian Forest Industries Council Officers: (a) Adam Zimmerman. (b) Tom Buell. (c) Ted Boswell. (d) Jake Kerr.

CFIC and I was its president and, in the words of Adam Zimmerman, "nursemaid, father confessor and voice of reason."

Once again, I found myself in the role of builder and sustainer of a consensus that was often difficult to keep intact. The Americans played divide-and-conquer with the Canadian lumber industry, splitting off the Maritime producers, who had a relatively small share of the US market, with lumber primarily produced from private lands. We were also not helped by some provincial governments – most noticeably, the Vander Zalm administration – that saw US efforts to drive up the industry's costs as a way to pull more revenue into their coffers, where it would certainly not be dedicated to more spending on reforestation and advanced silviculture. Nor did it help that our industry was seen to be a problem to be "fixed" so

The Canadian lumber industry is a mosaic: with firms big, medium and small, integrated and non-integrated, domestically owned and foreign owned, private and publicly traded. It is also an industry that seems to grow more than its share of independent thinkers. Getting them to work as a team, in cooperation with provincial governments of different ideologies and disparate ways of thinking, not to mention a federal government responsible for trade issues that would operate much more to our liking if we kept showing it a common front, was not an eight hours a day, five days a week kind of job. I spent a lot of time on the phone, calming people down, encouraging them to be patient, discouraging them from making those private, consensus-busting calls that politicians find so useful.

The technical side of things, talking with lawyers and expert consultants, was a lesser part of the operation but it did provide relief. No hired gun ever said to me, as the owner of a small efficient mill in the BC Interior once said, "Apsey, if I could lift you I'd throw you in the lake."

I got him calmed down. ▪

that Brian Mulroney and Ronald Reagan could get the trade deal that had become one of their must-do priorities.

In Softwood Lumber III, my role as everybody's Sancho Panza was made much easier by the understanding among companies and governments that we had to pull together or be pulled to pieces by the Americans. The coordination of research, legal action, government-to-government relations and lobbying efforts was sometimes a dizzying task, but always fascinating and hugely instructive. I worked with very good legal advisors, a number of different firms, and when they thought we needed specific expertise, they would bring in outside consultants. As head of CFIC, I spent forty million dollars on hired help. All told, including the cost of my own time, COFI's expenditures, the funds and time spent by our allies in the industry and in US sectors like housing, the battle to defend free trade against US protectionism cost hundreds of millions of dollars.

One very pleasant side effect of having spread tens of millions of dollars among Washington legal and lobbying firms was that Sharon and I received an invitation to the inauguration of the first President George Bush and tickets to the parade and one of the inaugural balls.

I am a small town boy from rural British Columbia who wandered into a forest and came out with a career that has had me rubbing elbows with premiers, prime ministers and presidents, not to mention captains of industry, and often I have paused in this progress to ask – as Cinderella must have wondered after the slipper fit – "Why me?" I believe I expressed this thought to Sharon at the inaugural ball, and I recall that her response was that I ought to stop posing rhetorical questions and lead her out onto the dance floor.

We had good seats for the President's inaugural speech from the steps of the Capitol and I recall thinking, "I wonder how many Canadians are sitting this close to the action?" Years later, whenever

I was in Washington on business and walking along some imposing avenue, it would not be unusual for a limousine to stop, a window to roll down and someone to call out, "Mike Apsey? What are you doing in town?"

Money not only talks in Washington, DC; it can also encourage a good memory. ■

I also spent many, many hours behind podiums and on planes flying to speaking engagements all over the world. The Canadian lumber industry is a global exporter. When the Europeans or the Japanese saw us squabbling with our biggest neighbour and customer, it was only natural for them to wonder how the dispute would affect them. What would an export tax, or a duty-free quota system, or a serious and lasting change in our cost structure, mean to their relationship with us? We could have left them to work out the answers for themselves, but that seemed an unnecessary risk. So in addition to speaking on both sides of the forty-ninth parallel, I was frequently out explaining to customers on other continents what it was all about and where we thought it was all going. I bustled about to so many speaking engagements that I somehow acquired the nickname in Britain as the "Stormin' Norman of the Canadian Timber Trade."

One thing I learned was that the dispute resolution mechanisms that Canada insisted be included in the FTA and NAFTA were a lifesaver. It did not matter that the US lumber coalition's allegations of subsidy were without foundation; US trade law is a highly malleable construct that can be made to do pretty much what US political forces want it to do.

Politics and trade are inextricably linked. Anyone who thinks that dealing with tariffs and non-tariff barriers is purely a business affair, to be settled on the basis of facts, figures and legalisms, hasn't played the game. The Americans are clearly leaders in connecting trade to politics.

One of my most memorable speeches was a time I threw away the prepared text and went toe to toe with John Ragosta, the chief lobbyist and spokesman for the US Coalition. We were part of a panel discussion before an audience of US buyers, wholesalers and retailers of lumber. The group seemed moderately friendly.

I was supposed to have gone first and had brought with me the usual kind of speech I gave in the US, a politely phrased explanation of the nature of the dispute ending with the equivalent of Rodney King's *Can't we all just get along?*

Then John Ragosta asked if he could lead off and I said that was fine by me. He delivered the kind of wild and woolly farrago of accusations and complaints that we had been hearing since 1982, the Coalition's Full Monty. The audience heard him out and gave him a muted response.

Then it was my turn. I held up my prepared text and said that I would leave it with the organizers if anyone wanted a copy. Then I tore apart John Ragosta's arguments, point by point, ignoring the trivial nonsense, and poking gentle fun at the tortured logic.

The audience ate it up. I concluded by telling the lumbermen that US law required that we submit a very detailed list of each and every company that was part of CFIC. But, through all the years of tribunals and panels and hearings, the one thing we had never been able to find out officially was: who were the companies that comprised the US Coalition for Fair Lumber Imports? The US authorities wouldn't tell us. Neither would Mr. Ragosta or his clients. An accused had a right to know who his accusers were. It would only be fair for them to let us know who was taking these actions against us.

Americans are the same as us in many ways. We both like a good fight but we like it clean. John Ragosta had to sit there with his jaw clamped while the very people he claimed to be protecting shouted at him to come clean. "Tell him!" they yelled. "What have you got to hide?"

Of course, he didn't tell them, and to this day no one knows for sure who is, and who is not, behind the Coalition. ∎

Because I was a member of the private-sector advisory groups that helped shape Canada's positions on NAFTA, I was invited to attend a ceremony in San Antonio, Texas, where the newly negotiated trilateral agreement would be initialled by the trade ministers of the three countries. The presidents of Mexico and the US as well as Brian Mulroney would also be there.

The event took place outdoors in a grassy area. Afterwards, there was a reception in another outdoor area, with security people everywhere. The dignitaries were lined up to shake everybody's hand and I was in the queue working my way toward them. A voice spoke in my ear: "You are about to meet the President of the United States of America. Introduce yourself, shake his hand and move on." I turned and saw a rock-jawed man with a ear plug in his ear.

I proceeded along the line. The first person I came to was Carla Hills, then the US Trade Representative. She gave me a quizzical look that said she vaguely knew me but couldn't place the face. She read my name tag and that seemed to help, but not enough for the

NAFTA initialling ceremony, San Antonio, Texas, 1992.

penny to drop. I said, quietly, "Softwood lumber." She dropped my hand as if it were contaminated and spoke to the next person in line.

Next, I came to President Bush and, as instructed, I introduced myself, shook his hand and said, just to be nice, "Good luck in the election, Mr. President." I must have raised the subject that was foremost in his mind that evening because instead of letting me go he opted to talk about how he thought things were going and his prospects for re-election. I stood there and listened – it was quite interesting – but from the corner of my eye I could see Brian Mulroney standing a few feet farther on with a look on his face that said, *What the hell is Apsey bending Bush's ear about?*

When I got to him he asked me, "Apsey, why do I see your name and face in the papers more often than my own?"

It is a matter of historical record that all three heads of government – Bush, Mulroney and Mexico's Salinas – found themselves out of office not long after. I'm pretty sure that shaking hands with Apsey had nothing to do with it. ∎

The Americans are certainly very colourful about it. One of my most memorable afternoons brought me face to face with the Montana Senator, Max Baucus, who was one of the most relentless peddlers of the subsidy canard. The Americans have a saying: my country, right or wrong. Max Baucus's motto would probably add an addendum: my constituents, come hell or high water. I may be unwise to admit it but I sometimes wish we had politicians who would stand up for Canada the way the Baucuses stand up for America.

But I was not eager to meet the man. When our Washington advisors said they had set up a meeting at his office, I said, "I'm not going. He doesn't like us."

"But, Mike," said our lobbyist, "he's always saying he's never met a Canadian who will look him in the eye and say we don't subsidize our lumber."

"And you want me to be the first?" I said with a slight shudder.

US Senator Max Baucus.

We were scheduled for a half hour with Baucus. Off I went, accompanied by two US colleagues. When we got there we learned that the
meeting would be no more than fifteen minutes long. That suited
me. We were shown into an anteroom. Five minutes later, the door
opened and a staffer came in and introduced himself as Michael – I
can't remember his last name. We chatted about inconsequentials
and then suddenly the door burst open and in strode Max Baucus.

He came straight over to me and we shook hands. I was prepared
to look him in the eye and say that our lumber was not subsidized
but it soon became clear that I might not get the chance. The Senator
began to express his views, quite forcefully, about how our stumpage
regimes constituted an outright subsidy. He went on and on, as if he
were delivering a stump speech.

The assistant kept looking at his watch and was obviously waiting,
as I was, for a break in the flow of rhetoric. Finally, the young man
made some remark about how we only had a few minutes. Baucus
turned to him and said sternly, "Michael, don't you ever interrupt
me when I'm speaking."

Then he went back to the harangue. As the phrases rolled onward,
with very little separation even for an intake of breath, I could see

US Senator Bob Packwood.

that our advisors wanted me to go, that this encounter had turned out to be not such a good idea. But by now I wanted to achieve what we had come for. I said, "What's a subsidy, Senator?" or words to that effect.

He stopped speaking, looked at me and said, "Michael, don't you interrupt me when I'm speaking." I could see he was now planning to leave, still able to make his boast about never having met a Canadian who'd stand up to him because he had filled all our allotted time with his own voice.

So I stared him in the eye and said, "Senator, Canadian stumpage does not constitute a subsidy."

He said nothing, just turned and left. I didn't change his position, but he did send me an autographed photograph.

I also had a session with Oregon Senator Bob Packwood, another of the die-hard advocates for the Coalition. He invited me to his office in the Capitol and said, "Mike, I would like to hear from you in twenty minutes why you Canadians think you are not subsidized."

I went through all the history and the arguments, chapter and verse. At the end of twenty minutes, Packwood said, "Thank you Mike. That's the finest explanation I've ever heard as to why you Canadians feel that you are not subsidized. And I, Bob Packwood, am even prepared to believe that you are not, in fact, subsidized.

"But Mike," he said, "I am going to get re-elected."

I was walking through the Capitol Building, that great domed monument to neoclassical architecture. The US lawyer accompanying me was showing me the sights: the wide rotunda, the chambers where the Senators and Representatives debate bills.

We passed along a panelled hall where carpenters were doing some renovation or restoration. There were scaffolds and ladders and stacks of very high grade lumber and plywood. My escort saw the direction of my gaze and said, "Mike, you will not talk to anybody about what you've just seen."

I agreed it would not be prudent. The finest quality wood products being carefully fitted to the walls of the US Capitol were stamped with the logos of Canadian firms. ■

A number of forest company CEOs and I were in Canadian Ambassador Derek Burney's office in the magnificent structure that is Canada's Washington Embassy. Through the window we could see the US Capitol. We were in the heart of downtown America, having a very good discussion of the lumber wars. At some point the question was asked, "Mr. Ambassador, what do you think the Americans want from us?"

Without a word, His Excellency rose from his chair, walked around his desk, dropped to all fours, crawled across the office and kowtowed to us. He couldn't have said it better. ■

September 5, 2003.

American politicians are shameless in their public rhetoric, but behind closed doors they are amiably cynical. More than once, a US senator or congressman told me bluntly, "Apsey, when will you Canadians start to understand, we're not asking you to do what we do, we're telling you: do as we say. It's heads we win, tails you lose."

The overall objective of establishing free trade, not just with the Americans and Mexicans, is the right goal for Canada and for the world. I don't expect to see it in my lifetime, but throughout my career it has been the great current on which both politics and

August 3, 2002.

economics have sailed and, despite the efforts of the Packwoods and Baucuses, it continues to gather strength.

Today, we don't have free trade, but we certainly do have freer trade. We're on course though we won't reach our destination any time soon. There are those who will throw up barriers because that is how they protect their interests, but there are other people whose interests require that the barriers come down, and over the past forty years there has been far more pulling down than putting up. Every time anyone ever built a wall, someone started thinking of how to get over it, or under it, or around it. We are an innovative species, and one of the most innovative of our subspecies is *homo business*.

November 16, 2004.

The Canadian forest sector, especially British Columbia's part of it, paid a price to get Canada the FTA and NAFTA. We were not the only ones to pay a price, but our ox was definitely gored. Even so, we were and are very strong supporters of free and unfettered trade. That has always been the basic philosophy of the industry, back to the days of "the Canadas."

CHAPTER TWELVE

Exercising My Dreams

When I left COFI in 1998, I said I was going to retire. Of course, the R-word can have a multitude of meanings. To some it means sitting around the house reading all the books they never had time for. For others it means an endless journey across manicured acres of herbicide-laden grass trying to coax small white balls into a series of eighteen holes – an activity best summarized by Mark Twain as "a good walk, spoiled."

For this lifelong Sancho Panza, it meant being able to select my own windmills. I could pick and choose the issues that I would address, the boards on which I would sit, the committees I would participate in. I did the picking and choosing according to two standards: that the work would embody the widest scope, and that it would be fun.

My involvement in the lumber wars continued but I let it gradually wind down. The people who were handling the file came and went; there were new faces and new approaches. The BC Lumber Trade Council asked me to continue to advise them and for a while I complied. But eventually I had to make a choice: my real interest was in cross-Canada forest initiatives – such as the National Forest Strategy – that were based on building a consensus among many different actors, while the lumber wars were having a divisive effect on the Canadian forest community; when I stood up to speak about these larger issues I did not want people wondering if my views might be coloured by my still being part of the BC industry's war band. So I eased myself out.

I decided to set up a small consulting firm – Michael Apsey Forest and Trade Policy Ltd. – and that led to some phone calls and letters asking me if I wanted to come on board at various corporations. The offers were flattering but they all implied a long-term relationship with the employer. I wanted only short-term consulting assignments, and then only if the job interested me. I was not open to doing anything just for the money. So sometimes the phone would ring and an old associate would say, "Mike, I have this terrible problem," and I would see what I could do, but sometimes I would say, "Gee, that's awful. Let me see if I can recommend somebody who can help."

The assignments that interested me most were those that offered the broadest scope, those that dealt with national and international issues of the forest. One of the first jobs came soon after I left COFI; the Canadian Forest Service asked me to study and assess the current governance of international forest issues and to spell out options for addressing any deficiencies. I couldn't have been happier than when I was putting that paper together and in fact I did more work than was specified in the contract. For decades I have been watching the world's forest take a beating. I have seen the evolution – slow and hesitant at best, though mostly it is just lacking – of the concept of international governance relating to the forest. I had developed some very strong views about the lack of meaningful international rules and standards for forestry issues.

The CFS study – its full title was *Assessment of the Current Governance of International Forest Issues and Options for Addressing Deficiencies* – looked at the history of governance, the current state of governance, and options I foresaw for the future. For me this was a labour of love and I sought out a great crowd of thoughtful forest people from around the world; some I had known over the years and some I was meeting for the first time. I plumbed their thoughts about where we were, where we had come from, and where we might go from here. As I expected, I found that there were many of us who wanted to see some form of international instrument – a convention, a multinational treaty – on the care and treatment of the forest. But, as I also expected, I continually ran into the unfortunate reality that we lovers of the forest, we professional foresters, collectively lack the political skills, and therefore the political clout, wielded by the champions of other issues – like freer trade, global warming, hunger and land mines – that have led to action by the international community.

It has always been, and remains today, very difficult to come to grips with the great forest issues facing our world. And yet, ironically, there is scarcely a major world issue that does not involve the forest. Global warming? The forest is a great consumer of carbon dioxide. Species extinction? The forest is the richest part of the biosphere. Energy? Half the world heats their homes and cooks their meals with wood from the forest. Fresh water? The forest is the vast sponge that holds rainfall in the soil. As I write this, hundreds of people on the island of Hispaniola have been drowned in catastrophic mudslides because the slopes above their town were stripped of the trees that used to soak up the rain.

I have long believed that the world needs an international convention on the forest. But in conducting the governance study I looked for a breadth of opinion, not just the views of the like minded. Canadians tend to favour the idea of international law imposing reasonable limits on the freedom of individual states, but there are those who think differently – I had met a few of them during the lumber wars – and no study of international governance would be complete without the opposing view. Even among those who were for an international convention, there were those who thought it should be created through the United Nations and others who said we should keep it out of the UN.

My own feeling was that the UN system works, but I wouldn't be too exercised if a movement to create an international instrument began outside the UN's ambit. A number of successful international initiatives have begun outside the UN and later found their way in. My main concern was that whatever we try to do, let us be bold. The age of "they should" has passed; we live in the era of "we must."

As I was developing a series of options to lay before the CFS, I received a call from a senior aide to UN Secretary General Kofi Annan. Word had got around about what I was doing and Annan's office wanted to know what options I was considering. I had no problem with the request and laid out the various directions I thought the world could choose from. One of my boldest ideas, or so I thought, was that the governance structure would involve a council of Ministers Responsible for Forests. The council would report to the UN's Economic and Social Council or its Commission on Sustainable Development.

Annan's aide said, "If you are going to be bold, why not have the group report to the General Assembly?"

I was surprised. That would mean that the world's forest had somehow moved considerably higher on the UN's agenda than I had thought. But as Kofi Annan's man said, people in the UN are starting to understand fully the importance of the world's forest to the security of the planet. But he wasn't just talking about food security, the supply of fresh water, or the other obvious headings. He was talking about security issues that range all the way from plagues to war. I found it heartening to know that within the UN system and in many countries around the world, thoughtful men and women have begun to think about the importance of the forest to the future of the globe.

That kind of thinking cannot come too soon. Each year, the world suffers a net loss of some ten million hectares of forest. Those figures take into account not only the forest land that is replaced by natural or human assisted regeneration, but the land that is turned over to industrial plantations. We live on a planet whose natural state is to be mostly covered by trees yet for centuries we have been removing the forest at an accelerating rate. We need to ask ourselves what the consequences of that removal will be, and how we, the nations of the world, can come together to deal with those consequences.

I delivered the study to the CFS in 1998 and it was available to the world through the Internet for quite a while. Canada's Department of Foreign Affairs supported the main thrust of my ideas, although the language has naturally evolved as diplomats have weighed in. The study generated some on-going discussions which I have followed closely, although I wish there were more concrete results than what Winston Churchill used to call "jaw-jaw." Among key actors like the UN, the World Bank, the regional development banks and other agencies, there has been some better coordination of thinking. But we still have such a long way to go, so much more to do. If we are to deal with some of the dire challenges we will surely face in this new century, the global forest must expand. Instead, it continues to shrink at an alarming rate.

Most of what I have done since leaving COFI has been pro bono work done for no recompense except expenses. I make no excuses if it sounds sentimental, but the forest has given a shape to my life – an endlessly fascinating puzzle to work out, and a truly noble cause to stand for – and I am determined to give back what I can. One of the ways I have worked to repay the debt has been my involvement in the National Forest Strategy Coalition, which I was proud to chair from 1999 through 2003.

The members of the NFSC are all organizations. When I retired from COFI I became a mere individual. The NFSC had to amend its rules to allow me to be a part of its work. I was deeply honoured that they thought that highly of my contribution. ■

NATIONAL   COALITION POUR
FOREST   LA STRATÉGIE
STRATEGY   NATIONALE
COALITION   SUR LA FORÊT

The NFSC is an ever-expanding collaboration among all those
who have something to do with the Canadian forest: federal, provincial and local governments, academia, industry and professional
associations, labour, Aboriginal organizations, research institutes
and the full spectrum of conservation groups. Every five years the
Coalition issues Canada's National Forest Strategy and the members
sign a new National Forest Accord. At each iteration of the Accord
a wider range of groups have put their signatures to its precepts and
action plan. I am immensely proud – as I believe every Canadian
should be – that Canada is setting the standard for the world in
bringing together our forest community around a series of goals that
meet the "Apsey test" of being *bold, doable and buy-in-able.*

The seeds of the process that creates a new National Forest Strategy every five years were planted way back in 1906 when the growing conservation movement prompted Canada's first National Forest
Congress. Prime Minister Sir Wilfrid Laurier presided, and out of
the Congress's deliberations came the first forest services and forestry schools. A good deal of history and development intervened
before the Canadian forest sector got together again in 1966 at the
Montebello Conference to consider how far we had come and where
the future might lead us. Then, in the late seventies, the sector came
together again around the issue of regeneration and by 1981 there
was the first Forest Sector Strategy for Canada. By the mid-eighties
a Canadian Council of Forest Ministers had appeared on the scene

Signing the National Forest Accord, 1998.

and in 1986 another National Forest Congress began the process that created 1987's new National Forest Strategy. From then on new strategies were created about every five years, in 1992, 1998 and 2003.

The evolution of these documents represents a continual pushing of the conceptual envelope among the ever-expanding membership of the Canadian forest community. The 1981 document was essentially about renewal of the timber supply and other economic considerations. By 1987, we were focused on scientific management of the resource with some consideration of environmental concerns. In 1992's strategy, the transformation from sustained yield of timber to sustainable forest management for a broad range of values was apparent, and by 1998 the inclusiveness of the process had broadened even further, both in the issues it addressed and in the growing number of partners who had joined this uniquely Canadian collaboration. By 2003, the strategy was still expanding to cover emerging forest issues.

As the scope of the National Forest Strategy steadily expanded, something else had been evolving at the same time: the process by which the NFS was translated from a statement of ideals into an action plan. Mechanisms were devised that provided an independent evaluation of progress toward the strategy's goals midway through each five-year period and again at the end of the cycle. A panel of capable, intelligent people, with great credibility in their own fields, were asked to look over what we said we would do and see how much of it we had actually done. That "double check-up" mechanism is the antidote to the perennial problem of "too much talk, too little action" that too often is endemic to the conference cycle.

It's not stretching things too far to say that the NFS is a Canadian national treasure. Not because of what's in the strategy, but because it exemplifies the Canadian genius for collaboration and consensus. Each strategy is not enshrined in law nor codified in regulations but it becomes the touchstone against which people and organizations throughout the forest community plan their activities and measure their accomplishments. It is a purely voluntary exercise in seeking the common good, and it is an example to the world.

And I believe there are many people in the world who are looking for just such an example. The concept of creating national forest plans and strategies is now, I believe, that most powerful of things: an idea whose time has come. Country by country, the outflow of action from that idea may assume different shapes and have different formal titles but more and more nations have, in essence, come to the conclusion that the forest needs longer-term, forward looking strategies.

Now I would like to see the Canadian process evolve to a new level. The mid-term and final check-ups have been good, but I would like to see if we can develop a mechanisms for continual monitoring of the NFS's progress. And let us not hide our successes. When we reach a milestone, let's talk about it. And if we encounter a contentious issue, let's go public and talk about that. The wider the community that we can involve in what's being done with and for the forest, the better the process will work. One truth that has become clear to me throughout my career is the need to tear down the silos that imprison our thinking and keep us focused on narrow goals. Certainly, we can have our own agendas and pursue our own interests, but when we think and act with an awareness of the wider context, we can adjust a detail or modify an approach here and there and contribute to a greater good – and better serve the forest.

I have come to believe deeply in the value of these strategies and have devoted a lot of my time to implementing the 1998–2003 strategy and developing the 2003-2008 version. As chair of the NFSC, I was invited to speak around the country and around the world. I've spent a lot of time on planes and on podiums, talking to meetings of ministers and deputy ministers and other groups that were inside or outside of the strategy process, to groups that we wanted to bring into the process, and to groups that needed to hear what Canada's forest community was doing.

It has been unpaid work, but I have never been happier. I'm going to keep doing it. The forest is one of the keys to the security of the planet.

Out of the National Forest Strategy process came FORCAST – a Coalition for the Advancement of Science and Technology in the Forest Sector – an initiative that was set up to champion the cause of forest-related science and technology in Canada. It was created by the Canadian Forest Service, the provincial forest services, research institutes and some elements of the industry and in 2000 I was asked to be its executive director on a part-time consulting basis. The NFS had called for an entity that could coordinate collaboration among the forest science-and-technology community to increase investment, foster further cooperation, facilitate communication and keep tabs on the results.

I have been involved in science and technology – or research and development as we used to call it – throughout my career. I have been a manager of research groups, have sat on the boards of research institutes, been a participant in national and international forums on science and technology with senior people from government and industry. Even as a forestry student measuring the heights and girths of red alder I understood the importance of research. So I went into FORCAST with hopes of that we would accomplish something.

But partway through the effort I had to ask myself, "Why are we still where we are in terms of developing science and technology for the Canadian forest sector?" I could compile a long list of commit-tees, task forces, forums, conferences, roundtables – process, process, process – convened to talk about sci-tech issues. I couldn't come up with a corresponding list of concrete results.

At a forum that I put together for FORCAST in Edmonton I looked at the discussion papers and thought, "Doesn't it all sound familiar?" At the next meeting of the FORCAST board, I made a pitch along these lines, "Over our careers we've all spent a considerable amount of time in preparing for forums, participating in deliberations, often sending our senior people. We come to some conclusions, make a set of recommendations, then we all look at each other and smile, say 'What a successful forum,' then we go home. A year or so later we get together to do it all over again, with much the same outcome. What's missing? A follow-up plan with firm commitments. Nobody knows who's going to do what to follow up on all the recommendations. So we work hard, think hard, write hard, then we go home and little or nothing changes."

I asked the FORCAST board to let me do a review of past efforts. They agreed, and with the assistance of the Canadian Forest Service, I went through the records of a slew of forums and conferences and, sure enough, my impression was backed up by the facts: plenty of talk leading to a similar set of findings, but little or no follow up. When all was said and done, there had been a lot more saying than doing. The outcome of my review was that I talked myself out of a job. At my request, FORCAST was shelved in 2003 – not killed outright but put in hibernation until it could serve a more useful purpose. Now there is the Canadian Forest Innovation Council, and I wish them every success in moving toward Mike Apsey's dream of a strong sci-tech sector being the heartbeat of the Canadian forest sector.

I will offer a couple of helpful observations beyond the need to develop a mechanism to turn more of our sci-tech talking into doing. I have come to realize that, within the Canadian forest sector (and without pointing a finger of blame at any particular group), there is no strong conviction that sci-tech comprises a core function of the sector. I am not saying it is a mere afterthought, but a cyclical industry – and, for that matter, cyclical governments – tend to produce cyclical thinking.

Inevitably, prices drop and when they do, sci-tech is one of first areas where budgets are cut and projects – and people – are dropped. There is not enough continuity of effort. The constant ups and downs mean we have difficulty in retaining the kind of people who can do first-class research. I would like to see a change in thinking – among both levels of government and the corporations – so that science and

Back when Paul Martin was finance minister, we met at a dinner in Vancouver and fell into a discussion of what the federal role in forest matters ought to be.

He said, "Mike, forests are a provincial resource. Why should Ottawa be involved?"

Here is the argument I made: Because every dollar generated by the forest sector gets divided into shares. The producing provinces get their shares in stumpage and other revenues. The companies get their shares from their profits. The workers get their share through wages and benefits.

And every one of those interests puts back some of what it gets out, in spending on infrastructure, in capital plant, in sweat equity. They do that to protect their investment in the sector because its viability is vital to their interests.

But the federal government also gets a piece of that dollar, in the income and sales taxes paid by the industry and its employees. That makes Ottawa a shareholder like the others, and it makes the continued health of the forest sector vital to Canada's interests.

And that's why the federal government needs to be a part of the Canadian forest sector's research community. ■

technology investments will become a core value, not an extra to be pumped up or down as balance sheets or political philosophies fluctuate.

I have also noticed that in other industrial sectors one of the factors leading to success is that the top people, the agenda setters, tend to be knowledgeable about the science and technology that affect their industry. Consider the fastest growing industries of the past decade or two, such as telecommunications or computers: would you expect to find people in the senior executive suites who aren't in close touch with what's happening in their own research labs, or who don't recognize that next year's earnings have a lot to do with what's on the laboratory bench today?

When I looked around the table at the FORCAST board, I saw intelligent, committed people. But I was not seeing deputy ministers or chief executive officers. They were not senior decision makers who could make commitments. Until science and technology become front-burner concerns of the forest sector's top people, we are not going to live up to our potential.

Over the years, I have sat on the boards of numerous groups that primarily dealt with the business side of the forest sector. The boards I have joined since retiring from COFI have had more to do with my very first love, the forest. They are all good causes and I fully support their aims.

I was on the board of the Pacific Salmon Foundation from its inception in the late 1980s until 2004. I am a member of the board of Sustainable Development Technology Canada and of the Canadian Forestry Association. I am past chair of Wildlife Habitat Canada and a past board member of the Forest History Society. As a past member of the Forestry Advisory Council to the President of the University of British Columbia I have been a staunch defender of an independent Faculty of Forestry, counselling against the kind of thinking that would fold the foresters into some other faculty.

Another favourite is the Tree Canada Foundation, of which I am immediate past chair. The TCF recognizes that, as one of the world's great forest nations, Canada is in the business of growing oxygen and taking up carbon emissions – its mottos are *Trees do their part… let's do ours* and *Grow Clean Air* – and therefore the TCF encourages the wilful planting of trees all over the country, particularly in the cities. From the Vancouver apartment that until recently I owned I could look out at the rooftops and see how many of them are now green with flowers, shrubs and trees. I was in downtown Vancouver but I was looking at a forest. The urban forest is beautiful to see, but greening the cities is important for more than aesthetic reasons; it is part of a better future for us and the forest.

At the time of writing, I am stepping off some boards, the better to concentrate my energies on global forest issues. I continue to work toward creating a Canadian chapter of the US-based Forest History Society. History has been my second love, after the forest, and I am painfully aware that with all the recent changes in corporate and government structures related to the forest, with pioneer foresters passing away, we may lose important parts of Canadian forest history that ought to be preserved. It doesn't matter where the journals

PACIFIC
SALMON
FOUNDATION

SUSTAINABLE DEVELOPMENT
TECHNOLOGY CANADA™

Tree Canada Foundation
Fondation canadienne de l'arbre
www.tcf-fca.ca

TECHNOLOGIES DU DÉVELOPPEMENT
DURABLE CANADA™

Wildlife Habitat Canada
Habitat Faunique Canada

**Canadian Forestry
Association
forestière canadienne**

since · depuis
1900

and photographs, the logbooks and records, are saved, whether it be by local regional or national agencies – it matters only that they not be lost for lack of attention.

One of the great pleasures of the later stages of my career was to have been invited to attend World Forestry Congresses. I've already mentioned Paris in 1991 but my favourite WFC was in Antalya, Turkey, in 1997. Besides having an opportunity to talk forest talk with some of the best foresters in the world – including people I'd met or worked with in forty-odd countries – I had time to be a tourist again, driving around in a rented car and visiting places that I love. I also saw the results of policy changes that, as a young man, I had had some part in shaping. The structure of the Turkish forest service had evolved, and the forest industry had expanded. I saw wonderful forests and great successful plantations.

In Antalya, I presented a paper entitled *An International Convention on Sustainable Forest Management: A Global Imperative*. It was well received and may have prompted the Canadian Forest Service to ask me to do the 1998 study on international governance. I was beginning to see more clearly the vision of a future for the world forest that is outlined in the next chapter.

I also attended the 2003 World Forestry Congress in Quebec City. Like Paris and Antalya, it was a great success. However, I was

I had one slightly scary time at a military checkpoint. I produced my Canadian passport. Suddenly guns were pointing at me, fingers on triggers. I remembered that Israeli agents carrying forged Canadian documents had recently been caught in an assassination plot in Amman, Jordan. It had been more than a quarter century since I had last spoken more than a half-dozen words of Turkish, but a glance into all those rifle muzzles restored my fluency in a moment. ■

embarrassed as a Canadian that neither our Prime Minister nor the Premier of Quebec saw fit to attend the Congress.

In mid-1999, after years of grating pain, I received a new left hip. The surgeon, Dr. Michael O'Neill of Victoria, did a superb job, as did the nurses at Royal Jubilee Hospital. The young woman who introduced me to the phenomenon of the sitz bath was especially to be commended. It was during that experience that I noticed a large black x on my left knee and was reminded of the marks timber cruisers put on trees that are to be cut. I asked Dr. O'Neill if such marks are really necessary. He said, "You really don't want to know."

After months of healing, walking, exercise and check-ups, I went for my final visit with the surgeon. He reminded me of all the measurements he had taken of the Apsey form before the operation. I told him I recalled them intimately. He then revealed that he had found me to be a half inch short on the left side and while I was under the knife he took it upon himself to rectify that lifelong imbalance.

"Really?" I said. "Then why didn't you go all the way and make me six-foot-one?"

I mention the operation because there is so much discussion in our time about the health care system. I can say only this: it was there when I needed it and it saved my lifestyle. The system has also been there for my family and my friends when they've needed it. It was there for my dear colleague, Ken Drushka, with whom I started this book, when he developed cancer. It made his life bearable while he was taking leave of it.

As Mike Apsey, citizen, I believe we have a very fine health care system. Let us not bitch and complain about it, rather let us recognize how good a system we have, then let us deal with its flaws and get on with life. Of course there are inefficiencies, so let us restructure the system to remove them, then spend the money we need to spend to make it the best system we can create.

If it needs a tweaking, let's tweak it. We have a lot of good people in health care, and we owe it to them as well as to ourselves to continue to improve the system. I wish we would apply that kind of thinking to all the assets we have in this great country of ours – to education, to the military, to the development of industry – identify the good, then work together to make it even better.

I've always travelled as part of my work. Even in the age of the Internet, you can't find out what is going on in the world from behind a desk. After leaving COFI, I continued to get out and see for myself what was happening.

As chair of Canada's National Forest Strategy Coalition, I was often invited to speak in various parts of the world. In 1999, I was in Paris to make a presentation to a major multinational panel of the European Parliament, the Council of Europe Committee on the Environment. The topic was Canada's progress toward sustainable forest management, under the recurring shadow of a threatened boycott of our forest products. When I had finished I took questions from the committee and the audience.

A senior representative of Greenpeace International had some questions. But first, he said, he wanted to put them in context. He said, "Mr. Apsey, we Europeans have destroyed our forests. You Canadians have not. We Europeans do not have options. You Canadians do have options. And we Europeans are going to make sure that you exercise those options, even if it means we have to boycott your products."

Once again, another reminder that context is everything. Many Canadians see people like that man from Greenpeace International as meddlers in our affairs. He sees himself as a champion of the world's forest, as entitled to exert pressure on us as we are to exert pressure on countries that continue to hunt whales. Does he have that right? Do we have the right to tell the world that what we do with our forest is no one's concern but our own? If we ever did, I believe we can no longer claim an untrammelled right.

The outcome of the Canadian delegation's appearance before the European Parliament's panel was that there has been no boycott of our forest products. The more we talked with each other, the more we discovered a desire for closer cooperation between Europe and Canada on forest issues.

The Barents Euro-Arctic Council is a group dedicated to improving relationships and contacts among the Russians and the other northern nations whose territories or interests touch upon the Barents Sea. They invited me to speak at an expert seminar on forestry at Petrozavodsk in the Republic of Karelia. I flew to Helsinki where I would meet some colleagues at a small private airport and we would continue on into Russia. While I waited at the airport, a group of distinguished looking Finns came in and I fell into conversation with one of them about matters of the forest. He asked some intelligent questions and I was enjoying a good discussion when some official-looking people came to escort my new friend and his party off to their plane. My own friends were just arriving. They wanted to know how I had come to be acquainted with the President of Finland.

We flew to Petrozavodsk in a twin-engine propeller plane, most of the way at low altitude so I had a good aerial view of parts of Russia I hadn't seen before. Petrozavodsk was a pretty city with friendly people, but on the way in I saw many small villages that had been abandoned and factories that had been closed. The Russians were on the move, migrating to the big cities under the pressure of a changing economy and society. Now they are coming out of their decades of torpor. They are becoming entrepreneurial, as are the Chinese. I believe that we in the developed world should engage these new economies with the latest technology, so that they can skip over the era of belching smokestacks and strip-mined ecologies, to leave a lighter environmental footprint than we did.

On shelves in my basement office are rows of big D-ring binders, each containing selected speeches I've delivered over the years. I've no idea how many times I've stood behind a lectern and unburdened myself of thoughts on forest policy, or international trade, or science and technology, or the foibles of the forest community, including this lifelong member. After I left COFI, however, the choice of subjects was entirely my own, and more and more I found myself speaking on behalf of the forest. And the more I spoke, the more I read and thought, the wider grew my scope.

A few years ago I was in Markham, Ontario, speaking at a congress on the urban forest on behalf of the NFSC. While I was preparing my comments it dawned on me that previous National Forest Strategies never mentioned the word urban. We in the forest community, even we foresters, tend to think of the forest as being "out there" somewhere. All over the world there are man-made boundaries, political boundaries, separating Canada from the US, one province from the next, cities from surrounding suburbs. Though they are just imaginary lines on maps, we take them very seriously, even to the point of killing and dying to prevent a line from being moved or erased.

But those lines are only of concern to us. The forest doesn't understand our boundaries, couldn't care less about them. Nor does the wildlife that lives in the forest. An urban coyote or a raccoon doesn't consider itself a city dweller. It lives, as it always has, in the forest. Is it a much modified forest? Yes, or at least temporarily. But if we stop mowing our lawns and patching the frost cracks in our asphalt, we would see how soon the forest came to reclaim what we have put our invisible lines around. In human terms, that "soon" might seem long

– years, even decades. From the forest's point of view, it would be no time at all.

In Markham, I was delivering such a message: that the lines we put around a forest, calling this part the Douglas fir forest, that part the Interior lodgepole pine forest, saying up there is the boreal forest, down here is the urban forest, those lines exist only in our minds. From the forest's point of view, Canada has only one forest.

I was in the middle of the speech, expounding on Canada's one forest when the obvious struck me. The line we draw around our part of the planet, saying this part is Canada, those parts are not, also exists only in the human mind. As far as the forest is concerned the globe has but one forest.

Ironically, the real barriers that nature placed between different parts of that one global forest have been steadily battered down by humankind. As we have spread across the world, as we have become able to leap from anywhere to anywhere in increasingly less time and with fewer and fewer hindrances, we have erased natural boundaries, put zebra mussels in the Great Lakes, rabbits in Australia, starlings across North America, and allowed invasive species to hitchhike all throughout the global forest.

We have but one forest, and the forest has a problem – us. The question is: can we also be the solution to the problem of us?

CHAPTER THIRTEEN

Bring On the Don Quixotes

As I write this, I am sixty-seven years of age. By my optimistic calcu-
lations, that means I have come through two-thirds of my lifespan.
That is far enough to be able to look back and see the direction in
which I have been heading since that day outside the Vernon Dairy
Drive-In when I threw in my lot with the forest. I see that I have been
moving along two complementary though seemingly contradictory
paths. One path has been the search for a wider scope; it has taken
me from the forest of British Columbia through the woodlands of
more than forty countries, until I now see the big picture of a world
that has but one forest. The other path has taken me deeper into the
holistic reality of the forest, showing me that beyond timber there is
wildlife habitat, and beyond that is biodiversity, and beyond that are
the linkages of forest and water, forest and food, forest and air. The
health of the forest is the health of the planet.

So now, two-thirds the way from the cradle to the grave, I can
take the perspective of a sixty-seven-year relationship with the forest
and use it to shape a vision of what is to come. And again, because I
am an optimist, I will express it as a positive vision.

I see a world in which the forest is recognized, as the man from
Kofi Annan's office recognized it, as an essential component in all
the great issues that face humankind in this new millennium. Our
numbers continue to grow. Soon we will be seven billion, then not

long after it will be eight billion and nobody knows – the expert projections vary widely – how many of us there will be by 2038 when I
turn one hundred. Where will we all live, what will we eat, will the
water be clean and the air unfouled? Will there be war, pestilence,
massacre and mass migration? Or will we find ways to work it out?

The forest will play a role in answering all of these questions. The
answers will more likely be positive if we have put ourselves into
a positive relationship with the forest, if we manage its resources
– all of them, the tangible as well as the intangible – in a sustainable
manner. I see two possible ways of establishing that relationship.

One is through a coming together of the world's forest nations in
a consensual strategy modelled on what Canadians have achieved
in our National Forest Strategy: a voluntary, collaborative exercise
in shaping mutual self-interest to serve the common good. Cynics
might call such cooperation a utopian dream, but Canadians have
shown that it can be done. More and more countries are now working toward their own forest strategies, though they may call them
programs or plans, and the natural next step of all this process, process, process should be to bring them all together under an international umbrella.

However, there are many indicators that that eventual umbrella
may unfold too late. Too often, when we face problems on an international scale, we don't recognize that we are heading for a cliff until
our front wheels are over the edge, and we don't start thinking about
a solution until we are halfway down the precipice. So I believe that
right now the most practical goal for the world forest community
is to work toward the establishment of a legally binding, holistic-
approach, international convention on the global forest. This would
be an instrument of international law setting out the definitions,
standards and commitments that the signatories would have to meet
in managing their portions of the global forest. It would provide
defenders of the forest with a legal tool to pressure their governments to do the right thing, and it would protect the world forest

from the unintended consequences stemming from an ever expanding number of international agreements on matters ranging from
biodiversity to desertification.

Cynics will also weigh in here to note that some forest nations
– certainly the United States, perhaps Brazil – would strongly resist
the effort to create the convention and would refuse to sign it. Of
course they would, at least initially, but so what? The US refusal to
accept the international convention against land mines – another
Canadian-led initiative, by the way – has not prevented scores
of other nations from signing it. The Americans also opposed the
International Criminal Court, but at the time of writing they had
ceased their annual effort to pressure the UN Security Council into
granting US peacekeeping troops a blanket exemption. The lesson:
when people of good will join together and press for change, change
will come.

My preference would be to see the collaborative strategy emerge
soon, as the peoples and governments of the world's forest nations
see the cliff's edge we are heading for, recognize that only cooperation will save us, and then rapidly come together. But even my irre-
pressible optimism has its limits. So I believe that we who care about
the forest should now bend all our efforts toward creating the legally
binding international convention. If the legalistic approach turns
out to be only a stepping stone to a true consensual regime, no harm
done. I believe it would act as a focusing mechanism to lead initially
recalcitrant forest nations toward the light.

In the preceding paragraph I used the phrase "we who care about
the forest." In a perfect world, that group would include every human
on the planet, since there is not one of us who will not be affected by
what happens to the forest and thus each of us should be part of the
effort to preserve it. This being a decidedly imperfect world, however, some of us are going to be called on to do more than others. I
would like to identify some of the people who I believe should be key
actors.

Ministers Responsible for Forests. In my time as a deputy minister, I argued that the ambit of the BC Minister of Forests should extend far beyond the timber content of the forest to include all the assets – wildlife, water, recreation and more – that are inherent to the resource. I would like to see that thinking take hold among the governments – national, regional or local – of all forest nations. And I would like to see each of those responsible ministers become a Don Quixote, fearlessly championing the forest.

Forest Corporations. The corporate world can be one of the most effective delivery systems for solutions to global problems. Consider the impact on the world of the connectivity revolution, from wireless cell systems to the Internet, all of it largely driven by corporations. They can react faster; in fact, they often have to react more quickly than governments because the marketplace can be far less forgiving than even the most angry electorate. My experience with how international boycotts led to a movement to certify sustainably managed forests tells me that the corporations can more easily climb the learning curve than governments. And today, with true economic globalization beginning to emerge, the mechanisms through which the corporate sector can collectively change direction – think of the role played by the annual Davos conference – are forming.

Non-Government Organizations. They are the other half of the equation that leads corporations and governments to change. I would like to see every forest-related NGO put the cause of establishing an international convention at the top of its to-do list. And I would like to see every individual supporter of these influential groups writing to elected representatives and letters-to-the-editor columns to put the issue on the public agenda.

Foresters. I leave my own profession to the last, not because we are the least important participants in this process but because I want to emphasize that the world's brotherhood and sisterhood of foresters – and I use the word in its broadest meaning – should be bursting with the loudest, feistiest defenders the forest could ever have. If foresters will not be Don Quixotes for the forest, who will?

We in the forester community are not known for our political clout. I can think of very few foresters who have run for office and even fewer who have achieved it. Among ourselves, in our associations and industry groups, we are not adept at moving the forest agenda forward, and moving it faster and further. We seem much better at putting in place process piled upon process when what is needed is action.

Every forester is trained to be a champion of the forest. It's true that, over the years since I was in school, the nature of the championing (and therefore the training) has changed. Once we managed the forest for timber, then for sustained yield, then for a wider range of assets, and now for holistic sustainability of all values, tangible or not.

But I do not see us presenting ourselves as champions. Too much of our effort goes into the narrowest possible view of the forest – the research paper focused on minutiae – while our participation in the public issues that really count is scant. I have always been an advocate of forest research, both pure and applied, but I recall a conference at which an academic forester got up and brandished a copy of the paper he was about to read, declaring, "Not one of you will understand what I am saying." I was too polite to ask, "Then what's the point of publishing?"

We should spend less time talking to each other about things that may matter a little and much more time talking to the public about things that definitely matter a lot. And we need to encourage more young people to join the profession. Young people considering a career in forestry today, and not enough of them do consider it, often picture the training as virtually unchanged from what a forester learned back when I was in school – timber management and bridge building – rather than the holistic approach to sustainable management.

In truth, we were always leading edge environmentalists; we knew what ecology meant before the other 99.999 per cent of the world caught on and we have evolved remarkably from my first class at UBC. But we have not explained our evolution to the public, and so we are seen as handmaidens of the forest corporations and governments rather than as the defenders of the forest that we are. It is no wonder that forestry school enrolment is declining around the world, nor that some schools have changed their names to get around the image problem.

We must do something to reverse the trend. The forest needs champions and if not us, then who? I believe we can restore our stature if we make an effort to tell our story. I hope this book is a small contribution to the cause, but I would like to see a communications component in every forestry school curriculum, both to train students in how to talk about the forest to the public and especially to the media and to make them aware that everything they do in and for the forest is part of a public issue.

If we can pull together all of these potential actors – forest ministers, corporate trailblazers, NGO activists and a growing corps of media-savvy foresters ready to tilt at a few windmills – out of this potent mix will come the political will to change the way the world deals with the global forest. Out of a sustained surge of political will can come an international strategy or an international convention or both.

One essential component of that strategy must be to close the glaring gaps in our knowledge of the forest. As we enter the third millennium we have a lot of information about the world's forest but we need a hell of a lot more. And we need a much deeper understanding of what the facts and figures mean. We need more research, especially local information gathering in the field. Here in Canada, where accurate reporting is dependable, there are still large blank spaces in the data; in some of the developing countries not only are the data holes vast, but many of the numbers we do get cannot be relied upon. That man in Turkey with his three hundred goats has his counterparts throughout the world's tropical forest zones, where illegal logging is scantily reported. Then there are places like Myanmar where a kleptocratic military junta is ruthlessly denuding the forest and shipping the wood to complicit mills in China and elsewhere.

We need a better statistical base and we need more sound science. Most of all we need to broaden our scope: we should be looking at the forest as an evolving holistic entity that is not just a collection of trees but a matrix of plants and animals, all interrelated one to the other, and all changing continuously; and we should look beyond our own national and cultural horizons to understand the forest as it exists in other parts of the world. Our context must be global.

Canada should be leading the way, through a more comprehensive effort to transfer skills and knowledge to where they are lacking. We cannot afford the luxury of disregarding problems in the world forest the way British Prime Minister Neville Chamberlain disdained the dismemberment of Czechoslovakia as a concern of "people in a far-away country about whom we know nothing." Global deforestation – that net loss of some ten million hectares per year – is a global problem and because Canada is one of the leading forest nations it is our problem. We must reverse the trend and create an annual net gain. It does not matter to me whether the forest comes back through natural regeneration, by human replanting of species in a natural mix, or by the spread of single species plantations with trees in neat and tidy rows. A forest is a forest.

Most of all, we need to rally the world's forest people behind the global equivalent of the vision expressed in Canada's National Forest Strategy: *The long-term health of Canada's forest will be maintained and enhanced, for the benefit of all living things, and for the social, cultural, environmental and economic well-being of all Canadians now and in the future.*

Change those words to read "the world's forest" and "all human-kind" and I believe we have a vision for every human being on the planet.

I would be remiss if I did not narrow my focus and offer some observations on the state and future of my first love, the British Columbia forest.

The BC forest is one of the world's most precious living jewels. Contrary to the tale told by propagandists, we have not destroyed it; instead, we have managed it responsibly. In hindsight, we see that we have not managed it perfectly but since the conservation movement took hold a century ago, foresters from H.R. MacMillan onward have done the best they could in keeping with the knowledge they had, and within the social, economic and cultural context of their time.

But if the past is some comfort, the future offers considerable concern. Our population is increasing, over four million now and every indication says it will continue to rise. Where will we all live? My guess is that there will be increased density in the major cities, where four-fifths of us now prefer to live. But there will also be expansion of the cities, of infrastructure and of industry, and much of that growth will come at the expense of the forest.

Over the past century, and particularly in the last decade, we have fenced in significant portions of the BC forest behind some of the invisible lines of which humankind is so fond, and declared the set-aside zones to be parks, wilderness and protected areas. Around other segments of the forest we have drawn lines that designate them as suitable for clearing and replacing with houses and shopping centres, highways and utility transmission corridors. Still other parts of the forest are delineated as farmland, private woodlots or Aboriginal territory.

What we have not done is to draw a line around the remaining publicly owned forest and say, "This is our natural and economic heritage and it will be managed scientifically and sustainably in the best interests of all."

The reader should not infer that I am talking about "the working forest" – i.e., a forest managed primarily for commercial timber values. The definition of the working forest evolves over time. When I was young the working forest of British Columbia did not include the lodgepole pine forest of the Interior. Now it does. As science and wood-utilization technology improve, species that now have little or no commercial value may come to be included in the steadily widening definition.

Of course, a significant portion of the public forest may indeed be best managed primarily for timber. Forest products remain the backbone of the provincial economy, although I believe the industry should focus more closely on our advantages, turning our many unique species into unique products. I will not describe those products as "value-added;" too often, adding value also involves adding costs which diminish the final economic outcome, whereas the real goal should be to add more margin.

The BC forest should be sustainably managed for a range of values, indeed a wider range than many of us now recognize as inherent to the forest. There are many goods in the woods. Beyond timber, recreation, wildlife, water and aesthetics, there are non-timber commercial products like mushrooms, Christmas trees and salal. We should also consider the contribution the forest makes to the health of the planet by taking carbon from the atmosphere. Perhaps under some future version of the Kyoto Protocol, British Columbia will someday be paid by the world for this essential service. Perhaps too we will levy an economic charge on forest values now provided for free – like the scenic beauty of SuperNatural British Columbia that supports a tourist industry, or the service the forest provides to municipalities by soaking up rainwater so that it can find its way to aquifers and reservoirs instead of running back into the sea.

We must see the forest in its wholeness and we must manage it holistically. Part of that management requires an end to hit-or-miss decision-making on the use of the forest. If there is to be a change in the use of any part of the forest – including urban expansion, new transportation corridors, opening farm land – the proposal should go through a meaningful test to establish that the change in use is best for all. Then we could come to rational decisions: this piece of land is best suited to growing public trees, that piece would be better managed as a private woodlot, that stretch of river valley works best as a wilderness preserve, this territory should be restored to the holders of its Aboriginal title.

For that part of the BC forest devoted mostly to timber production, we also need a clear understanding that we are engaged in a partnership between a public resource and private capital, invested in plant, facilities, forest management, taxes and employee wages and benefits. We, as owners of the resource, all benefit from that investment, and have done so throughout the building of our province. In recent years, new stakeholders have established themselves at the table – including those Europeans who want us to avoid making the mistakes they made – but we have created processes that deal with the wider world's involvement.

I have faith that the BC Treaty Process will bring the Aboriginal peoples of BC to their rightful place at the table, creating stability and certainty as to the long-term future of the resource.

The task before us now is to ensure that we have a clear definition of responsibilities between the owners of the resource and those who are using it. Part of the clarity will be a tenure system that fairly meets the needs of all stakeholders. Even more, we need a useful structuring of the provincial agencies responsible for overseeing the partnership. Given the forest sector's importance to the province and given the need to deal with the forest holistically, I believe that there should be a BC Ministry of the Forest to which should accrue responsibility for the other assets – water, wildlife, recreation and so on – that extend from the forest. Under the current format, sustainably and holistically managing the forest requires interconnections among several different branches of several different departments. The result is process, process, process, and all of it adds up to inefficiency.

But since I have seen the view from the industry's side of the table as well as that from the government's side, I must wonder if the role of governments in our new century is becoming almost secondary. As much as anything else, forest management practices in recent years have been driven by demands from the world's consumers that the forest products they buy come from certified forests.

The other dynamic driving forest policy in Canada, and especially in BC, has been trade law cases brought by a handful of lumber firms in the US. One long-term solution to the continual harassment by the US lumber lobby is market diversification. Programs to bring in new customers have always been a good investment, and I applaud the new versions that are now in place or in development. We should remember that the market for BC forest products is the globe, not just North America. By all means, we should continue to serve our longstanding non-North American markets, but we should be looking hard for new opportunities in the economies of China, Taiwan and other Asian countries.

Our governments and industry must reaffirm their commitment to full free trade. At the moment, we do not have free trade in lumber – the best we have achieved lately is freer managed trade – and I doubt that I will live long enough to see it become truly free. But it is not just a case of the US lumber lobby's efforts to keep the price of lumber artificially high. Around the world, as the WTO and other agreements break down tariff barriers, we are continually confronted by a host of non-tariff barriers, such as idiosyncratic building codes and standards, and spurious concerns about plant health. We require a continuous, concerted push through all channels, national and international, by governments, by the industry and by our allies – US home builders, for example – to get what will best serve us all: free and unfettered trade.

I also believe we British Columbian forest folk should be world leaders in safety, efficiency and environmental systems. To that end, I would like to see more investment in new science and technology, and not just the usual practice of throwing money at research when prices are up and downsizing as soon as prices slide. Science and technological innovation should be a fundamental component of any modern business person's world view. That should be especially true of an industry blessed with access to one of the greatest natural resources the world offers. There's an old saying that the best time to plant a tree is twenty years ago, and the second best time is now. The same applies to science and technology. I would like to see every major forest corporation engaged, directly and indirectly, in continuous research and development. I would also like to see more research into markets and where we stand in relation to competing industries around the world. We need to look around us more often and with sharper vision, to see who is moving up and to know why. And, though it would be the ruin of many consultants like me, I would like to see that research information shared as widely as possible. We are an industry; we should think and act like one.

Finally, the perennial question asked of people like me in times like these: is it time for another Royal Commission into the British Columbia forest sector? I have given the matter a great deal of thought and have spoken with a number of knowledgeable people who have also pondered over where we are and where we might be heading. My answer is: no. My reasoning: another Royal Commission will not do what needs doing. We need something much bigger and much more far-reaching.

We need an inquiry with the authority of a Royal Commission but with wider scope than was available to Commissioners Sloan or Pearse in the slower, simpler times in which they deliberated. The process cannot deal only with what goes on in BC. We are a small open economy in an increasingly global marketplace, and a small democratic society in a world polity that is more and more knit together by international obligations. The inquiry's purview must encompass a bigger picture, both in space and in time. It must look beyond our borders and it must look into the short-, medium- and long-term futures.

And the picture must move. The inquiry must not only look at a much wider range of issues than any previous Royal Commission – including economics, the environment, social and political factors, trade, taxation, and much more – but must look at them as a matrix whose elements are all organically evolving in relation to each other. There can be no "silo thinking."

Nor can all of this information be filtered through the view of one, two or three Commissioners, no matter how wise they may be. The process may be directed by one or a few capable individuals, but its active membership must be broad and inclusive. The widest possible base of stakeholders must not only be heard from but must be active participants in shaping a consensus.

The inquiry mechanism must find a way to combine: the power of a Royal Commission; the broad consensual approach of a round table; and the simultaneously deep-focused and wide-angled view of a first-rate think tank. Moreover, it must be a permanent entity, continuously re-evaluating its subject and itself, as does Canada's National Forest Strategy, and as did the revolving resource analyses and programs that used to be part of the governance of the British Columbia forest.

The kind of institution – let us call it British Columbia's Permanent Commission on the Forest – that could undertake such a continuing inquiry does not exist, to my knowledge, anywhere in the world. Therefore we must bring it into existence.

That would be a bold initiative. But we British Columbians are a bold people; if we were not, we could not have created Canada's first constituent assembly and given it the daunting task of redefining our electoral system. If we are audacious enough to experiment with the way we govern ourselves, we can be enterprising enough to take a new approach to the most significant element of our physical, economic and cultural landscape – the forest.

So let us assume that such a permanent commission can be established, because we are the kind of people who can do what has not been done before. And if its membership were properly broad, so that all stakeholders were included and empowered, its action plans would be acceptable to all. Therefore it meets the three criteria of an Apsey vision: it is bold, it is doable, and it is buy-in-able.

And thus, after two-thirds of a lifetime of experience on several sides of the forest community's table, after consultation with many people who have spent their lives thinking about the forest, and after considerable reflection in the tranquility of semi-retirement, that bold, doable, buy-in-able vision is my recommendation to those who love the forest of British Columbia: let us establish a Permanent Commission that will do what is right for all of us, and right for the forest.

There is a certain finality to closing a memoir, a sense that "here endeth the lesson" and now the story is told. I do not feel any finality. This book is only a chapter in a story that I hope will go on for some time yet.

I am intrigued by the future, especially the future of the world's forest. But I keep it in mind that though we are all bound for the future, the future is not a destination at which we will ever arrive. It just keeps on going and going, as we keep on going and going, as the forest keeps on growing and growing.

Every day brings the possibility of new adventures, of whole new worlds to encounter. I look forward to all of them.

– THE END –

ACKNOWLEDGMENTS

I have been blessed throughout my life with the support of many people: family, friends, teachers, colleagues, mentors and associates, as well as the kind folk I met along the way. Some of them were to be found in high office in the world's great cities, others lived in jungles or in barrios. I am the product of all the help, instruction, counsel and care that they willingly gave to me. I am grateful for all the gifts and to all the givers.